A
Journey

through

GREEK
mythology
Revised Printing

monica cyrino
University of New Mexico

Kendall Hunt
publishing company

www.kendallhunt.com
Send all inquiries to:
4050 Westmark Drive
Dubuque, IA 52004-1840

Copyright © 2008 by Kendall Hunt Publishing Company

ISBN 978-0-7575-8910-2

Printed in the United States of America
10 9 8 7

CONTENTS

PREFACE

How to Use This Guidebook

A Journey through Greek Mythology is a guidebook intended to accompany students in an introductory Greek mythology course. This guidebook serves as a practical and versatile introduction to the study of the major Greek gods and heroes, as it lays the groundwork for an exploration of the representation, interpretation, and influence of the classical Greek myths. Using this guidebook, students are able to consider how the gods and heroes functioned as objects of deep religious awe and reverence for the ancient Greeks, and yet at the same time how they were portrayed as colorful, unpredictable, subjectively "anthropomorphic" characters in the popular art and literature of classical antiquity. The guidebook offers an opportunity for students to investigate how archetypal figures and narratives emerge in Greek mythology and how these patterns develop in different representational media and literary genres. The guidebook also encourages students to discover how the Greek myths continue to influence our contemporary culture today.

The chief aim of this guidebook is to give students a familiarity with the major Greek myths and how to appreciate them. The book's twenty chapters cover a wide range of the principal ancient Greek myths about the most important and fascinating gods, heroes, and events in Greek mythology. First there is an introduction outlining different ways to understand and interpret myths, followed by chapters on noteworthy topics ranging from the Greek narratives of the birth of the universe, through a detailed survey of all the powerful Olympian gods, and finally to a consideration of some of the major Greek hero sagas. Each chapter introduces the subject at hand and outlines the goals for that unit of study, by introducing and explaining key terms, motifs, and themes within the topic. Each chapter offers a thorough exploration of the subject, and presents several significant concepts within example boxes throughout the discussion. Each chapter concludes with a collection of bibliographic sources useful for further study, with both recommended primary and secondary sources, as well as a section offering some suggestions for popular culture resources that may be explored and enjoyed alongside the main subject matter of the chapter. Finally, each chapter ends with a self-quiz that allows students to challenge their acquisition of key concepts and terminology. At the end of the guidebook, students will also find an extensive glossary of Greek names and terms for quick reference.

This guidebook is designed in such a way that it may best be used in conjunction with readings from the ancient Greek primary sources. In an introductory survey of the principal ancient myths, it is important to understand how the myths are presented in the original literature of the ancient Greeks. It is highly recommended that readings from ancient Greek literary works be assigned to accompany this guidebook, in particular Hesiod's *Theogony* and *Works and Days*, several of the *Homeric Hymns* to the major gods, as well as selections from Homer's *Iliad* and *Odyssey*. It is also suggested that students be encouraged to view images taken from ancient Greek vase paintings and sculptures, so that they may examine the representations of the gods, heroes, and myths in their own contemporary visual and cultural context.

Now, on to the journey!

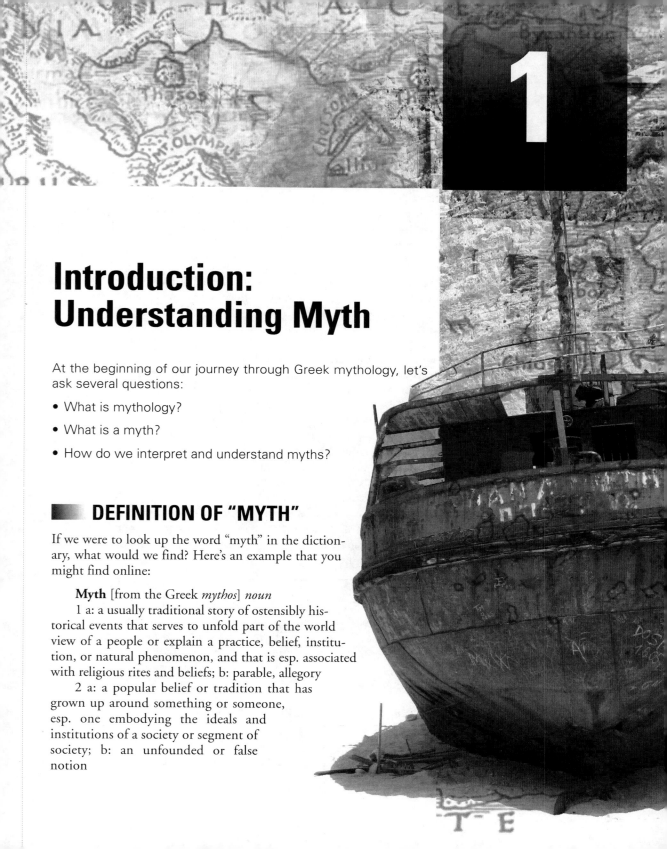

Introduction: Understanding Myth

At the beginning of our journey through Greek mythology, let's ask several questions:

- What is mythology?

- What is a myth?

- How do we interpret and understand myths?

DEFINITION OF "MYTH"

If we were to look up the word "myth" in the dictionary, what would we find? Here's an example that you might find online:

> **Myth** [from the Greek *mythos*] *noun*
>
> 1 a: a usually traditional story of ostensibly historical events that serves to unfold part of the world view of a people or explain a practice, belief, institution, or natural phenomenon, and that is esp. associated with religious rites and beliefs; b: parable, allegory
>
> 2 a: a popular belief or tradition that has grown up around something or someone, esp. one embodying the ideals and institutions of a society or segment of society; b: an unfounded or false notion

3: a person or thing having only an imaginary or unverifiable existence
4: the whole body of myths
synonyms Myth, Legend, Saga: a traditional story of ostensibly historical content whose origin has been lost.

(source: *Merriam-Webster's Online Dictionary*)

This definition is all-encompassing, fairly broad, and general, but ultimately somewhat confusing. This definition also reveals some rather sweeping assumptions about the nature of myths and mythology. Many of us hold some of these same assumptions, but are they true? In fact, not all of these assumptions are true all or even some of the time. Let's review some common suppositions about what "real" myths are supposed to be.

Assumption 1: "Myths are born, not made."
The assumption here is that real myths must be ancient, and that their origin must be both entirely unknown and anonymous—that is, we don't know where the stories came from or who composed them.
Assumption 2: "Myths explain natural phenomena."
The assumption here is that all myths are essentially explanatory "nature stories"— that is, they must explain something in the natural world around us.
Assumption 3: "Myths are always about divine or supernatural events."
The assumption here is that real myths always contain a divine element—that is, they must be about gods and supernatural beings.
Assumption 4: "Myth represents actual religious ritual."
The assumption here is that real myths represent something like an actual script for the performance of religious rites—that is, ancient peoples used myths mainly to celebrate their gods and other religious beings.
Assumption 5: "Myths were once really believed by some primitive societies, but modern people are too smart to believe myths anymore."
The assumption here is that real myths are unsophisticated and unscientific explanations for things—that is, the society that originated the myth was not smart or sophisticated enough to come up with a better explanation, and modern society no longer believes such silly, made-up stories.

That's Incredible!

This notion of the "incredible" aspect of myth sounds biased and definitely lacks nuance, yet notice that it fits well with the common usage of the words "myth" and "mythical" today, to mean something implausible, far-fetched, or downright untrue.
This meaning is quite prevalent today on contemporary magazine covers, for example:
"The *Myth* of Male Sensitivity" or "The *Mythical* 5-Day Diet."
Or how about this catchy headline:
"Bigfoot: *Myth* or Real?"

How do we make sense of all these varying definitions, assumptions, and ideas about myths and mythology? Let's see if we can get to the heart of the matter and come up with a more workable definition.

First of all, let's introduce a couple of useful terms.

Mythology is a set or system of myths.

Also, the study of mythology means that we analyze the form, purpose, meaning, and function of myths.

> *Mythos* = the ancient Greek word for "an utterance, word, something said or spoken." It can also refer to a story, tale, or speech.

In the ancient Greek context, a *mythos* is the product of the storyteller's art, something that is subject to spontaneous change and revision with each retelling. So always keep in mind the oral/verbal nature of Greek mythology.

Also, remember that Greek mythology has a literary character: the ancient Greek writers and poets used their culture's myths as the principal subject matter for their literary creations. This is where we go to find what survives of the stories of Greek mythology: myths can be found in epic poetry, poetic hymns, and dramatic plays.

Now let's look at some names given to the various types of stories we will encounter on our journey through Greek mythology. These are the traditional categories that scholars use to make distinctions between different types of stories. But remember that these are loose categories; when we apply them to actual Greek myths "out in the field," the boundaries may blur and some of the types will merge into one another.

STORY TYPES

- True myth/myth proper
- Saga
- Legend
- Folktale
- Fable

True Myth/Myth Proper

True myth and **myth proper** are terms usually used to refer to stories that deal primarily with the major gods. These stories mainly involve the gods' relationships and interactions with each other, and they also deal with human beings' relationships and interactions with the major gods. Many of these stories reveal an interest in defining human existence in connection to that of the divine.

Saga

Saga is a term used to describe a story seemingly rooted in a sense of history. No matter how creative or fantastic, the saga purports to refer to actual human persons and events.

The people involved in a saga are usually royal, aristocratic, or singled out in some way. Very often, the term refers to the collected tales of a particular city, family, or royal house.

For example, the "Trojan saga" refers to all the stories told about the founding of the city of Troy, its many important inhabitants, and, of course, the famous Trojan War and the fall of Troy. Another famous story cycle is the "Theban saga," which refers to the stories about Oedipus, King of Thebes, and his dysfunctional family.

Legend

Legend is a term that may be used in a general sense like the term *myth*, but more often it is defined closer to the meaning of *saga*. That is, a legend usually refers to a story with a connection to real persons and historical events.

Consider, for example, the "legendary" character Achilles—is there any evidence that he was a "real" warrior? Or was Odysseus a "real" hero?

Folktale

Folktale is a term that describes popular tales of adventure with the primary purpose of entertainment. Folktales generally star a clever, down-to-earth hero whose ingenious schemes save the day. The folktale hero interacts with fanciful and often stereotypical beings of the popular imagination such as giants, witches, and monsters. The folktale contains elements of magic, mystery, and the grotesque. The term *fairytale* is often used interchangeably with *folktale*.

Note that folktale elements as just described can be interwoven into the narratives of myth, legend, and saga. For example, the story of the adventures of Odysseus contains many typical folktale elements, patterns, and figures.

Fable

A **fable** is an animal tale that delivers a "moral" at the end of the story. The fable was not a favored narrative form in classical Greek mythology, and only became popular later in antiquity.

Remember that these categories are not strict, and that many stories will contain aspects of each.

Traditional Tale

The most useful definition for myth is to call it a *traditional tale*.

This emphasizes the narrative quality of myth—it is a dramatic story with a beginning, middle, and end—and it is a story that says something significant and meaningful enough about a certain culture or society to be handed down from generation to generation and retold over and over again in different formats.

Myth Time

The ancient Greeks believed in "myth time." Keep in mind, perhaps more so than other myth systems, that Greek mythology contains a strong historical element. This means that the ancient Greeks believed in their mythic past—they believed that there was a time when gods and humans communed more openly and with more familiarity with each other, from the beginning of the Creation time through the Age of Heroes. But since that time had passed, they believed the gods only spoke to humans through oracles and dreams.

Also, some scholars believe that certain myths have a foundation in real historical fact, and indeed some myths would appear to be corroborated by literary, historical, or archaeological records.

For example, the story of the Trojan War is a famous epic saga, but can it also be based on real history? Archaeologists seem to think so.

Near Eastern Influence on Greek Mythology

Let us also look out for the influence on Greek mythology of the much older cultures and civilizations of the Near East, particularly from Egypt, Mesopotamia, and even ancient Crete. Certain Greek myths reveal this influence, especially in the realm of monstrous and fantastical elements.

 # THEORIES ABOUT MYTH

Now that we have come up with a workable definition of myth and examined some of its properties, let's consider how people over the centuries have interpreted myths and their origins, function, meaning, and purpose.

A number of different theories have been devised to understand and explain the significance of myths. These theories emerge out of all the various academic disciplines you can find around campus: anthropology, psychology, sociology, religious studies, even biology. Sometimes it seems like there are as many theories as there are myths! No single theory will work to explain every myth, and very often it is beneficial to combine theories when attempting to analyze certain myths.

Theory of Rationalization

This is where a natural explanation or cause is given for a supernatural one. For example, you are offering a rationalizing explanation when you say all the gods and heroes are actually just exceptional human beings who were deified for doing great deeds. Or if you say that Pegasus, the beautiful winged horse of Greek myth, is "just a really fast horse."

Although the tendency toward rationalization would seem to be a modern one, in fact the inclination to apply this theory to myths started in ancient times and not surprisingly was popular with the Greek natural philosophers. So while debunking ancient tales or explaining them away is still a popular activity even today, especially on television, the theory of rationalization remains an uninteresting and rather limited method for understanding the dynamic and often complicated nature of myths.

Metaphorical Interpretations

Let's turn to those theories that seek to find deep, multilayered meanings in myths—that is, every myth *stands for* some profound universal truth. This is the opposite of the literal view, in that the myth cannot be taken at face value, but rather must be carefully unpacked because the myth *symbolizes* something else.

Theory of Allegory

The theory of allegory is one of the most informative and useful of the metaphorical interpretations. This is where the narrative of the myth presents its various components and details—people, places, actions—and they all function as symbols of something else. Allegory also uses figurative language; that is, it uses metaphor and simile to enhance its meaning.

For example, in an allegory, all the gods are symbols of human qualities and emotions, and so their myths portray the workings of those activities and emotions.

Aphrodite = "sexual lust"
Ares = "war"
So when Aphrodite seduces a willing Ares in Greek myth, her action in effect is saying "Make love, not war"!

Or, another allegory example is when a myth tells of a hero who wrestles with Death or goes to the Underworld while still alive and returns unscathed. This allegory symbolizes the universal human desire to conquer death and the possibility of attaining immortality.

Internalist Theories

Other metaphorical interpretations connect myths to the human mind—that is, "it's all in your head." These theories see myths as direct products of internal psychological processes, such as thoughts, fantasies, wishes, and dreams. So, if myths are spontaneous expressions of the human psyche, myths must be intimately linked to human mental processes. It should come as no surprise that this is a favorite theory of psychologists and psychoanalysts for understanding myths.

Sigmund Freud
Sigmund Freud (1856–1939) was an Austrian psychologist most famous for his theories about the unconscious mind, especially dealing with the mechanisms of repression and

sexual desire. In his work on the unconscious mind and especially dreams, Freud discovered the importance of dream symbols as reflections of unconscious desires, and then he developed the similarity between dreams and myths. Freud believed that myths reflect the efforts of waking people to make sense of the jumbled visions and impulses of their sleep world. That is, myths are connected to and derive from a person's dreams.

Freud also thought that dreams, and their waking counterpart, myths, allowed the human mind to relieve psychic tension by violating certain taboos in safely displaced contexts. According to Freud, one of the earliest and most basic patterns of dream/myth wish fulfillment in the human psyche is paralleled in the story of Oedipus.

> In Greek mythology, Oedipus is the king and great hero of Thebes who saves the city from the ravages of the murderous she-monster, the Sphinx. But Oedipus is also the cursed mortal who unknowingly kills his own father and then marries his own mother, having four children by her. When he discovers who he really is, a patricidal committer of foul incest, he gouges out his own eyes to atone for the two crimes.

Freud connected the Oedipus myth to a stage in human psychosexual development where the child experiences feelings of aggression and hostility to the parent of the same gender, while seeking the exclusive love of the parent of the opposite gender. Freud called this the **Oedipus complex**. In his later work, Freud went on to connect the experience of Oedipal desires to various other social, ethical, and religious themes. For example, Freud concluded that the sense of guilt felt by males for wanting to kill or remove their father-rivals gives rise to the concept of the Supreme Being, or God, as an angry father who must be constantly appeased.

Freud's approach to the connection between myths and the human mind provides numerous insights in understanding many Greek myths where family psychodrama plays a big part, such as the bloody chain of family vengeance, sex, and murder in the saga of the House of Atreus; or myths that deal with persistently repressed human emotions, fears, and desires, such as the tale of the monstrous Minotaur hidden in the labyrinth on the island of Crete. And as we shall see, the theme of jealousy toward the father is one of the most prevalent motifs in Greek myths of creation, as well as in stories about the rise of the great god Zeus, and the father-rivalry motif appears as well in several stories of heroes as they strive to achieve the goals of their quests.

Carl Jung

Carl Jung (1875–1961) was a Swiss psychiatrist whose widely influential work connected psychology to the realms of art, religion, and mythology. Once a student and friend of Freud's, Jung's work went further in the connection of human dreams and myths. Jung noted that certain figures and narrative situations were common to dreamers of all cultures, races, and nations. As well, he noted that myths from different cultures and times reveal similar figures and story patterns. Jung theorized that myths are a projection of what he called the "collective unconscious" of the entire human race—that is, myths show the persistent psychological tendencies of all members of human society.

In his work on the collective unconscious, Jung also advanced the notion of *archetypes*. These are innate, generic, idealized patterns and images that are universally accepted to represent a common idea, whether a person, object, event, activity, or even a concept. Jung noted that archetypes appear in the dreams of individuals, and in the myths of societies. Thus, archetypes represent the traditional, universal expressions of symbols that are common to us all, no matter when or where we live.

Examples of Jungian archetypes in myths are:

- The hero
- The wise old man
- The great mother
- The trickster
- The divine child

Archetypes can also take shape in common myth story patterns:

- The hero's quest
- The flood
- The succession myth
- The sacred marriage
- The conquest of death

In Greek mythology, we will see how many of the gods and heroes represent archetypal characters, while the myths themselves reflect archetypal situations and actions, such as the story of the greatest Greek hero, Herakles, and his labors.

Jung's approach to understanding the comprehensive nature of myth is fascinating and useful because it shows how all societies depend psychologically upon their myths, and how all cultures are intricately connected. Furthermore, Jung's work on archetypes influenced one of the most important and publicly well-known scholars of comparative mythology in recent times, Joseph Campbell (1904–1987). Campbell applied many Jungian concepts to his study of the archetypal patterns in the journey of the hero, what he called the *monomyth*, a story pattern that he believed conveyed universal truths about the individual's search for self-discovery and a person's role in society. In turn, Campbell's work on the hero archetype greatly influenced several modern filmmakers, including George Lucas, creator of the *Star Wars* films. (Note: The figure of the archetypal hero is explored in Chapter 16).

Externalist Theories

Let's move on now to look at some interpretive strategies for myth that follow an external approach—that is, these **externalist theories** understand myth as a reaction to our external, both physical and cultural, environment. These theories are sometimes referred to as *anthropological approaches* to understanding myth, since they focus on the natural, cultural, and social environments surrounding human beings. These theories view myth as an attempt to explain natural phenomena, or offer explanations for social, political, and religious customs and institutions; that is, myth explains the outside world.

Modern Use of Archetypes

Even in today's contemporary world, we readily relate to archetypes. In popular culture contexts, whenever a group is portrayed, each member of the group will usually represent a single archetype. Pop music groups will often present the individual members of the group as separate archetypes: for example, the "cute one," the "bad one," or the "quiet one." Two extreme examples of groups that marketed their individual members as archetypes include the notorious 1970s band the Village People and the teen-pop 1990s group the Spice Girls. Archetypes are effective because they allow people to recognize and thus relate to the separate group members as unique "characters." This is especially true in the narratives of television shows or films that depict large groups of cast members, whether it's on television series such as *Gilligan's Island* (1964–1967) or *Lost* (2004–present), or in films such as *Ocean's 11* (2001). The use of archetypes in dramatic fiction—film, television, novels, and plays—is valuable for artists because almost everyone in the audience unconsciously recognizes the archetypal characters and situations, and thus will have a basic understanding of their motivations, desires, and goals; sometimes the audience can even recognize the plot itself. Viewers more readily identify with, and thus buy into, images and stories they can understand.

As we explore the way societies use myth to explain their external world, we must beware of labeling societies that have working, developed myth systems as "primitive," "naïve," or even "unsophisticated." It is a common misstep to say that a society that composed myths used them as explanatory principles because they couldn't figure out "science." In fact, in classical Greek society, myth and science existed side by side. Although Greek mythology as it appears in classical Greek literature obviously developed from something earlier and perhaps less refined, it does not indicate that such an earlier society was "simple" or "crude" in any way. Another descriptive term for such earlier societies is "instinctive" or, even better, "prescientific."

Nature Theory

Nature theory says that myth explains meteorological and cosmological phenomena—that is, myth deals with weather, seasons, and cosmology. Myth explains such questions as "Why is it raining?" Although some Greek myths deal with weather—and the great god, Zeus, is prominent among weather gods—as a rule most Greek mythology pays scant attention to nature and natural forces.

Charter Theory

Charter theory says that myth is connected to human social customs and practical life. Myth confirms existing institutions by providing a charter, or foundational principle, for present-day beliefs, practices, customs, and conventions. The charter story is validated because it emerges from the genuine mythical tradition. In this theory, myth explains such questions as "Why do we sacrifice animals to the gods?" While the charter theory helps us analyze some Greek myths, it can sometimes be a limiting approach because it does not take into account the more imaginative or metaphysical elements of myth.

Aetiological Theory

Aetiological theory is closely related to the charter myth theory, in that this theory interprets myth as an explanation for the cause or origin of a particular object or place, such as an animal, plant, mountain, river, constellation, musical instrument, weapon, and many other items.

The Greek word *aetion* means "origin, cause, reason."

In Greek mythology, many myths contain aetiological elements—that is, there will be an *aetion* or "origin" element expressed in the narrative of the myth, but the theory is not usually comprehensive.

Spider-Woman

For example, the myth of Arachne provides an *aetion* for the web-spinning spider.

Ritualist Theory

Ritualist theory says that all myth is connected to religion—that is, myth describes or explains specific religious practices, rituals, or events. The connection of myth and religion helps elucidate some myths, such as those concerning the Greek god of wine and rebirth, Dionysus. Yet while this has been a very popular and influential theory with some scholars, such as the poet Robert Graves, the approach fails to cover the great variety of Greek myths.

Structuralist Theory

Structuralist theory says that the most informative part of myth is its structure, that is, the way the various constituent elements of the myth fit together. According to this theory, the structure of myth is made up of pairs of opposites, and myth is constantly mediating between and trying to reconcile these contradictory elements. So myth is understood as a mode of communication—that is, societies use myth to resolve conflicts and tensions that otherwise would go unresolved. So the purpose of myth is the reconciliation of opposites for the benefit of society.

Examples of these oppositions include:

- Male/female
- Mind/body
- Nature/culture
- Hunter/hunted
- Life/death

This theory also maintains that the underlying structure of myth reveals certain patterns that recur in other myths. That is, similar myths will show similar patterns with similar constituent elements, sometimes even following the same narrative order or sequence. For example, as we shall see, the Greek hero tales reveal several common elements, as do the stories of the mortal lovers of Zeus. Finding similar patterns and sequences of elements that recur in separate stories helps us to organize our study of myths and allows us to compare individual myths to each other.

While this theory can be very useful in understanding myth, especially in viewing the parallel development of different myths, the structuralist scheme can be too fixed and linear and not very flexible. Thus, it does not apply to all Greek myth, which is often complicated by the presence of a strong historical dimension as well as many successive layers of narrative development. For example, the Trojan War saga may contain real "historical facts" independent of the strict structure outlined for such a myth. Furthermore, almost all Greek myths are very highly developed—that is, they have experienced a long period of development, during which the original structure could have been modified over time to fit the context or circumstances of the time of retelling.

On our journey through Greek mythology, let's apply a combination of theories and approaches as we explore the Greek myths.

Let's bear in mind that Greek myths show many layers of development, and often have a historical dimension.

Let's remember that Greek myths are dynamic and constantly changing, and that myths vary according to who is telling them and also according to the time and mode of telling.

Let's note the importance of the audience for Greek myth—that is, myth has an important function to respond to the needs of its listeners and/or viewers. That's why myth can and often does and even should change every time it is retold: there is *no one single version* of any Greek myth!

So, let us revise our earlier definition to include a reference to the importance of the application of myth, that is, how myth is used and in what context:

Myth is a *traditional* tale applied for *popular* use.

As we shall see throughout our journey through Greek mythology, modern movies, television shows, graphic novels, commercial advertisements, and other popular culture applications of myth help us to understand the ever-changing, ever-renewable, ever-dynamic nature of myths and mythology.

◼ SOURCES FOR THIS CHAPTER

Bremmer, Jan. (Ed.). (1986). *Interpretations of Greek Mythology*. New York: Barnes & Noble.

Campbell, Joseph. (1972). *The Hero with a Thousand Faces*. Princeton: Princeton University Press. First published in 1949.

Csapo, Eric. (2005). *Theories of Mythology*. Oxford: Blackwell.

Dowden, Ken. (1992). *The Uses of Greek Mythology*. London and New York: Routledge.

Edmunds, Lowell. (Ed.). (1990). *Approaches to Greek Myth*. Baltimore: The Johns Hopkins University Press.

Freud, Sigmund. (2006). *The Interpretation of Dreams*. Translated and edited by J. A. Underwood. London and New York: Penguin Books. First published in 1899.

Graf, Fritz. (1993). *Greek Mythology: An Introduction*. Translated by Thomas Marier. Baltimore: The Johns Hopkins University Press.

Jung, Carl G. (1991). *The Archetypes and the Collective Unconscious*. Volume 9.1 of *The Collected Works of C. G. Jung*. Translated by R. F. C. Hull. London and New York: Routledge. First published as essays from 1933 to 1954.

Lefkowitz, Mary. (2005). *Greek Gods, Human Lives: What We Can Learn from Myths*. New Haven: Yale University Press.

Morford, Mark P. O., and Lenardon, Robert J. (2007). *Classical Mythology*, 8th ed. Oxford: Oxford University Press.

Young, Robert M. (2001). *Oedipus Complex: Ideas in Psychoanalysis*. Cambridge: Icon Books, Ltd.

◼ POPULAR CULTURE REFERENCES

Films

Star Wars (1977). Director: George Lucas.
Bill & Ted's Excellent Adventure (1989). Director: Stephen Herek.

Television

Joseph Campbell and the Power of Myth (1988). Documentary interview with Bill Moyers, PBS.
MythBusters (2003–present). The Discovery Channel.

Online

Encyclopedia Mythica (www.pantheon.org)
Joseph Campbell Foundation (www.jcf.org)

Self-Quiz for Chapter 1

1. What is the definition of the Greek word *mythos*?

   _____

   _____

   _____

   _____

2. What kind of tale is a "true myth"?

   _____

   _____

   _____

   _____

   _____

3. What is meant by *saga* or *legend*?

   _____

   _____

   _____

4. What is the theory of rationalization?

   _____

   _____

   _____

   _____

5. What is an allegory?

   _____

   _____

   _____

6. What is the Oedipus complex?

_____

_____

_____

_____

7. What is the collective unconscious?

_____

_____

_____

_____

_____

_____

8. What is meant by *archetype*?

_____

_____

_____

_____

_____

9. What is aetiological theory?

_____

_____

_____

_____

_____

10. What is structuralist theory?

_____

_____

_____

_____

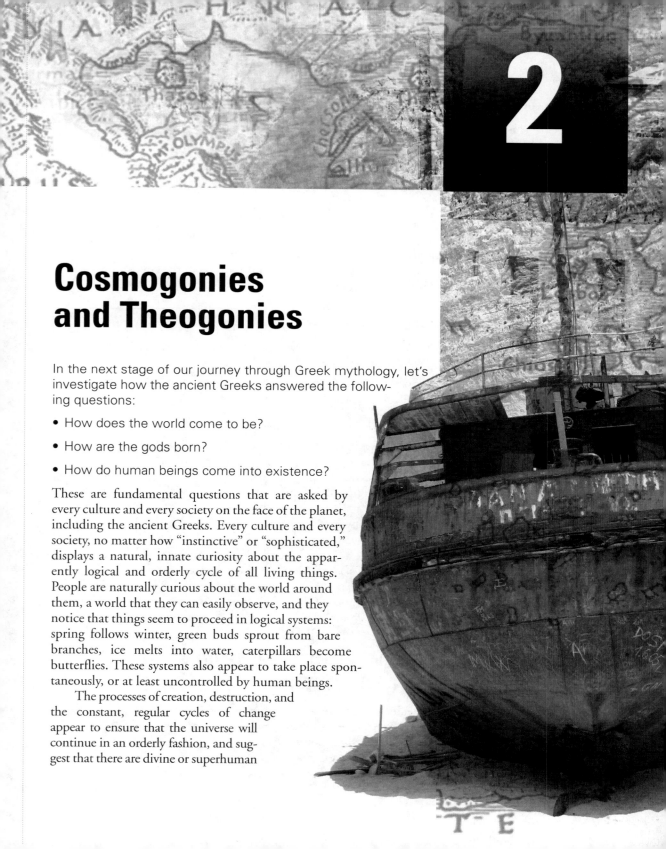

Cosmogonies and Theogonies

In the next stage of our journey through Greek mythology, let's investigate how the ancient Greeks answered the following questions:

- How does the world come to be?

- How are the gods born?

- How do human beings come into existence?

These are fundamental questions that are asked by every culture and every society on the face of the planet, including the ancient Greeks. Every culture and every society, no matter how "instinctive" or "sophisticated," displays a natural, innate curiosity about the apparently logical and orderly cycle of all living things. People are naturally curious about the world around them, a world that they can easily observe, and they notice that things seem to proceed in logical systems: spring follows winter, green buds sprout from bare branches, ice melts into water, caterpillars become butterflies. These systems also appear to take place spontaneously, or at least uncontrolled by human beings.

The processes of creation, destruction, and the constant, regular cycles of change appear to ensure that the universe will continue in an orderly fashion, and suggest that there are divine or superhuman forces persistently operating to ensure the continuation of all the forms of life and all the natural systems in the world.

People observe that there is an *essential system* in the natural world that reveals:

• Order

• Perpetuity

• Divinity

So every culture and every society has inherited or composed their own creation myths, stories that describe the origins of the world, the gods and other divine powers, and human beings—stories that reveal the essential order in the universe. These myths respond to our natural human curiosity about the causes of the world and the manner of its creation.

A creation myth is called a *cosmogony*. The term comes from the Greek words *kosmos* "order" + *genesis* "birth." Thus, cosmogony = "birth of the universe."

Kosmos in the English Language

When American astronomer and humanist Carl Sagan refers to the "cosmos," he means the universe as an ordered system.

A person who is "cosmopolitan" is a citizen of the world.

"Cosmetics" help you put your face in order!

Cosmogonies tell about the creation of the world, how the "cosmos" or universe began and developed, how the gods came into the world, and how human beings were born.

Cosmogonies also describe the creation of gods and other supernatural beings. This aspect of the tale is called a *theogony*. The term comes from the Greek words *theos* "god" + *genesis* "birth." Thus, theogony = "birth of the gods."

The ancient Greeks had many myths of creation in their narrative, artistic, and literary traditions. These myths contain many elements that can be found in the creation myths of other cultures and societies around the world, such as the Egyptians, Babylonians, Sumerians, Hebrews, Hindus, and Native Americans. These common motifs occur in several different cultural traditions and may rightly be called "archetypal" in a Jungian sense, in that they are universally accepted and repeated images or patterns.

Let's look at some of these common motifs in cosmogony myths.

▨ COSMOGONY THEME 1: THE UNION OF HEAVEN AND EARTH

In this motif, one of the first events to occur in the creation of the world is when the Earth is joined together with the sky, or heaven. Often this is depicted as a "marriage" between the Earth and sky/heaven, where the Earth is (usually, but not always) seen as the sacred female principle and the sky is the sacred male. Often the Earth is seen as the sacred mother who gives birth to various principles—natural phenomena, gods, humans—out of her earthly body.

COSMOGONY THEME 2: THE IMPORTANCE OF PRIMAL WATERS

In this motif, the creation of the world comes about because of the presence of primal, life-giving waters. Often the water or the sea is the source of creation itself, or there is a sea deity who is prominent in the narrative of the creation story. This is to be expected. Because creation myths are essentially allegories—that is, metaphorical stories—for human birth, the presence of primal waters suggests something like the amniotic fluid surrounding the "baby" universe.

COSMOGONY THEME 3: STRUGGLE IN HEAVEN

In this motif, the creation myth narrates the tale of a war or struggle in heaven between gods or groups of divinities. Out of the divine conflicts emerges a chief god, and often it is the child of the previous god who proves to be superior in the struggle.

Divine Conflict = Younger Generation Beats the Older

When the child-god proves to be stronger and takes over from the parent-god, this is known as the *succession motif.*

COSMOGONY THEME 4: CIVILIZATION IS A DIVINE GIFT

In this motif, the creation myth shows that the gods have a purpose for the creation of human beings as part of the divine plan to restore order over disorder. The divinities plan to give "civilization" as a gift from gods to humans, and thus it can be taken away if humans do not behave themselves. Often the creation myth will tell the story of how humans fell from a state of perfection in the eyes of the gods and thus must be restored to their previous state of grace.

Let's now look at how these motifs manifest themselves in the ancient Greek literary versions of cosmogonies and theogonies.

The earliest Greek account of the creation is a brief mention by the great Greek epic poet Homer (ca. eighth century BC), who wrote the *Iliad* and the *Odyssey* (more on these epic poems in later chapters). Homer suggests that two Titans, Oceanos and his sister-wife, Tethys, were involved in the process of bringing the Olympian gods to power (*Iliad* 14.201—although it must be noted that this story comes as part of an outright lie that the goddess Hera tells to trick the goddess Aphrodite!). As his name implies, the god Oceanos was conceived of as the stream of "ocean" water that surrounds the flat disc of the Earth, which is set in the middle like a scoop of ice cream in a root beer float. Oceanos encircles and supports the Earth, so he can be said to sustain and even nurture the Earth itself and the gods who rule over it. From this geographical image comes the significance of the primal water in this Homeric creation myth.

But the most complete and important Greek version of the creation myth comes from the Greek poet Hesiod (ca. seventh century BC), in a long mythological poem he wrote called the *Theogony*. Some important details are added in another poem by Hesiod called *Works and Days*. Most scholars consider Hesiod's account to be the classic Greek version. The rest of this chapter will focus on Hesiod's account of the origin of the universe, the gods, and human beings.

Remember, a *Theogony* story primarily tells the "birth of the gods" and offers a divine genealogy of how the gods came into existence.

Hesiod's *Theogony*

The purpose of the *Theogony* is to provide a divine genealogy.
The major theme of the *Theogony* is to show how order comes out of conflict.
The main focus of the story is the primacy of rule of the great god Zeus.

Hesiod begins his story by calling on the Muses to help him tell the tale of how the gods came into being (*Theogony* 1–115). This long invocation of the Muses indicates the enormity of the poetic task at hand and how much help Hesiod will need in narrating the story of the *Theogony*.

Who are the Muses? The Muses are the nine lovely daughters of the great god, Zeus. Their mother is Mnemosyne, the goddess of memory. The Muses are the goddesses of the various arts, and they represent the ultimate source of artistic and intellectual inspiration. The Muses inspire artists and writers in their crafts. Some people believe that the Muses may have originally been fountain spirits, with the idea being that they give something like a gush of artistic creativity into the willing artist.

Mne(mo)- in the English Language

A *mnemonic device* helps you remember something.
When you have *amnesia*, you have no memory of anything.
Amnesty is an official act of forgetting, or pardon.

Hesiod gives us a beautiful description of the Muses' birth and their graceful dancing and singing. Then he describes how the Muses appear to him and inspire him to reveal the truthful account of the genesis of the gods. The Muses grant Hesiod divine ability and tell him what he must do in his poem: above all he must exalt their father, Zeus.

A Beautiful Allegory

Memory (Mnemosyne) + Divine Authority (Zeus) = Artistic Inspiration (Muses)

Hesiod names all nine Muses: Cleio, Euterpe, Thaleia, Melpomene, Terpsichore, Erato, Polyhymnia, Urania, and Calliope.

THE FIRST PRINCIPLES

In his genealogical account, Hesiod begins by outlining four important principles that come before all other beings (*Theogony* 116–122).

1. Chaos

"First Chaos came into being." What is meant by *Chaos* in Hesiod's story? The word *chaos* in Greek means "space, or yawning void," and is related to the word *chasm*, as in a big canyon or ravine. Although we can't be exactly sure what Hesiod meant by *Chaos*, it is clear that it is an explanatory concept or first principle, and not necessarily "disorder," as in the modern meaning of the word. It most likely means just a big open space.

2. Gaia = Earth

Next comes Gaia, also known as Ge, the Earth. She is the primordial mother of all living things. She is described as "broad-breasted" and is called "the secure place of all things." It is not clear whether Gaia comes out of Chaos as offspring, but it seems more likely that she just comes next, as an equal principle.

3. Tartaros = Pit of the Underworld

Next comes Tartaros, a dark place already figured as a pit deep in the Earth. We will return to a discussion of Tartaros when we visit the Underworld (in Chapter 14), but its presence here as one of the first principles may indicate that Hesiod wanted to give a moral dimension to his story by mentioning up front this notorious place of punishment.

4. Eros = Sexual Desire

Next comes Eros, who is called "the most beautiful among the immortal gods." Hesiod describes how Eros works on our minds and bodies to bend us to his will. Eros explains the existence of sexual attraction. Notice that Eros is one of the first principles: the force of sexual desire is seen as a cosmic power. Why do we need Eros now? Eros, the force of procreation, is the basis of Hesiod's genealogical model. We need Eros now to make sure all the divine beings are born!

GAIA AND OURANOS = THE SACRED MARRIAGE

After Hesiod lays the groundwork with his first four principles, he turns his focus to Gaia, the primordial mother Earth. Notice that from here on, the story tells of gods who are more fleshed out and personified: they "marry," "conceive," and "give birth."

Gaia is considered the oldest Greek god, and one of the most essential Greek deities. She signifies the importance of the idea of the primal female. She represents the power of fertility, reproduction, and procreation. She is the great giver and supporter of all things.

Gaia is so powerful that her first act is to produce her own consort, or husband, Ouranos, the sky, or heaven (*Theogony* 126–128). The birth of Ouranos from Gaia suggests the original separation of these two elements, which visibly interact whenever one gazes out on the horizon. He emerges from Mother Earth "as an equal to her," and she produces him for a specific purpose, "that he may cover her all around and be a secure place for the blessed gods." So, while Gaia is the source, Ouranos is born to be her equal partner.

Note that Gaia produces Ouranos without any sexual activity.
This process is called *parthenogenesis,* meaning "maiden birth."

Now Gaia, the primal female, goddess of the Earth and fertility, joins in sweet love with her husband, Ouranos, the primal male, sky god and symbol of the heavens. Mother Earth is covered by her husband, Father Sky, who lays himself upon her, as he rains down and impregnates her receptive body. The union is a fundamental allegory for the process of agriculture, which was a vital concern and source of wonder for people of ancient cultures everywhere. The worship of Earth and sky goes back to very early times.

This personification of Earth as the female/mother goddess and sky as the male/father god, and their joining together in physical lovemaking, is an essential, widespread, and re-curring theme in Greek mythology. This motif is called the *sacred marriage*, or in Greek, the *hieros gamos*. We will see this motif recur many times in the depiction of male sky gods and their interactions with the many female divinities who represent the basic power of fertility, procreation, and motherhood.

Sacred Marriage = *Hieros Gamos*

Father Sky showers Mother Earth with his love.

The Children of Gaia and Ouranos

The union of Mother Earth and Father Sky now produces three sets of offspring (*Theogony* 132–153).

First are the twelve beautiful Titans (in order of birth): Oceanos, Coeos, Crios, Hyperion, Iapetos, Theia, Rhea, Themis, Mnemosyne, Phoebe, Tethys, and (the last-born) Cronos.

Next come two sets of monsters:

- The three Cyclopes ("Circle-Eyes"): Brontes, Steropes, and Arges.
- The three Hecatoncheires ("Hundred-Arms"): Cottos, Briareos, and Gyes.

Who are the Titans? The Titans are mainly to be considered as representing the di-vine aspects of various natural phenomena, as we have already seen with Oceanos, who represents the stream of water surrounding the disc of the Earth. Note how the Titans are often spoken of in male-female pairs—such as Oceanos and his sister-wife, Tethys—and these couplings produce offspring who play major roles in Greek mythology. So, while the Titans don't have many stories associated with themselves, we can trace most Greek deities back to an original Titan. Indeed, most of the Titans give birth to very important offspring, and we shall meet many of them in future chapters during our journey through

Greek mythology. Thus, the Titans are considered significant as the generation before the great Olympian gods (more on them later).

Trouble in the Earth-Sky Household

Hesiod continues the *Theogony* story by describing how Ouranos hated his offspring and, as each one was born, he shoved them back inside Gaia. This greatly upset Mother Earth: she groans in pain and anger, and plans her revenge against her cruel husband. Gaia creates the element of *adamant*, a mythical metal of incredible hardness, and from it fashions a sickle, a curved sword (often used as an agricultural implement to harvest grain). She asks all of her children to help her execute her vengeance plan, but none had the courage to help her, except her youngest Titan son, Cronos, who hated his father ever since birth. Gaia happily gives him the sickle and hides him in an ambush. That night, when Ouranos spreads himself upon Gaia to make love to her, Cronos leaps out of the ambush and cuts off the genitals of Ouranos, flinging them away (*Theogony* 154–182).

The castration of Ouranos is the primeval crime of Greek mythology, and it reflects a whole range of deep, unconscious human desires, feelings that are at the same time sexual, social, familial, and political. Not surprisingly, there are many complex Freudian interpretations of this myth. From the father who is jealous of his children and the affection his wife lavishes on them; to the mother who manipulates her sexuality as well as the devotion of her youngest child in her marital conflict with her husband, the child's father; to the son who wants to take his father's place in his mother's affections and the hierarchy of the family household—this is truly an Oedipal triangle many generations of "myth time" before Oedipus!

Also at work in this story is the Freudian "castration complex," where the male has an unconscious fear of being deprived of his sexual potency due to a sense of guilt over his repressed sexual desires. Ouranos gets rid of his children because he fears their potential power, and rightly so: Cronos not only literally deprives him of his sexual potency (by cutting off his genitals), but he also takes away his father's status as the supreme sky god. It is no mere detail that Ouranos is conquered when he is about to make love to Gaia: that moment of the expression of male power becomes the moment of his greatest vulnerability. The son whom he feared achieves both sexual and political power, and total freedom, by removing his father-rival with a clean slice, as he throws his father's power away.

> As a political allegory, the story of Cronos is an example of the *succession motif*, in which the younger god conquers the older one and assumes his power.

What Happens to the Sky God's Genitals?

The severed genitals of Ouranos still contain their procreative force—they produce offspring even as they are thrown away (*Theogony* 182–206). From the cut end of the genitals, drops of blood fell upon Gaia and impregnated her, and she gave birth to the Erinyes, or Furies, who are the Greek spirits of vengeance and punishment. Here is a stark allegory: the blood from Gaia's act of revenge produces the Furies, the bloodhounds of Greek mythology who relentlessly pursue those guilty of blood crimes, especially against members of their own family (more on the Furies in later chapters).

The sky god's genitals themselves are cast upon the surging sea, where the flesh is surrounded by seafoam, in Greek called *aphros*. From this immortal mixture is born a great goddess, Aphrodite, goddess of love, beauty, peace, and smooth sailing.

Hesiod tells us she is called "foam-born," because she was born from the *aphros*.

She is called "Cythereia," because she floated past the island of Cythera.

She is called "Cypria-Born," because she was born near the island of Cyprus.

She is called "Genital-Loving," because she sprang from the sky god's genitals. (Note that this title is close to one of her more usual titles, "Laughter-Loving.")

Aphrodite is accompanied by Eros, god of desire, and Himeros, god of longing.

We will consider this mighty goddess more fully in her own chapter (Chapter 8), but for now consider the bold allegory that is manifest in this story: Aphrodite's birth from the male genitals relates to her role in sexuality and reveals her aggressive sexual nature. Also, the birth of Aphrodite is significant at this point in Hesiod's genealogical model because she signals a new, harmonious universal order where love eases the way.

But Ouranos has the last word, as he promises his Titan children that they in turn will get their just deserts (*Theogony* 207–210). This promise will come true with the rise of the great god Zeus.

On our journey through Greek mythology, let's remember these important motifs that appear in the ancient Greek cosmogony myth:

- The first principles
- The sacred marriage
- The succession motif

SOURCES FOR THIS CHAPTER

Clay, Jenny Strauss. (2003). *Hesiod's Cosmos*. Cambridge: Cambridge University Press.

Lamberton, Robert. (1988). *Hesiod*. New Haven: Yale University Press.

Lombardo, Stanley. (Trans.). (1993). *Hesiod: Works & Days, Theogony*. Indianapolis: Hackett Publishing Company.

Lombardo, Stanley. (Trans.). (1997). *Homer: Iliad*. Indianapolis: Hackett Publishing Company.

Morford, Mark P. O., and Lenardon, Robert J. (2007). *Classical Mythology*, 8th ed. Oxford: Oxford University Press.

POPULAR CULTURE REFERENCES

Television

Cosmos: A Personal Voyage (1980). PBS series hosted by Carl Sagan (13 episodes).

Online

Greek Mythology Link (www.maicar.com/GML/)

Self-Quiz for Chapter 2

1. What is a cosmogony?

   _____
   _____
   _____
   _____

2. What is a theogony?

   _____
   _____
   _____
   _____

3. What is Chaos?

   _____
   _____
   _____
   _____

4. Who is Gaia?

   _____
   _____
   _____
   _____

5. Who is Eros?

   _____
   _____
   _____
   _____

6. Who are the Muses?

_____

_____

_____

_____

7. Who is Mnemosyne?

_____

_____

_____

_____

_____

8. What is the sacred marriage?

_____

_____

_____

_____

9. How does Ouranos lose his power?

_____

_____

_____

_____

_____

10. How is Aphrodite born?

_____

_____

_____

_____

3

Upstarts: Prometheus and Pandora

As we continue along our journey through Greek mythology, let's consider how the Greek creation myth explores the following themes:

- The succession motif
- The sacred marriage between Earth and sky
- Divine conflicts in heaven
- Rebellions vs. the divine order

In this chapter, we will explore how these themes appear in the narrative of the rise of the great god Zeus, especially the succession motif. Just as Cronos overcomes his father, Ouranos, by castrating him with a sickle, in turn, Zeus will overcome his father, Cronos, after a series of long wars in heaven. Both Ouranos and Cronos fear being overthrown by their children, and both systematically attempt to destroy their children at birth. Both are ultimately defeated when alliances are formed between their wives and children— that is, the mothers (and grandmother) join with the children against the fathers.

So let's investigate the rise of Cronos to supreme god; the conflict between Cronos and his children; the struggle of Zeus against his father, Cronos; and the rebellion against Zeus of the god Prometheus, along with the tale of Pandora, the first woman.

CRONOS AND RHEA

After he overthrows his father, Cronos, the youngest male Titan, now takes supreme rule of heaven. Cronos assumes his father's role as the sky god in charge of the universe. As the sky god, Cronos must have a consort: so he takes as his wife Rhea, his Titan sister. Here we have another incarnation of the sacred union of an Earth goddess and a sky god.

The Titans: Cronos and Rhea

Sacred Marriage = Version 2.0

Cronos and Rhea essentially take over the divine rulership roles of their parents, Ouranos and Gaia, but they have some more specific aspects to them as well.

Cronos (in Roman mythology = Saturn) is depicted as a gloomy old man, carrying the curved sickle he used in his infamous punishment of his father. In appearance he is much like our notion of the "Grim Reaper," a somber, dark-robed figure who foreshadows the coming of death. Sometimes his name is mistakenly associated with the Greek concept of *chronos*, or "time," so he is also seen as "Father Time"—this is especially true at the end of the year, when we see the elderly, sad "Old Year" going out, and the cheeky baby "New Year" coming in. However he is depicted, Cronos represents the transitional stage in Greek mythological divine power between his father, Ouranos, and his son, Zeus.

Rhea is the Titan Earth Mother, and she basically takes over the role of the supreme Greek goddess. She is another manifestation of the great goddess of fertility and procreation. Rhea is important as the mother of the six original Olympian gods.

TROUBLE IN THE TITAN HOUSEHOLD

As Hesiod relates the story, Cronos as a parent fundamentally reenacts his own father's brutality toward his children (*Theogony* 453–467). After their marriage, Rhea, like a good fertility goddess, begins to have babies. She gives birth to the first five Olympians (in the following order): Hestia, Demeter, Hera, Hades, and Poseidon.

But Cronus was afraid of his children, since he knew well that he was destined to be conquered by his own child. So, not wanting to lose his status as supreme god, Cronos swallows each one of his children as it is born. The act of swallowing his five infants gives rise to the Freudian interpretation of the smothering parent who suffocates his children with his overwhelming attentions. But the most obvious interpretation is that Cronos feared the inevitable repetition of the succession motif.

Rhea, like her mother Gaia before her, is terribly upset by her husband's brutal treatment of their children. When she finds herself pregnant for the sixth time, she decides to take action (*Theogony* 468–491). Rhea goes to her parents for help in devising a scheme to trick Cronos—one can only imagine what that family gathering was like! Gaia and Ouranos know that Cronos is destined to fall, so they instruct their daughter to go to the island of Crete to give birth to her sixth child in secret. And Gaia takes a stone wrapped in diapers and gives it to Cronos, who swallows it whole, not knowing that his last and most important child is being born in secrecy and safety on the island of Crete.

Baby Zeus is born in a secret cave on the island of Crete, surrounded by protective guardians and watched over by his grandmother, Gaia. He is tended by local nymphs, and nursed with the milk from a magic goat named Amaltheia. In the story of Zeus' babyhood, we see the first expression of the *divine child motif*, which will appear many times during our journey through Greek mythology.

The Divine Child Motif

In this recurring motif, a baby god or hero
who is in danger from outside forces
grows up in safety close to nature
and goes on to achieve great things.

ZEUS' RISE TO POWER

When young Zeus has grown to manhood, he sets out to depose his father, Cronos. He is helped by his mother, Rhea, and his grandmother, Gaia, who tricks Cronos into vomiting up the five original Olympians, who now are "reborn" from their father in reverse order: Poseidon, Hades, Hera, Demeter, and Hestia. Cronos also vomits up the stone that Gaia used to trick him when Zeus was born: Hesiod tells us that Zeus placed the stone as a sacred item in the shrine at Delphi (*Theogony* 498–500), which was later seen by ancient tourists who visited the oracle there.

The five brothers and sisters of Zeus, the original Olympians, now join with Zeus to do battle against Cronos and the Titans. Zeus also sets free from the Earth his father's brothers, the Cyclopes, who are so grateful for their freedom that they forge for Zeus his signature weapons of thunderbolts and lightning (*Theogony* 501–506). As the supreme sky god, Zeus imposes order with his powerful thunderbolt and lightning.

Succession Myth = New Supreme Being Conquers Old One

Zeus must now overcome his father, Cronos, as he rises to
power as the new sky god.
Zeus must bring order to a disordered universe.

REBELLION VS. ZEUS: PROMETHEUS

Before the Olympian family can be established under its new supreme head, Zeus must face a series of challenges and threats to his nascent authority. Since Zeus is such an important god, not surprisingly, there are many versions in Greek mythology of these struggles for leadership in heaven, and these divine conflicts are not always carefully arranged in precise "myth time" order. So let us begin where Hesiod does, with the rebellion of Prometheus. (We will return to the battle against Cronos and the Titans in the next chapter).

In Hesiod's narrative of the tale, Prometheus engages in a colossal struggle against Zeus, while the poor human race gets stuck in the middle and pays a terrible price as "collateral damage" in the divine conflict (*Theogony* 507–616). The tale of Prometheus is a central feature of Hesiod's account—note the emphasis on the ruling command of Zeus.

Prometheus, whose name means "Fore-thinker," is the son of the Titan Iapetos; his mother is either the Titaness Themis, or Clymene, an Oceanid (daughter of the Titan Oceanos), so he is "Titan" on both sides. As the story goes, Prometheus was very fond of human beings, and felt compassion toward them when they sacrificed their best cuts of meat in their worship of the Greek gods. So, he tricks Zeus into accepting the inferior portion of the sacrificial offering. First he slaughtered an ox, and divided it into two parts: he wrapped the good flesh in the ox's hide, and then he took the bones and wrapped them up in the appetizing white fat. Prometheus wanted the poor, hungry humans to keep the better portion of the meat hidden in the ox hide. Zeus, being omniscient, knew he was being deceived, but he chose the fatty portion anyway, and he became enraged that Prometheus would try such a trick on him.

The myth of Prometheus tricking Zeus with the sacrifice is an *aetiological* myth, since it provides the cause or explanation for the way humans sacrifice to the gods. It also can be called a *charter* myth, in that it charts the origin of the human custom of sacrifice. Food was very scarce in the ancient Greek world, so when people sacrificed to the gods, they would keep the meat for themselves and burn the white fat as an offering to the gods—the greasy, delicious-smelling smoke would curl up to heaven and please the gods.

> Prometheus tricks Zeus in the sacrifice—this is an
> *aetiological*/charter myth to explain ritual of sacrifice.
> Religious Sacrifice = Barbecue Time!

But Zeus was still angry, so he decided to take the gift of fire away from human beings. Prometheus sees the wretched humans shivering in the dark, eating their food cold, and he feels bad for them. So he goes up to heaven and steals fire, hiding it in a hollow fennel-stalk with a wick tucked inside, and gives fire back to humans.

Symbolism of Fire

The notion that fire is a gift from the gods and must be stolen away from heaven shows that fire is considered divine, something that belongs in heaven and not necessarily on Earth. Fire is a symbol of wisdom, the arts and sciences, because it gives the basis for material culture: warmth, light, cooking, working with metals. Fire is a powerful symbol of civilization, because it grants dominion over harsh nature. Fire gives humans the power to control the cold, dark natural forces. Fire is a great gift to humans.

Zeus realizes that it is dangerous to the gods if humans possess the power of fire, because it *narrows the gap* between gods and humans: fire makes humans godlike!

Prometheus is probably in origin a fire god, as well as a culture god, the deity who brings civilization in the form of all the arts and sciences to human beings. Although he was not formally worshipped by the ancient Greeks, Prometheus was always very popular as a folk hero, a patron of the "little guy," and a friend to humans. Prometheus is the supreme Jungian archetype of the divine trickster figure, the clever hero, who always has his wits about him and knows all the right strategies.

Archetype of the Clever Hero or Trickster

Characters fitting this archetype include Prometheus, Hermes, Odysseus, and the Native American Coyote.

Contemporary pop-culture clever heroes include
the Professor on *Gilligan's Island* and
Angus "Mac" MacGyver on *MacGyver*.

Punishment of Prometheus

The story of Prometheus sounds positive, since he is a great benefactor to human beings. But the consequences of Prometheus' major help to humans are readily apparent in Hesiod's account of the tale. Because of his supreme trickery, Prometheus is severely punished by Zeus. The great god Zeus chains Prometheus to a rock high up in the Caucasus Mountains, where every day an eagle comes and eats away Prometheus' liver—since Prometheus is divine, his liver grows back every night, and the eagle comes back the next day and eats it again.

The suffering of the archetypal culture hero is a common motif in Greek mythology, and occurs in other myth systems as well. The culture hero is sometimes seen as a "scapegoat" figure, in that he takes on the misery so humans don't have to suffer.

The suffering motif is tied to the motif of punishment
against those who commit acts of audacity, or *hubris*.

The theme of punishment for acts of *hubris* is a major aspect of myth, and we shall come across this motif many times during our journey through Greek mythology (see especially Chapter 13). Every trick or scheme or attempt to challenge the gods brings with it a compensating punishment, to the perpetrator of the *hubris* and often those around him as well. This "double-barreled" punishment is what happens in the Prometheus story.

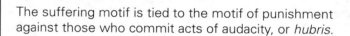 THE CREATION OF PANDORA

Hesiod tells us that Zeus was so angry that he immediately contrived "an evil thing" for human beings in exchange for their possession of fire. Zeus orders his son, Hephaestus, the blacksmith god, to fashion out of earth and water the figure of a maiden, the first woman, who is named Pandora. Hesiod tells the story at *Theogony* 570–616, and another version with some significant details, including her name and the details about her extraordinary jar, is at *Works and Days* 47–105.

Pandora is created out of the Earth, and she represents another aspect of the female fertility goddess. Her name means "All Gifts"—this may signify her origin as an Earth goddess, the "all-*giving*" deity who gives her bounty to the world. Hesiod also explains her name as the one who "*receives* all gifts," since each one of the Greek gods gives her some trait or attribute to make her beautiful, alluring, skillful, intelligent, and curious, but she is also made to be devious, greedy, and painfully seductive.

> Zeus promises Pandora will be
> "an evil thing men take pleasure in embracing" (*Works and Days* 58).

No matter how beautiful she is, the lovely, clever, demanding Pandora is intended as a punishment from Zeus, something to bring humans down, just as fire had raised them up. To make matters worse, Zeus gives Pandora as a gift to Epimetheus, Prometheus' dim-witted brother, whose name means "After-thinker." Zeus makes sure that Epimetheus wouldn't know what hit him, even though he is warned by his brother, Prometheus, not to accept gifts from Zeus—as the saying goes, hindsight is 20/20. Like the misleading sacrificial portion chosen by Zeus, where the appetizing outside hid an inedible interior, according to Hesiod's account, Pandora looks deceptively good on the outside, but she hides something not so good on the inside.

Pandora's Jar

The first woman brings with her a jar, in Greek called a *pithos*, a large earthenware storage vessel for oil or wine. The word *pithos* later (probably in medieval times) became confused with the Greek word for box, a *pyxis*, and so the popular idea of "Pandora's box" was born. Whether jar or box, the symbolism is the same—the container belonging to Pandora represents the capacity of the female to produce life, with its complex mixture of blessings and evils. The jar/box is a symbol of the female womb, the power of conception and procreation, and the irresistible lure toward sexual knowledge.

Aetiological Myth

In Hesiod's account, when Pandora opens her jar, out fly all the pains and evils, the *kaka* or "bad stuff" (in Greek) of the world. The myth of Pandora's jar provides an *aetiology*, or explanation, for the existence of "bad stuff" in the world. But one element is stopped from emerging from the jar into the world. At the lip of the jar, only the winged goddess Hope remained in the house with humans. The status of Hope in the story is utterly ambiguous: is Hope a bad thing like the rest of the jar's contents, because it can give humans false expectations, deluding us into "false hopes"? Or is it a good thing, because Hope inspires us to get through the daily grind of our lives? Is Hope a blessing or a curse? Good or bad, Hope is the only thing humans can still control.

Themes in the Pandora Story

The Greek Pandora is similar to the archetypal "Eve" figure familiar from the Judaeo-Christian biblical tradition and to many other primal female figures from other myth systems. In these narratives, the first female is depicted as the origin or cause of a new phase of human life, a departure from childlike innocence and a "growing up" into human adulthood. This new phase of human existence is filled with a mixture of blessings and evils. This includes a new knowledge of sexual desire, for the woman's beauty and intelligence kindles sexual desire in humans for the first time. Sexuality is seen as both positive and negative: procreation is good and pleasurable, but sexual relationships are full of troubles, and life itself—which woman creates—is full of hardships. The first woman initiates this wisdom about life and an accompanying loss of innocence, which is often in these myths blamed for an exile from paradise, also known as the primal fall.

> The first woman initiates knowledge and wisdom, but sometimes "ignorance is bliss."
> With the creation of woman, the human race "grows up" and experiences the loss of childlike innocence.

Theme of New Regime of Zeus

Hesiod's account indicates that the great god Zeus must prove his leadership through a series of challenges (and we shall see more of these tests in the next chapter). The story of Prometheus also suggests that at this early stage of Zeus' reign, he was afraid, like his grandfather and father before him, of the succession threat: Zeus is justifiably fearful that he might suffer the same fate as Ouranos and Cronos and be overthrown by a younger god. The glorious figure of the Titan Prometheus would be enough to scare any new divine leader! Indeed, in a later version of the myth, we are told that the "Fore-thinker" knew a shocking secret that put Zeus in great danger: Prometheus knew that the beautiful sea goddess Thetis was destined to have a child greater than its father, yet he doesn't warn Zeus to avoid her in his erotic pursuits. So that is why Zeus reacts so strongly in this situation: his very survival depends on his ability to control the defiant, brilliant Prometheus.

> Zeus imposes order on the world through just punishment.
> Zeus also gains experience, wisdom, and maturity through challenges and trials.

▬ THE AGES OF HUMANKIND

The ancient Greeks had several different stories about how human beings were created and came into existence. So although we have heard Hesiod's account of the creation of the first woman, Pandora, there is no fixed tale in Greek mythology about the creation of men, or human beings in general. Some accounts say that Zeus created humans, some say that Prometheus created them, and some accounts say gods and humans are born from the same source (as Hesiod suggests, *Works and Days* 108). Perhaps the lack of a fixed tale indicates that the ancient Greeks assumed some kind of correlation or even parity in the existence of immortals and mortals.

But Hesiod does give an account of the Ages of Humankind (*Works and Days* 106–201). Hesiod says there are five distinct stages of human history, which includes the traditional four "metallic" ages: Gold, Silver, Bronze, and Iron; then between the last two metallic ages, Hesiod intriguingly inserts a fifth age, the Age of Heroes. This addition reflects Hesiod's awareness of history, and demonstrates the frequent presence of the historical element in Greek mythology (as we discussed in Chapter 1). Hesiod describes each age in the distant past in mythological terms down to the Bronze Age, which historically ended with a series of military conflicts around the Mediterranean area, perhaps even including the Trojan War. So Hesiod inserts an Age of Heroes to reflect that time of those famous warriors involved in battles and raids. Then he reaches his own time, the Iron Age, which he describes as a very difficult and brutal time for humans.

Theme of Human Decline

Note the emphasis on the progressive deterioration of the human race, where each age gets a little worse than the previous one. In Hesiod's account, this decline is only temporarily stopped by the anomalous Age of Heroes. Like many cultures, the ancient Greeks looked back with fascination upon a legendary Golden Age, a time of greatness when humans mingled with the gods in a true paradise. Even today, people like to speak of "the good old days," when things were a whole lot better.

Hesiod's bleak vision of the current Iron Age proves humans need Zeus to impose order on the world of human disorder.

▄▄▄ THE FLOOD MYTH: DEUCALION AND PYRRHA

The theme of a new world order coming out of disorder and destruction appears again in the myth of the flood. As we will see, the Greek flood myth has much in common with the biblical story of Noah's Ark. Almost every culture on the face of the planet has its own flood myth, which indicates that this is a very important shared archetype. The flood is a universal symbol of the cycle of death and rebirth, the idea of total destruction that precedes new creation, and the notion of purification by water.

The flood myth archetype has a dual nature:

Death = the flood destroys old forms.

Life = the flood represents the rebirth of new forms.

There is also a personal dimension of flood myths that corresponds to the purification or baptism rituals found in many ancient and modern religions. The word "baptism" comes from the Greek word *baptizō*, which means "to immerse in water." The flood is a larger cultural version of what happens to an individual during religious baptism or purification by water. In the rite of baptism, the water cleanses the soul of its old patterns, sins, and troubles, and from the water a new soul is "born again" to a new life.

In the flood myth, there is always a central hero figure who is spared destruction, who survives the deluge—sometimes with his family and friends (and pets)—and who emerges from the waters into a brand new existence. The hero of the flood myth represents the hope for a new beginning that all humans seek. The flood myth reminds us that all life depends on death, that the one is tied to other in an inexorable cycle.

The Greek flood myth features Deucalion, the son of Prometheus, and his wife, Pyrrha, the daughter of Epimetheus and Pandora. Deucalion and Pyrrha were warned by Prometheus that Zeus was angry at the impiety of humans and planned to destroy and cleanse the entire human race with a colossal flood. Like the biblical story of Noah, the Greek flood myth emphasizes the idea of the sinfulness of humanity, and the fact that the flood is a divine punishment, a harsh but eventually constructive act of God.

In the Greek version, Zeus gathers all his thunder clouds and sends storms and torrents of rain down on the world, in order to destroy the world and "wipe the slate clean." All living things on Earth—people, animals, plants—drowned or starved as a result, except for Deucalion and Pyrrha, who were warned by Prometheus to save themselves and their family in a boat. The god Zeus allowed them to be spared because they were the most pious of human beings. After the flood waters receded, Deucalion and Pyrrha land their boat atop Mt. Parnassus at the shrine of the great Titan goddess, Themis, who instructed them to repopulate the empty Earth. The couple picked up stones and tossed them over their shoulders: from Deucalion's stones came a new race of rock-solid men, and from Pyrrha's stones came a new race of strong women.

There is a political *aetiology* in this myth: the son of Deucalion and Pyrrha, Hellen, gives his name to the Greek people, as they call themselves *Hellenes* and their country is called *Hellas*; and their grandsons and great-grandsons give their names to the various branches of the historical tribes of ancient Greece.

An *Allegory* in the Flood Myth

The boat is like the mother's womb from which
a new age of humanity is born.

 On our journey through Greek mythology, let's keep in mind the following themes and motifs as we follow the rise of Zeus and the formation of the Olympian circle:

- Conflicts in heaven
- The succession motif
- The divine child motif
- Theme of punishment
- Order comes from disorder

▇▇ SOURCES FOR THIS CHAPTER

Dougherty, Carol. (2006). *Prometheus*. In the series *Gods and Heroes of the Ancient World*. London and New York: Routledge.

Dundes, Alan. (Ed.). (1988). *The Flood Myth*. Berkeley: University of California Press.

Kerényi, Karl. (1997). *Prometheus: Archetypal Image of Human Existence*. Trans. by Ralph Manheim. Princeton: Princeton University Press.

Lombardo, Stanley. (Trans.). (1993). *Hesiod: Works & Days, Theogony*. Indianapolis: Hackett Publishing Company.

Morford, Mark P. O., and Lenardon, Robert J. (2007). *Classical Mythology*, 8th ed. Oxford: Oxford University Press.

Panofsky, Dora, and Panofsky, Erwin (1991). *Pandora's Box: The Changing Aspects of a Mythical Symbol*, 3rd ed. Princeton: Princeton University Press.

Phillips, John A. (1984). *Eve: The History of an Idea*. New York: Harper & Row.

▇▇ POPULAR CULTURE REFERENCES

Film

Lara Croft Tomb Raider: The Cradle of Life (2003). Director: Jan de Bont.
Evan Almighty (2007). Director: Tom Shadyac.

Television

Hercules and the Circle of Fire (1994). Director: Doug Lefler.
Xena: Warrior Princess (1995). Syndicated series.
    Season 1, Episode 4: "Cradle of Hope."
    Season 1, Episode 7: "The Titans."
    Season 1, Episode 8: "Prometheus."
Mystery of the Megaflood (2005). NOVA series, PBS.

Online

Greek Mythology Link (www.maicar.com/GML)

Self-Quiz for Chapter 3

1. Who are Cronos and Rhea?

   _____

   _____

   _____

   _____

2. How is Zeus born?

   _____

   _____

   _____

   _____

   _____

3. What is the divine child motif?

   _____

   _____

   _____

4. Who is Prometheus?

   _____

   _____

   _____

   _____

5. How does Prometheus trick Zeus?

   _____

   _____

   _____

6. How does Zeus punish Prometheus?

_____

_____

_____

_____

7. Who is Pandora?

_____

_____

_____

_____

_____

_____

8. What is the symbolism of Pandora's jar?

_____

_____

_____

_____

9. What are the Five Ages of humankind?

_____

_____

_____

_____

_____

10. Who are Deucalion and Pyrrha?

_____

_____

_____

_____

4

The Olympian Circle

Let's continue on our journey through Greek mythology, and let's follow the early career of Zeus as he rises to be the supreme lord of the universe, and gathers around him the group of gods known as the Olympian circle. Keep these key themes in mind:

- New regime of Zeus
- Formation of the Olympian circle
- Victory of order over disorder

ZEUS VS. THE TITANS

Just as Zeus faced the rebellion of Prometheus, now he must face several other conflicts to prove himself the supreme leader of the gods. In his account, Hesiod next narrates the struggle of Zeus and his allies against the Titans, the first offspring of Ouranos, led by the youngest male Titan, Cronos, in an epic war that lasted ten years (*Theogony* 629–735). Zeus and his brothers and sisters fought from Mt. Olympus— hence comes the term "Olympians"—while Cronos and his allies fought from Mt. Orthrys.

Battle vs. Titans = *Titanomachy*
machos = Greek word for "battle"

Zeus sets free from imprisonment under the Earth his father's brothers, the Cyclopes, who forge for him the thunderbolt and lightning, Zeus' signature weapons; and he also releases the Hecatoncheires, whose hundred-armed missile power Zeus harnesses in the fierce battle against the Titans.

After the ten-year battle, Zeus and the Olympians are triumphant over the Titans. The rebel Titans are punished by being imprisoned in Tartaros, the deep, dark pit of the Underworld, where they are guarded by the Hecatoncheires. An important leader on the Titan side was Atlas, brother of Prometheus, who receives a special punishment: Atlas is punished with having to hold up the entire world!

"Atlas" in Contemporary Language

An *atlas* is a volume or collection of maps.
An *atlas* "supports" the geography of the world.

◼ REBELLION OF THE GIANTS

After the *Titanomachy*, Zeus and the Olympians have to face the rebellion of the Giants, the monstrous offspring of Mother Earth, Gaia, who were also known as the *Gegeneis*, "Earth-born Ones." There are many different versions of this story in Greek mythology, and the depiction of the struggle of the Olympians against the Giants was a very popular visual theme in ancient Greek art and architecture. The image of the beautiful Olympians battling with and eventually conquering the hideous Giants adorned numerous temples throughout the Greek-speaking world.

Battle vs. Giants = *Gigantomachy*

The Titans and Giants are often confused in the traditional tales of Greek mythology: both are seen as monstrous creatures born from Mother Earth who set out to depose the brilliant Olympian gods and who suffer punishment as a result. Like the Titans, the Giants are punished by being stuck underground, and they are usually described as located underneath mountains in volcanic regions around the Mediterranean.

◼ ZEUS: DRAGON-SLAYER

Hesiod tells us that Zeus had only one more battle to fight before he could attain supreme power: he had to defeat the dragon-monster, Typhon, also known as Typhoeus (*Theogony* 820–880). Typhon was the love-child of Gaia and Tartaros, and he is the last-born child of Mother Earth. Typhon is a terrible dragon-monster, with a hundred snaky heads that flash burning fire, and he roared and barked like a menagerie of wild animals. Hesiod describes how Zeus and Typhon fought a violent battle, shaking and scorching the Earth, until Zeus zapped him with a thunderbolt and burned all his snaky heads. Like other rebels against Zeus, Typhon is imprisoned beneath the Earth, either in Tartaros (in Hesiod's account), or underneath a volcano, Mt. Aetna, in Sicily (in later versions).

Themes in the Typhon Story

In this myth, Zeus achieves his position as the supreme god by performing an archetypal feat: the slaying of a dragon-monster. In the myth systems of many cultures, the greatest god or hero performs this symbolic feat in order to attain high status and various rewards. The dragon-monster represents the powers of monstrosity, savagery, and disorder, while the god-hero's victory over the dragon-monster proves the superiority of civilization, harmony, and order. We shall come across this supremely important theme many times in our journey through Greek mythology.

Archetypal Dragon-Slayers

Zeus vs. Typhon
Apollo vs. Python
Herakles vs. Hydra, and Ladon
Marduk vs. Tiamat
Siegfried vs. the Dragon
St. George vs. the Dragon
   (Great Hero/Patron Saint of England)

As we proceed along our journey through Greek mythology, let's keep in mind these themes and motifs intrinsic in the character and career of the great god Zeus.

- The divine child motif = special protection of young god/hero
- The succession myth = pattern of divine struggle
- Victory of order over savagery

Challenges to Zeus' Authority

Prometheus
Titans
Giants
Typhon

■ DEVELOPMENT OF THE OLYMPIAN CIRCLE

Now Zeus assumes supreme power over the universe, and he is the CEO of the world, with authority over all gods, humans, and beasts. But he does share certain powers and privileges with his family, first with his brothers and sisters, the five original Olympians, then with his numerous children as they are born. This is how the Olympian circle develops, with Zeus at the head of the circle as the patriarch. The Olympian circle is a **family** of extremely powerful deities, whose powers mostly complement each other but also sometimes come into conflict. We shall meet and get to know each one of these major Olympian gods on our journey through Greek mythology.

As his special area, Zeus takes the sky, since he is the heir to the role of supreme father and sky god, the position once held by Ouranos and then Cronos in rapid succession. Zeus' brother, Poseidon, takes the sea as his special sphere, and his brother, Hades, takes the Underworld. As we shall see, Zeus has several erotic liaisons with major and minor goddesses, but as his official wife, he takes his sister, Hera, who rules by his side as his queen (more on the first couple in the next chapter). Hesiod tells us that grandmother Gaia approves Zeus as supreme lord and the division of prerogatives (*Theogony* 883–885). Thus, the Olympian gods unite as a family, as each deity assumes certain powers and spheres of influence.

Olympian *Pantheon* = Fourteen Major Gods
Pantheon means "all (the) gods together."

Zeus and Hera
Poseidon, Hades, Demeter, Hestia
Ares, Hephaestus, Apollo, Hermes
Aphrodite, Athena, Artemis, Dionysus

Canon of twelve = only twelve official thrones on Mt. Olympus

Hades and Hestia sit elsewhere:
Hestia keeps her seat at the hearth;
Hades stays in the Underworld.

WHO ARE THE OLYMPIANS?

Let's take a look at the nature of the Olympian gods, this most powerful ruling family in Greek mythology. For the ancient Greeks, the Olympian gods have two primary roles, and these simultaneous functions are complementary to each other: the gods are both objects of devout religious worship and the featured players in the majority of the Greek myths. While most modern religions usually don't feature the god or gods they worship in stories or myths, this was generally not a problem for the ancient Greeks, who by and large accepted this coexistence in the unique nature of their Greek gods. The ancient Greeks genuinely worshipped their gods and, at the same time, enjoyed and learned from their gods' appearances in their myths.

Anthropomorphism

anthropos = human being + *morphe* = shape, form
thus, anthropomorphism = "the quality of having the shape or form of human beings"

Anthropomorphism

The ancient Greek idea of divinity is basically *anthropomorphic*—that is, the gods are thought of as being like human beings in form and character, but in real terms, they are actually *more intense than* normal human beings. The gods are bigger, faster, better-looking, and more powerful than mere humans. They are also experts at being sneaky, greedy, lustful, cruel, jealous, and vain. Like humans, they suffer guilt, physical pain, and the pangs of love. So it would be truthful to say that the Greek gods are idealized, exaggerated, or even *extreme* versions of regular humanity.

Immortality

The major difference between the Greek gods and the mere mortals they resemble yet rule over is that the gods are immortal. That is, while humans grow old, wrinkled, and weak, and eventually die, the major Greek gods remain young and beautiful forever, and they live for all eternity. Through their immortal veins flows the divine substance called *ichor*, a fluid lighter and clearer than human blood. The gods eat *ambrosia*, which literally means "immortal stuff," and they drink *nectar*, although they also like to drink wine.

Powers

The Greek gods are extremely powerful. They can be invisible or change their shape whenever they wish, and take on the guise of other gods or even mortals. As we shall see, all the major gods are associated with birds and other animals—like Zeus' eagle—that often represent them in various myths.

All the Gods Are Versatile, Powerful, Knowing

Zeus and Apollo are omniscient = "all-knowing,"
but only Zeus is omnipotent = "all-powerful."

Location

The major Greek gods live on the high peaks of Mt. Olympus, a lofty mountain that reaches up to heaven. But each god also has his or her special, favorite places throughout the world, as we shall see as we get to know each god and goddess. The gods are worshipped at their particular temples, shrines, groves, and other sacred areas, and humans honor them by building sanctuaries, carving statues of wood and stone, singing hymns, and offering sacrifices. The gods sometimes repay these rituals and services by communicating with mortals through dreams, visions, and oracles.

The ancient Greeks believed that gods and humans are inextricably bound together.
For the ancient Greeks, mythology and religion existed side by side.

CATEGORIES OF DIVINITY

As we shall see, the Olympian gods occupy the top rung of the divine hierarchy in Greek mythology. The Olympian *pantheon* was like an aristocratic family ruling over everyone else. But we shall also encounter several other categories of minor gods, nature spirits such as nymphs and satyrs, and various monsters. There is also a category of demi-gods and heroes, who are usually the offspring of one of the major gods and a mortal lover; these "mixed-race" beings, such as the great Herakles, figure prominently in hero tales.

Another category of deities holds sway in the nether regions of the Underworld, called *chthonian,* or *chthonic,* gods, from the Greek word *chthonos,* meaning "ground, earth." These powerful deities rule over the mysterious forces of death, vengeance, and punishment. We shall encounter many of these supernatural beings in our journey through Greek mythology.

The Olympian family of gods,
with Father Zeus at the top,

is like a powerful governing aristocracy.

In the next few stages of our journey through Greek mythology, we will encounter and study all of the major Olympian gods. For each one of the Olympian gods, you should be familiar with and be able to name:

- Names and titles
- Sacred places
- Attributes (items associated with the god)
- Animals, birds, trees, plants
- Parents
- Major offspring

SOURCES FOR THIS CHAPTER

Burkert, Walter. (1985). *Greek Religion.* Trans. by John Raffan. Cambridge: Harvard University Press.

Larson, Jennifer. (2001). *Greek Nymphs: Myth, Cult, Lore.* Oxford and New York: Oxford University Press.

Lombardo, Stanley. (Trans.). (1993). *Hesiod: Works & Days, Theogony.* Indianapolis: Hackett Publishing Company.

Mikalson, Jon D. (2004). *Ancient Greek Religion.* Oxford: Blackwell.

Morford, Mark P. O., and Lenardon, Robert J. (2007). *Classical Mythology,* 8th ed. Oxford: Oxford University Press.

Pedley, John. (2005). *Sanctuaries and the Sacred in the Ancient World.* Cambridge and New York: Cambridge University Press.

Price, Simon. (1999). *Religions of the Ancient Greeks*. Cambridge and New York: Cambridge University Press.

Sissa, Giulia, and Detienne, Marcel. (2000). *The Daily Life of the Greek Gods*. Trans. by Janet Lloyd. Stanford: Stanford University Press.

POPULAR CULTURE REFERENCES

Film

Dragonslayer (1981). Director: Matthew Robbins.
Clash of the Titans (1981). Director: Desmond Davis.

Online

Greek Mythology Link (www.maicar.com/GML)
Here Be Dragons (www.draconian.com)

Self-Quiz for Chapter 4

1. What is the Titanomanchy?

   _____

   _____

   _____

   _____

2. What is the Gigantomachy?

   _____

   _____

   _____

   _____

3. What happens to Atlas?

   _____

   _____

   _____

4. Who is Typhon?

   _____

   _____

   _____

   _____

5. What is a pantheon?

   _____

   _____

   _____

6. What is anthropomorphism?

_____

_____

_____

7. What flows in the gods' veins?

_____

_____

_____

_____

8. What do the gods eat?

_____

_____

_____

_____

9. What do the gods drink?

_____

_____

_____

_____

_____

10. What is meant by *chthonian* gods?

_____

_____

_____

_____

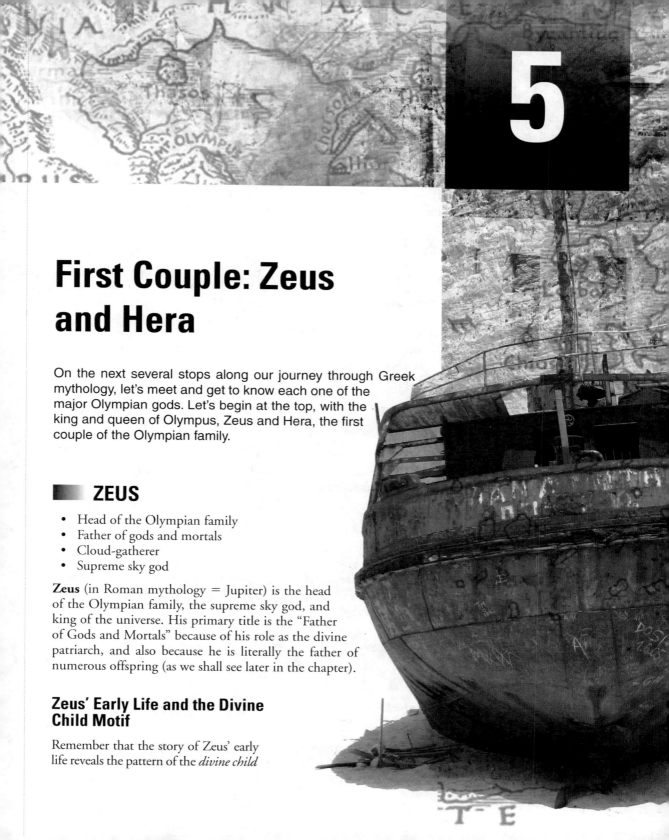

5

First Couple: Zeus and Hera

On the next several stops along our journey through Greek mythology, let's meet and get to know each one of the major Olympian gods. Let's begin at the top, with the king and queen of Olympus, Zeus and Hera, the first couple of the Olympian family.

ZEUS

- Head of the Olympian family
- Father of gods and mortals
- Cloud-gatherer
- Supreme sky god

Zeus (in Roman mythology = Jupiter) is the head of the Olympian family, the supreme sky god, and king of the universe. His primary title is the "Father of Gods and Mortals" because of his role as the divine patriarch, and also because he is literally the father of numerous offspring (as we shall see later in the chapter).

Zeus' Early Life and the Divine Child Motif

Remember that the story of Zeus' early life reveals the pattern of the *divine child motif.* This is an archetypal pattern in Greek mythology where a young god or hero is both endowed with exceptional blessings and at the same time vulnerable to great dangers. The divine child grows up close to nature and animals, receives special care and training, and finally emerges as a great god or hero who is ready to face his destiny and conquer all foes.

This is just so in Zeus' case: Baby Zeus was threatened by his father, Cronos, who voraciously swallowed all his brothers and sisters. So Zeus' mother, Rhea, and his grandmother, Gaia, devised a scheme to keep young Zeus safe in a cave on the island of Crete. There young Zeus is nurtured by a magic goat and protected by nymphs, until he can grow up and challenge his father for supremacy over the universe.

King of the Gods

Zeus is depicted as a tall, physically robust, regal, bearded man in the prime age of his life. Zeus is often shown seated on a throne, holding a scepter and/or a thunderbolt, the symbols of his divine power and influence. As king and father, Zeus is charged with protecting political and social institutions, especially those in which the male expresses his authority and control: kingdom, tribe, clan, and family. He is also charged with protecting the relationship between guests and hosts, a very significant and sacred institution in the civilization of the ancient Greeks.

Sky God

Zeus is the god of the sky, and everything that happens in the sky. He is the god of weather, rain, storms, clouds, hurricanes, tornadoes, thunder, and lightning. Zeus is called the "cloud-gatherer" because he gathers the clouds together whenever he wishes to create a storm. He is often shown about to hurl his thunderbolt, his preferred method of enforcing his divine authority and punishing rebels and scofflaws.

Aegis-Holder

Zeus is also depicted as the bearer of the sacred *aegis,* a magic shield with special protective properties. Anyone who wears the *aegis* is invulnerable to attack, as the *aegis* cannot be penetrated. The word *aegis* means "goat-skin," and originally may have been just a rustic type of cloak. Later, as we shall see (in Chapter 10), Zeus gives the magic *aegis* to his favorite daughter, the warrior-goddess Athena.

Aegis in Contemporary English Usage

"Under the *aegis*" of something or someone means under its protection or defense.

Zeus' Symbols

Zeus is primarily associated with the majestic eagle, the alpha-predator among all birds and soaring king of the skies. Like Zeus, the eagle is fierce, determined, and always in control.

Zeus is often shown with the eagle at his side, and he sometimes assumes the form of an eagle in some of his myths. He sends the eagle to punish Prometheus after the Titan's rebellion. The eagle is a symbol of strong, ruling entities throughout human history, from the Roman Empire to the United States government. Zeus is also associated with the oak tree, one of the most imposing and magnificent trees, and the strongest wood in the natural world. At his oracular shrine at Dodona in northern Greece, Zeus would deliver his divine prophecies through the rustling of the leaves of a great oak tree.

Zeus' Sacred Attributes

- Thunderbolt
- Throne and scepter
- Clouds
- Eagle
- Oak tree

Zeus' Sacred Places

Zeus' main sacred place is Olympia in southern Greece, where there was a temple and statue dedicated to the great Olympian Zeus. The sanctuary at Olympia was also the host of the ancient Olympic Games, which began in 776 BC, founded by Zeus' son, the great Greek hero Herakles. The Olympic Games celebrate the authority of Zeus and were held in his honor. Zeus also had an oracular shrine at Dodona in northern Greece.

Father Zeus

The supreme god is extremely lusty, and his frequent sexual conquests form a major recurrent theme in Greek mythology. Zeus is depicted as the idealized image of the divine lover, sexy and irresistible. Zeus mates with numerous goddesses, minor female deities, and even mortal women, and since Zeus has supreme sexual and procreative potency, he also has offspring pretty much every time he has sex. The god Zeus has legions of children. We will encounter plenty of stories about Zeus' erotic exploits and his many offspring on our journey through Greek mythology.

Sexual Promiscuity of Zeus

Zeus' erotic antics provide glorious genealogy for divine and human families.

"Zeus juice" enriches the mythological gene pool!

Zeus' Sexual Conquests

As we shall see, Zeus enjoys "role-playing" in his many erotic exploits. That is, Zeus often takes the form of animals, natural elements, and even other people when he seduces his various lovers. Perhaps this is an essential expression of his ultimate divine power, his ability to take control over any form he wishes.

Some examples of Zeus' sexual role-playing include the following myths:

- Metis and the fly (Zeus)
- Europa and the bull (Zeus)
- Leda and the swan (Zeus)
- Alkmene and her husband (Zeus)
- Danae and the "golden shower" (yes, Zeus)

Ganymede

Zeus also loved a boy, the young Trojan prince Ganymede. Zeus fell in love with the boy's youthful beauty, and so the great god assumes the form of an eagle—his sacred bird—and swoops down to Troy to abduct him. In other versions of the tale, Zeus takes the form of a whirlwind to snatch Ganymede away. Zeus takes Ganymede up to Mt. Olympus, where he keeps him by his side at all times.

The Moons of the Planet Jupiter
Named for the sky god's many lovers, the moons of the planet
Jupiter include Europa, Io, Callisto, Metis, Leda,
and Ganymede (the biggest moon).

Offspring of Zeus

Keep in mind that the theme of Zeus' sexual promiscuity is not only an entertaining part of Greek mythology, it is also a narrative construct used to enrich the genealogies of mortals and immortals. So, as we shall see throughout our journey, Zeus is father to many important gods, supernatural beings, and heroes.

The three *Moirae,* or **Fates,** are (in some versions of Greek myth) said to be the children of Zeus and the Titan goddess Themis. The Fates are originally birth spirits that influence the course of human life, and then they come to be seen as three old women who weave the destiny of each individual as if it were the "fabric" of one's life.

- Clotho = "Spinner"; she spins out the thread of a life.
- Lachesis = "Measurer"; she measures out the length of the thread.
- Atropos = "Unbending"; she snips the thread at the end of life.

Big Question in Greek Mythology
Does Zeus have ultimate say?
Or do the Fates have the "final cut"?

 HERA

- Wife of Zeus
- "First Lady" of Olympus
- Queen of the gods
- Goddess of marriage

Hera (in Roman mythology = Juno) is the wife and consort of Zeus, the queen of the Olympian family, and the personification of female social power. In classical Greek mythology, Hera's power and authority come primarily from her association with Zeus, that is, her marriage to the supreme sky god and king of the gods. Her role can be compared to that of the First Lady in the American government, who derives her power from her conjugal relationship to the president. But Hera's influence goes well beyond that, and she has her own well-developed characterization in Greek myth.

Great Goddess

Hera is associated with the city of Argos in southern Greece, and she is probably in origin a great mother goddess from that area. Hera is another manifestation of the great goddess of the Earth, and her marriage to Zeus is thus another reenactment of the sacred marriage of Earth and sky.

The Olympians, Hera and Zeus
Sacred Marriage = Version 3.0

Marriage to Zeus

In Greek myth, the story is told that Hera was reluctant to marry her brother, Zeus, and so she fended off his advances. But Zeus used one of his clever sexual role-playing tricks to deceive Hera: he came to her in the form of a little cuckoo bird, who hopped around her lap until Hera was charmed and kissed him on the beak. The story also says that her wedding night with Zeus lasted three hundred years—perhaps this number reflects the amount of time it took for the idea of the sacred marriage to achieve religious significance among the early peoples of ancient Greece.

Queen of the Gods

Hera is the highest-ranking female Olympian, and she is depicted in majestic queenly fashion. Hera is shown as a very tall, beautiful, regally robed woman in the prime age of her life. Hera is often shown seated on a throne, holding a scepter and wearing a rich crown, the symbols of her divine power and authority. As the queen and divine matriarch, Hera is charged with protecting political and social institutions that are important to women, especially those functions in which the female attains social status: queenship, marriage, household, successful childbirth, and family.

Hera's Poetic Epithets

Poetic epithets are descriptive phrases associated with certain characters in myth and epic poetry.
"Hera of the White-Arms" and "Ox-Eyed Hera"
are common epithets used to describe the queen of the gods.

Hera's Symbols

Hera is primarily associated with the peacock, the elegant and dignified bird who takes pride in his beautiful appearance, especially the brightly spotted feathers of his tail—the peacock does act a bit pompous! Hera is also associated with the cuckoo bird, as Zeus first seduced her in that guise. Another animal associated with Hera is the cow, perhaps reflecting her origins as a great mother goddess.

Goddess of Marriage

Hera's main function in Greek mythology is to protect and enforce the tradition of marriage, the social institution most important to ancient Greek women. As a goddess of civilization and order, Hera defends the rules of marriage, which is considered by many cultures to be a stabilizing force in society. Hera is associated with the wedding veil, a symbol of female chastity, as the barrier between the bride and her groom. Hera is often shown lifting her veil, to enact the moment when the bride gives herself fully to her new husband.

Modern Wedding Customs Are Very Ancient!

June (from Juno) is the favorite wedding month.

The bride wears a veil, which is lifted at the moment of marriage.

Hera's Sacred Attributes

- Crown
- Throne and scepter
- Wedding veil
- Peacock, cuckoo bird
- Cow

Hera's Sacred Places

Hera is associated with the city of Argos in the Peloponnese in southern Greece, which may also be her place of origin as a great goddess. Hera had a grand temple and sanctuary on the island of Samos in the southeastern Mediterranean Sea. She was also worshipped as the patron goddess of the magnificent city of Carthage in North Africa.

Wrath of Hera

The theme of Hera's jealousy and anger over Zeus' affairs is major motif in Greek mythology. Just as Zeus engages in many erotic exploits as part of his divine characterization, Hera reacts to his philandering with ferocious rage to defend the sanctity of marriage, her own primary sphere of influence. While she cannot strike at the all-powerful Zeus himself, Hera often strikes with cruel retribution against her husband's many mistresses and his legions of bastard offspring.

The Story of Io

One of the most prominent tales of Hera's fury over one of Zeus' love affairs is the tale of Io. The lovely Io was one of Hera's own priestesses, so Hera easily figured it out when Zeus started having an affair with her. So to protect her, Zeus changes Io into a little white cow. But he doesn't fool his wife, who asks him for the cow as a gift. Zeus couldn't say no! Hera places her faithful servant, Argus, in charge of guarding Io, so Zeus wasn't able to save his mistress. Argus was an especially good guard, as he had one hundred eyes, only fifty of which would ever go to sleep at any given time. Determined to help Io, Zeus sent his tricky son, Hermes, to tell Argus stories until he bored him to sleep. When all his eyes finally closed, Hermes killed Argus and set the little Io-cow free. Hera was enraged by the loss of her devoted servant Argus, so to commemorate his loyalty, she placed his myriad eyes on the tail of her bird, the peacock. And she sent a vicious gadfly to sting Io and chase her all the way to Egypt, where Zeus finally changed her back into a woman. Io suffers greatly at the hands of Hera's anger, but she fulfills her destiny in Egypt, as she is associated there with the goddess Isis.

Hera Represents Female Social Status

Wifehood = *not* Marital Love

Motherhood = *not* Motherly Love

OFFSPRING OF HERA AND ZEUS

As the principal couple in the Olympian version of the sacred marriage, Hera and Zeus join together in a fertile pairing, and they have four children. They have two sons, the Olympian gods Ares and Hephaestus, whom we shall meet in upcoming chapters on our journey through Greek mythology. Hera and Zeus also have two daughters, who, while they are not among the major Olympians, do have significant mythological and cultural roles:

1. **Eileithyia:** Their first daughter is Eileithyia, the goddess of successful childbirth. The ability to give birth to healthy, living children was considered by the ancient Greeks an important measure for the female social role of wifehood and motherhood. Like her mother Hera, Eileithyia protects the status of women through their ability to provide legitimate heirs and thus ensure the continuation of the family. Eileithyia is sometimes depicted as a midwife, helping women with successful childbirth.

2. **Hebe:** The second daughter of Hera and Zeus is Hebe, the goddess of youth, whose name literally means "the bloom of youth." Unlike most of the Greek gods, Hebe actually has a job: she serves as the cupbearer of the gods as they party on Mt. Olympus. We are told that Hebe gives up her job as the Olympian waitress when she marries the great hero Herakles—notice the allegory here, as the hero

attains "eternal youth" in exchange for all his labors (more in Chapter 17). After Hebe resigns, Ganymede takes over her role as divine cupbearer.

As we continue on our journey through Greek mythology, we will meet more Olympian gods and study their important myths, relations, and attributes.

The Olympian Circle
The Olympian circle is a family headed by father Zeus.

SOURCES FOR THIS CHAPTER

Dowden, Ken. (2006). *Zeus*. In the series *Gods and Heroes of the Ancient World*. London and New York: Routledge.

Leeming, David, and Page, Jake. (1994). *Goddess: Myths of the Female Divine*. Oxford and New York: Oxford University Press.

Leeming, David, and Page, Jake. (1997). *God: Myths of the Male Divine*. Oxford and New York: Oxford University Press.

Morford, Mark P. O., and Lenardon, Robert J. (2007). *Classical Mythology*, 8th ed. Oxford: Oxford University Press.

Slater, Philip E. (1992). *The Glory of Hera: Greek Mythology and the Greek Family*. Princeton: Princeton University Press.

Young, David. (2004). *A Brief History of the Olympic Games*. Oxford: Blackwell.

POPULAR CULTURE REFERENCES

Film

I Still Worship Zeus (2004). Director: Jamil Said.

Television

Xena: Warrior Princess (2000). Syndicated series. Season 5, Episode 12: "God Fearing Child."

Online

Greek Mythology Link (www.maicar.com/GML)

Self-Quiz for Chapter 5

1. What are Zeus' primary titles?

   _____
   _____
   _____
   _____

2. Where are Zeus' sacred places?

   _____
   _____
   _____
   _____
   _____

3. What is Zeus' sacred bird? tree? weapon?

   _____
   _____
   _____

4. What are Hera's primary titles?

   _____
   _____
   _____
   _____

5. Where are Hera's sacred places?

   _____
   _____
   _____

6. What is Hera's sacred bird? What other attributes are associated with Hera?

_____

_____

_____

_____

7. Who are the Moirae?

_____

_____

_____

_____

_____

_____

8. Who is Io?

_____

_____

_____

_____

_____

9. Who is Ganymede?

_____

_____

_____

_____

_____

10. Who are Eileithyia and Hebe?

_____

_____

_____

_____

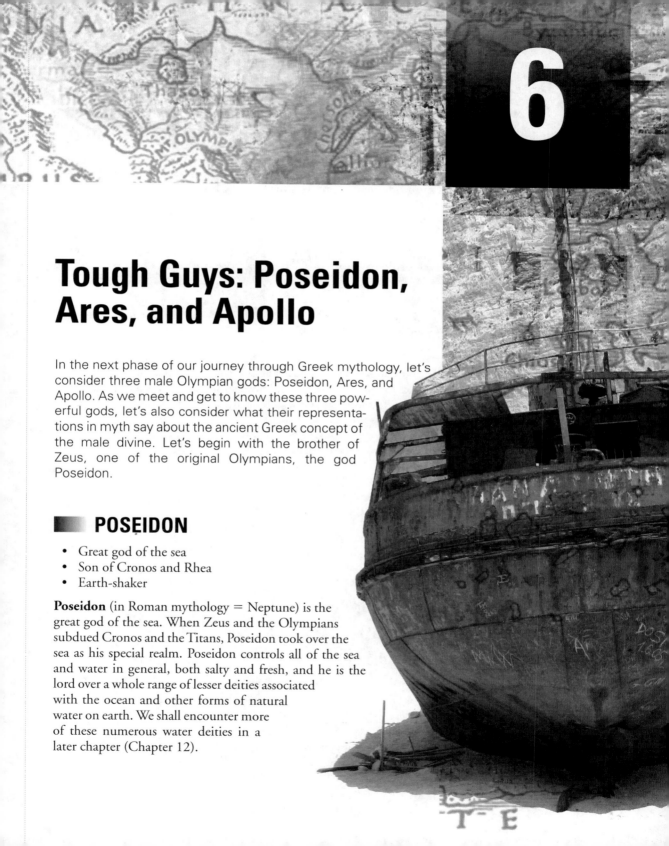

6

Tough Guys: Poseidon, Ares, and Apollo

In the next phase of our journey through Greek mythology, let's consider three male Olympian gods: Poseidon, Ares, and Apollo. As we meet and get to know these three powerful gods, let's also consider what their representations in myth say about the ancient Greek concept of the male divine. Let's begin with the brother of Zeus, one of the original Olympians, the god Poseidon.

POSEIDON

- Great god of the sea
- Son of Cronos and Rhea
- Earth-shaker

Poseidon (in Roman mythology = Neptune) is the great god of the sea. When Zeus and the Olympians subdued Cronos and the Titans, Poseidon took over the sea as his special realm. Poseidon controls all of the sea and water in general, both salty and fresh, and he is the lord over a whole range of lesser deities associated with the ocean and other forms of natural water on earth. We shall encounter more of these numerous water deities in a later chapter (Chapter 12).

God of the Sea

Poseidon is depicted as a mature, imposing, bearded god, like his brother Zeus, but Poseidon is shown to be rather rough around the edges, shaggy, even uncouth-looking. In temperament Poseidon is volatile, unpredictable, quick to rage, and dangerous, like the sea itself. Like Zeus, Poseidon is often shown seated on a throne, but he is usually under water and accompanied by fish, dolphins, and other sea creatures. His main attribute is the trident, a three-pronged fisherman's fork used for spearing fish.

Earth-Shaker

Poseidon is also the god of earthquakes, tidal waves, and tsunamis. In Greek mythology, the explosive violence of Poseidon is considered the cause of these natural disasters: he merely strikes the sea with his trident to cause the seabed to quake and huge waves to come crashing ashore, destroying everything in their path.

Poseidon's Symbols

In origin, Poseidon has many of the characteristics of a robust male fertility spirit. His association with the gushing movement of water and waves suggests that he can be seen as an emblem of male sexual force. Poseidon is primarily associated with horses and bulls, animal symbols of male strength, potency, and sexual virility. In many myths, Poseidon takes the form of a horse or a bull, or creates them at will.

Poseidon and Horses

He creates the horse
in the shape of a breaking wave.
He seduces Demeter
in the form of a stallion.

Poseidon's Sacred Attributes

- Trident
- Horse
- Bull

Amphitrite, Queen of the Sea

Poseidon marries Amphitrite, a sea goddess, daughter of the Old Man of the Sea, Nereus. She is called a *Nereid,* which means "daughter of Nereus," and we shall meet more of her kin in a later chapter. Nereids are notoriously disinclined to marry and give up their freedom, and Amphitrite is no exception. Poseidon and Amphitrite assume roles similar to that of Zeus and Hera, within their realm of the sea. Poseidon is a very lusty god, and has countless affairs with goddesses, mermaids, and sea nymphs, while Amphitrite is always expressing her anger and jealousy over his erotic adventures, and takes vengeance against his mistresses and bastard children.

> Poseidon and Amphitrite = King and Queen of the Sea

Triton

The son of Poseidon and Amphitrite is Triton, a merman with a human body above the waist and fish tail below. Triton is known as the "Trumpeter of the Sea," as he is often depicted blowing on a conch shell to summon sea creatures together.

Contest for Athens

One of the most famous myths of Poseidon is the story of his competition with the goddess Athena for the patronage of the city of Athens. The two gods meet upon the Acropolis in Athens, where a panel of citizen judges is set to rate their respective gifts to the city: whoever bestows the better gift wins the role of patron. Poseidon strikes the ground of the Acropolis with his trident, and out gushes a spring of water; but the water is salty, so Poseidon is disqualified. Athena grants the city the gift of the olive tree, and is named the clear victor. This is an *aetiological* myth, as it explains the political reality of Athena's patronage of her city, and the historical importance of the olive tree and its by-products in the economy of ancient Athens.

> On the Acropolis today, one can still see the marks of Poseidon's trident and the olive tree of Athena!

ARES

- God of war
- Son of Zeus and Hera
- Spirit of bloodlust

Ares (in Roman mythology = Mars) is the great god of war. In Greek myth, Ares is the son of Zeus and Hera. While Ares—as Mars—was a very important and revered deity in the martial culture of ancient Rome, the Greek Ares is less of a well-developed god, as he is primarily a symbol of brutal, bloody warfare. Ares is the personification of bloodlust, the desire to do battle, fight fiercely, and slaughter one's enemies.

God of War

Ares is depicted as a physically powerful man in the prime of his youth with chiseled male beauty. His primary attributes are his weapons and armor: his shield, spear, and helmet. Ares is strong, with well-built muscles, incredibly handsome, and purely masculine—in today's terms, he would be considered the peak of male *machismo*. Ares is seen as the impulsive passion of bloodlust, more of an emotion than an actual god. He is pitiless, vengeful, and fearsome, but extremely good-looking.

Ares' Sacred Attributes

- Weapons, spear
- Armor, helmet, shield

Noble Aspects of War

The ancient Greeks considered righteous conflict, strategy, and victory to be noble aspects of war.
In Greek mythology, these belong to the goddess Athena.

Ares' Sacred Places

Ares is primarily associated with northern Greece, especially Thrace, and the kingdom of Macedonia, which has a famously martial culture. Ares had a major cult in the city-state of Sparta, which also had a strongly military society. Ares can be found on all battlefields throughout the world.

Like bullies everywhere, Ares is surrounded by a posse of tough-guy companions.

Ares' Buddies

Phobos = "Fear"
Deimos = "Terror"
These names—Phobos and Deimos—are also the names of the moons of the planet Mars.
Eris = "Strife"
This spiteful goddess is sometimes his girlfriend!

Spirit of Bloodlust

The recognition that humans seem to be hard-wired to do battle and violence to their enemies is a very ancient human belief, and ancient societies, including the Greeks, often found themselves at war. The god Ares represents this drive toward violence and battle. But in Greek mythology, Ares is sometimes shown in a negative light, and he is often shown to be a poor warrior and a sore loser. Ares is seen fighting indiscriminately on either side of battle, not caring about the reasons for war, as he is merely the blind impulse of savage bloodlust. Most of the other major gods dislike and disrespect him: Ares is gloomy, brutal, bloodthirsty, and accident-prone.

Modern Expression of Ares

Road Rage!

Aphrodite and Ares

There is one Olympian goddess who enjoys the company of the *macho* warrior god: Ares is Aphrodite's favorite lover. In stark contrast to Aphrodite's crippled, soot-covered husband, Hephaestus, the blacksmith god, Ares is physically vigorous, healthy, and well-endowed. In Greek mythology, Ares and Aphrodite appear together in many stories, and they shared many joint cults and temples throughout ancient Greece. The idea seems to be that love and war are two sides of the same coin: both are passions that can enter and seize a person completely and cause one to act blindly. So while Ares is a rather low-status Olympian, his intimate association with Aphrodite, great goddess of love and beauty, shows that bloodlust can be a strong, seductive, all-encompassing power.

Ares and Aphrodite have many children.

The most famous is Eros, whose name means "sexual lust."

Love and war are two sides of the same coin.

Love is a battlefield.

▰▰ APOLLO

- God of light, the sun god
- Phoebos = "Bright One"
- God of prophecy
- God of music
- God of medicine
- Archer god, Far-striker

Apollo (in Roman Mythology = Apollo or Phoebus) is the classical Greek god of light and the sun. In intellectual terms, he is the god of the pure Greek ideals of reason, self-knowledge, and self-discipline. Apollo is one of the most important gods in the Greek pantheon, and as we will see, he has many significant titles, attributes, and spheres of influence. Apollo is depicted as a handsome young man in the youthful prime of his life, usually beardless, with long hair, sparkling eyes, and a tall, athletic body.

Birth of Apollo

Apollo is the son of the great god Zeus and the goddess Leto, who is the daughter of the Titans Coeos and Phoebe. One of the most important myths about Apollo is the story of his birth on the sacred island of Delos (as told in the *Homeric Hymn to Apollo* 1–178). As the story goes, the pregnant Leto wandered all over Greece looking for a refuge to give birth to the mighty son of Zeus. But because of Hera's jealous wrath, no place would give her shelter in her hour of need. When Leto finally comes to Delos, she promises the island everlasting fame as the sacred birthplace and sanctuary of a great god, so Delos allows her to rest there. Grasping the trunk of a palm tree, Leto gives birth to Apollo, who blesses the island with his power and glory.

Delos

Delos was an important cult site of Apollo.
Music festivals, athletic contests, and religious rituals were held in his honor.

Twin Brother of Artemis

Apollo is the twin brother of the Olympian goddess Artemis, who was born first. In some versions Artemis also is born on Delos, or in other versions, on the small island of Ortygia, near Sicily. It is said that Artemis helped her mother deliver her younger twin, Apollo, which is in keeping with her function as a goddess of childbirth. The Olympian twins, Apollo and Artemis, are joined together in many myths. They love their mother, Leto, and are shown defending her in a number of stories. We shall consider Artemis more fully in a later chapter (Chapter 9).

Shrine at Delphi

Apollo's most sacred place is his oracular shrine at Delphi. The *Homeric Hymn to Apollo* (179–546) tells the story of how Apollo establishes his holy Delphic Oracle. As the story is told, Apollo goes to found his shrine near Mt. Parnassus, the same site where Deucalion and Pyrrha landed after the Great Flood. There Apollo slays a fierce she-dragon named *Python*. Some interpret this act of slaying a female dragon as the moment when the male god Apollo seizes the holy site from the great goddess Themis, one of the original female Titans. Themis is an important ancient Greek goddess whose name means "justice," and she is associated with the ideas of justice, fairness, and the right way, concepts that are also important to Apollo as the god of reason.

The god is called **Pythian** Apollo
because he slew the dragon *Python*.
Apollo = Heroic Dragon-Slayer

Apollo Delphinios

Next, Apollo establishes his cult at the shrine by recruiting priests to serve him there. As the *Homeric Hymn* tells the story, Apollo sees a ship sailing over the dark sea with a crew of Cretan sailors, so he leaps onto the ship in the form of a dolphin and then kidnaps them to serve as attendants at his sanctuary. This is an *aetiological* myth that explains the name of the shrine and the cult title of Apollo: *delphis* is the Greek word for "dolphin," and thus the name Delphi comes from the story of the god's miraculous appearance as a dolphin. Apollo is sometimes known as a god of sailors and colonists, who would consult the sacred oracle before setting out on their journeys over the sea to establish new colonies.

Delphi = Location of the *Omphalos*

Omphalos = "Belly-button" of the Earth

The ancient Greeks considered this spot to be the actual physical center of the universe.

God of Prophecy

Apollo's shrine at Delphi was the most important and influential shrine in ancient Greece because of the presence of the god's oracle. People would come from all over the ancient world to ask for and receive answers from the god Apollo on questions ranging from the personal to the political. In the god's temple was his medium, a priestess called the *Pythia*—her name was given in honor of Pythian Apollo. The *Pythia* sat upon a tripod, a high three-legged chair, and would go into a frenzied trance, during which she would hear the prophetic voice of the god. Inspired by Apollo, she would utter the prophecies in garbled words to the priests, who would then translate and explain them to the petitioners seeking the god's advice.

What Caused the *Pythia* to Hallucinate?

Theories to explain the trance-like state of the *Pythia* include:

The priestess inhaled toxic fumes that came from under the temple.
The priestess smoked or chewed laurel (bay) leaves.
The priestess was chosen for her natural psychic abilities.

Pan-Hellenic Site of Delphi

As the most important religious sanctuary in ancient Greece, Delphi was considered a "Pan-Hellenic" site; that is, it belonged to "all the Greeks." Another important Pan-Hellenic site was Olympia, the sacred shrine of the great god Zeus. A Pan-Hellenic site was a center of religious worship, but it was also significant as a place where ancient people gathered to celebrate music, poetry, and athletic events such as foot and chariot races.

Pan-Hellenic sites every four years held festivals, games, and contests to celebrate the physical and intellectual accomplishments of the Greek people. At Delphi, the celebration was called the Pythian Games.

A Pan-Hellenic site always has:

- Temple: for religious activity
- Theater: for literary/musical activity
- Stadium: for athletic activity

The Laurel

The victor at the Pythian Games would be crowned with a wreath of laurel leaves.

The laurel wreath was also a symbol of honor for poets and heroes, hence the phrase "to rest on one's laurels."

baccalaureate = "laurel berry" = university degree

poet laureate = officially appointed by the government

Apollo's Loves

Like his father, Zeus, Apollo is a very amorous god, and there are many tales in Greek mythology about Apollo's erotic affairs. As these stories indicate, Apollo is attracted to nymphs, mortal women, and mortal boys. However, these stories also suggest that Apollo is rather unlucky in love. Typically, Apollo becomes interested in someone, who rejects him out of fear or disinterest, and then the beloved ends up cursed, dead, and/or turned into a plant or a flower. Some see Apollo's bad luck in love as a "humanizing" aspect of the god, but since most of his lovers experience tragic endings, it may also suggest Apollo's devastating power.

Some examples of Apollo's doomed lovers are the following:

- Cassandra, Trojan priestess = cursed with prophecies that were never believed
- Daphne, nymph = turned into a laurel tree (sacred to Apollo)
- Hyacinthus, Spartan boy = killed by a discus, turned into flower
- Cyparissus, Cean boy = mourned to death, turned into a cypress tree

God of Medicine

Apollo is the healer god, and rules over the profession of medicine. Several myths emphasize his healing skills and his ability to save the lives and protect the bodies of humans he cherishes. His role as the god of medicine is manifest in the story of his son, Asklepios (in Roman mythology = Aesculapius), the greatest physician of the Greek mythological world. Asklepios was trained as a young man by the centaur Chiron, and became such an expert healer that he could even raise dead souls back to life. But this interference with the natural order angered Hades, who complained to Zeus, and the great god zapped Asklepios down to the underworld with a thunderbolt.

Apollo = God of Science and Exploration

Apollo Program = NASA's manned spaceflights from 1961–1975

"Houston, we have a problem. . ."

God of Music

Apollo is the god of music, and he takes ferocious pride in his musical skills. His primary instrument is his lyre, a seven-stringed instrument, and his favorite accompanists are the Muses, goddesses of the creative and fine arts. In Greek mythology, Apollo's proficiency as a musician is often tested in stories of competition, where someone foolishly challenges Apollo to a musical contest, inevitably loses, and is brutally punished by the god. One such tale is the story of Marsyas, a satyr (a male nature spirit) who becomes a skilled flute player and then boldly challenges Apollo to a contest. Apollo of course wins the contest, and skins poor Marsyas alive—his blood flowed together with the tears of his mourners to create the River Marsyas.

Archer God

Apollo is known as the "Far-striker," because he always has his bow and arrows, which he uses to enforce his divine will. In stories of war, Apollo is responsible for bringing swift death in battle with the unerring shafts of his arrows. Apollo the Archer is also associated with hunting, and he may in origin be linked with tribes of nomadic hunters, as is suggested by another one of his cult titles: Apollo *Lykios*, or "Wolf God." But Apollo's associations with flocks, and his powers of medicine and music, may also suggest his origins come from the pastoral culture of ancient Greece, as he seems to fit the archetype of the "good shepherd." Apollo is indeed a god of great complexity and there are many layers of characteristics in the nature of his divinity.

Apollo's Sacred Attributes

- Bow and arrows
- Laurel tree and wreath
- Palm tree
- Lyre
- Swan, raven, dolphin, wolf
- Delphic tripod

Apollo = God of Many Contradictions
Gentle/Violent, Healer/Destroyer, Lover/Killer

Apollo Teaches Self-Restraint:
"Know Your Limits"

On our journey through Greek mythology, we will meet many more male gods, demi-gods, and heroes whose myths and attributes will reveal significant resonances with the three Olympian gods we have met in this chapter. Let's keep in mind these important aspects of the Greek male divine:

- Power
- Fertility
- Wisdom

SOURCES FOR THIS CHAPTER

Clay, Jenny Strauss. (1989). *The Politics of Olympus: Form and Meaning in the Major Homeric Hymns*. Princeton: Princeton University Press.

Fontenrose, Joseph. (1978). *The Delphic Oracle*. Berkeley: University of California Press.

Leeming, David, and Page, Jake. (1997). *God: Myths of the Male Divine*. Oxford and New York: Oxford University Press.

Miller, Andrew. (1986). *From Delos to Delphi: A Literary Study of the Homeric Hymn to Apollo*. Leiden: E.J. Brill.

Morford, Mark P. O., and Lenardon, Robert J. (2007). *Classical Mythology*, 8th ed. Oxford: Oxford University Press.

Riggs, Michael. (2006). *Edicts of Ares: 13 Absolute Rules of Warfare*. Philadelphia: Xlibris.

Ruden, Sarah. (Trans.). (2005). *Homeric Hymns*. Indianapolis: Hackett Publishing Company.

POPULAR CULTURE REFERENCES

Film

Apollo 13 (1995). Director: Ron Howard.
Mars Attacks! (1996). Director: Tim Burton.
Poseidon (2006). Director: Wolfgang Petersen.

Television

Star Trek (1967). Original series.
   Season 2, Episode 31: "Who Mourns for Adonais?"
Xena: Warrior Princess (1995–2001). Syndicated series.

Online

Greek Mythology Link (www.maicar.com/GML)

Self-Quiz for Chapter 6

1. What are Poseidon's main titles?

   _____
   _____
   _____
   _____

2. What is Poseidon's main attribute?

   _____
   _____
   _____
   _____
   _____

3. Who is Amphitrite?

   _____
   _____
   _____

4. What are Ares' main titles?

   _____
   _____
   _____
   _____

5. What are Ares' main attributes?

   _____
   _____
   _____

6. What are Apollo's main titles?

_____

_____

_____

_____

7. Who is Leto?

_____

_____

_____

_____

_____

_____

8. What are Apollo's main attributes?

_____

_____

_____

_____

_____

9. What is Apollo's sacred place?

_____

_____

_____

_____

_____

10. Who is Asklepios?

_____

_____

_____

_____

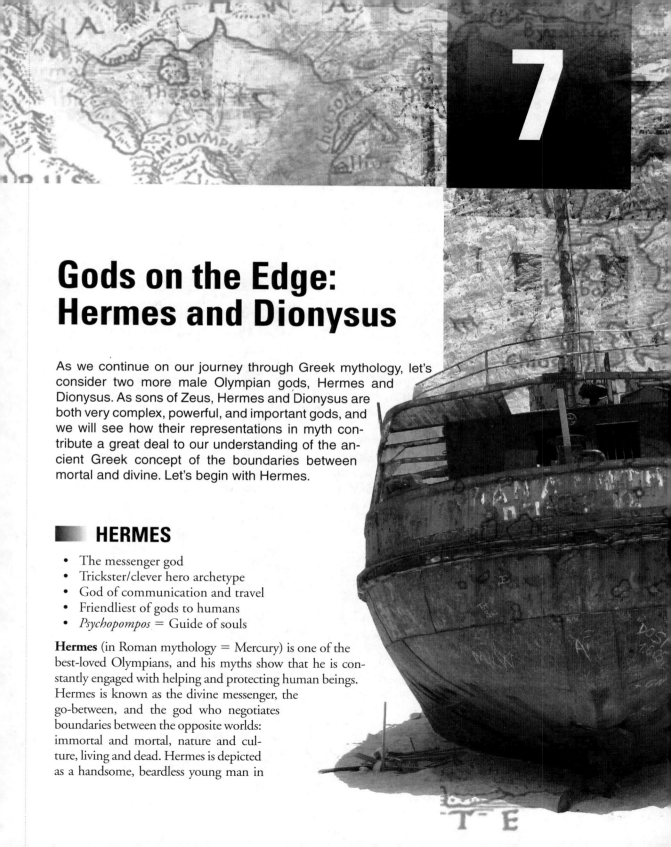

7

Gods on the Edge:
Hermes and Dionysus

As we continue on our journey through Greek mythology, let's consider two more male Olympian gods, Hermes and Dionysus. As sons of Zeus, Hermes and Dionysus are both very complex, powerful, and important gods, and we will see how their representations in myth contribute a great deal to our understanding of the ancient Greek concept of the boundaries between mortal and divine. Let's begin with Hermes.

HERMES

- The messenger god
- Trickster/clever hero archetype
- God of communication and travel
- Friendliest of gods to humans
- *Psychopompos* = Guide of souls

Hermes (in Roman mythology = Mercury) is one of the best-loved Olympians, and his myths show that he is constantly engaged with helping and protecting human beings. Hermes is known as the divine messenger, the go-between, and the god who negotiates boundaries between the opposite worlds: immortal and mortal, nature and culture, living and dead. Hermes is depicted as a handsome, beardless young man in the boyish prime of his adolescence, a slightly younger version of his elder brother, Apollo, with whom he shares much in common. Hermes is most often shown in motion, with his lithe, athletic body poised in movement or flight. Hermes is a god on the go.

Mercury

Mercury = smallest, fastest planet

Mercury = the element of "*quicksilver*" that

measures temperature in thermometers

Birth of Hermes

Perhaps one of the most important and wonderfully charming myths about Hermes is the story of his birth in a cave on Mt. Cyllene in Arcadia in southern Greece (as told in the *Homeric Hymn to Hermes* 1–580). Hermes is the son of the great god Zeus, and the goddess Maia, who is the daughter of the Titan Atlas. Maia is a minor goddess or mountain nymph associated with the season of spring; she is also the eldest and most beautiful of the Pleiades, seven sister nymphs who give their names to the springtime star cluster. Maia, whose name in Greek means "Mommy," is another expression of the great mother goddess, as she is identified with springtime, divine fertility, and motherhood.

Divine Child Motif

As soon as he is born, as the *Hymn* tells us, Baby Hermes leaps from his cozy cradle and sets out to establish himself as a fully fledged Olympian god. Of all the Olympians, Hermes receives the most detailed story of his infancy, and the story manifests all the aspects of the *divine child motif.* Baby Hermes is indeed very precocious! As the tale goes, the one-day-old Hermes steals cattle belonging to his brother Apollo, and then lies about it to protect himself from their father's wrath. But Zeus is utterly charmed by his new son's clever, cunning ways, and even Apollo is ultimately won over when Hermes presents him with the new instrument he invented, the tortoise-shell lyre. In the story of his babyhood adventures, Hermes displays all the talents and attributes of his nature, as he establishes his divine spheres of influence.

Baby Hermes = First Inventor

Hermes' inventions include the
lyre, sandals, fire-sticks, and shepherd's pipes.

Trickster God

Hermes is the glorious Olympian representation of the archetypal trickster god. As his myths show, Hermes is clever, childish, sneaky, creative, witty, inventive, and one of the most expert liars around. Like all tricksters, Hermes is a lover of practical jokes, and even enjoys being the butt of such pranks. Hermes especially likes naughty jokes, and he can be something of a smart-ass. As a god he rules over the purely physical sphere, and he is in charge of the lower bodily functions. His own myths show him to be a sexually promiscuous god, although this is quite a common trait among the male Greek gods. Hermes also embodies the characteristics of the clever hero archetype as he is charming, amiable, and always helpful to humans.

Messenger of the Gods

Hermes is the divine messenger, primarily working for his father, Zeus, but Hermes delivers messages for many other deities and people as well. Later on our journey through Greek mythology, we will meet Iris, another messenger of the gods. Hermes protects messengers and heralds, known for their speed and ingenuity on the job. Because messengers and heralds were often vulnerable to danger in ancient Greek society, never knowing how their messages would be received, Hermes reaches out to protect them in particular. The staff carried by messengers and heralds is the symbol of their office and a signal that they are not to be harmed, since they are under the protection of the god Hermes.

Symbols of Protection and Healing

Caduceus = winged herald's staff entwined with two snakes
Rod of Asklepios = staff with one snake

Both are used as symbols of modern medical organizations.

God of Communication

Hermes protects people who make their living using words and communication—in particular he helps teachers, lawyers, politicians, journalists, writers, postal workers, and all public speakers. Hermes also protects those engaged in commerce, such as traders, merchants, auctioneers, and businesspeople. Hermes even reaches out to protect people who dwell on the edge and whose livelihoods depend on trickery, lies, and deception, such as gamblers, con-men, thieves, and magicians. Since Hermes is always actively engaged on the human sphere, he is noted as the friendliest of gods to humans.

Hermes is the patron of athletes.

Statues of Hermes were found in ancient Greek *gymnasia*.

Gymnasion in Greek means "naked place," and is the source of our modern word *gymnasium*.

Hermes and Apollo

Hermes is closely linked with his elder brother Apollo in both their myths and visual representations. They are both young male gods who symbolize two sides of the same divine coin, where Hermes represents the more physical aspects of deity and Apollo represents the more intellectual and spiritual sides. Both gods appear to have their origins in the pastoral society of ancient Greece, as they are both associated with flocks (cattle and sheep), music, medicine, protective powers, and fertility. Hermes in particular is associated with flocks and shepherds, and he protects shepherds as another class of people who live their lives on the outskirts of society.

God of Travel

Since he is constantly in motion, Hermes is associated with travel, roads, and borders. Hermes wears special sandals, which are often depicted with wings on them to denote the quickness of his movement. To depict him as a fast-moving wanderer, Hermes also has a special hat, a wide-brimmed traveler's hat called a *petasos*, which is also sometimes tricked out with wings. Always willing to help humans, Hermes acts as a guide for travelers all over the world. Hermes is a god of paths, journeys, exchange, and transitions. Hermes is especially mobile at night, the time of sleep, death, and dreams.

Herms

Herms are statues of Hermes in the form of a pillar with head and genitals. The ancient Greeks set *herms* up at crossroads and borders, and they are considered to be phallic good luck symbols.

Psychopompos = "Guide of Souls"

One of Hermes' most significant functions is to guide recently dead souls across the boundaries to the Underworld. As a god of transitions, Hermes helps the newly dead "cross over" to the other side. In some myths, Hermes also leads a soul back to the land of the living, as in the cases of Persephone and Eurydice. Hermes negotiates the boundaries between the mortal and the immortal realms.

Hermes' Sacred Attributes

- *Caduceus* = herald's staff
- Winged sandals and hat
- *Petasos* = traveler's hat
- Ram
- Cattle

Hermes and Aphrodite

Hermes is joined with the goddess Aphrodite in numerous cults and rituals. The two gods share a number of similarities: they are both very mobile, physical, and friendly to human beings. Their association in religious worship is symbolized by their child, Hermaphroditus, who has both male and female sexual body parts. As the story is told,

Hermes and Aphrodite, being the good-humored parents that they are, got a hearty laugh when they first saw their "doubly-endowed" child.

> Now let's turn from
> Hermes = Boundary Crosser
>
> And move on to
> Dionysus = Boundary Breaker

DIONYSUS

- God of wine and intoxication
- Twice-born god
- God of resurrection
- God of drama
- God of nature and vegetation

Dionysus (in Roman mythology = Bacchus, Liber) is the great god of wine and intoxication in general. In Greek mythology, he is also known as Bakchos and Iakchos. Dionysus is an exceptionally complex and powerful god. In his myths and worship, Dionysus fulfills the role of the dying and rising god archetype. Dionysus is a god of resurrection because he is reborn inside his worshippers. Dionysus presides over all "out of body" experiences: intoxication, ecstatic dancing, and drama. Dionysus is depicted as a beautiful young man, sensual and languid, with smooth limbs and long, curling hair.

> **Dionysus = God of Drama**
>
> Drama involves impersonation for the audience.
>
> Tragedy and comedy were performed
>
> at the *Great Dionysia* festival in Athens.

Birth of Dionysus

One of the most significant myths for understanding the nature of Dionysus is the traditional story of his birth. Dionysus is the son of the great god Zeus, and the mortal woman Semele, the daughter of Cadmus and Harmonia, king and queen of Thebes. As the story goes, when a suspicious Hera finds out about the affair, she visits Semele in the disguise of an old woman and tricks her into challenging the identity of Zeus. So Semele persuades Zeus to swear an oath to grant her a wish, but the great god's heart sank when his lover asked him to prove his supreme deity. When Zeus revealed himself in his total divinity, poor Semele was incinerated by the fiery brilliance. Zeus saves their baby from the pile of smoking ashes, sews him into his thigh, and brings him to full term. Thus Dionysus is born from the groin of Zeus, an allegory or metaphorical relationship that establishes his identification with male fertility and productivity.

> Dionysus is called the "Twice-born god"
> because he was born from Semele and then from Zeus.
>
> Thus he is a symbol of resurrection and rebirth—a
> god who dies and is reborn.
> This serves as an analogy for human worship.

Baby Dionysus

Father Zeus puts Baby Dionysus under the protection of Hermes, to keep the baby away from the jealous eyes of Hera. For safe-keeping, Hermes entrusts baby Dionysus to old Silenus, an elderly male nature spirit. In Greek mythology, there are many nurses associated with the infant Dionysus, especially the nymphs of the legendary Mt. Nysa. Other versions of the tale have the baby raised by Ino, the sister of Semele, and so the maternal aunt of Dionysus. In art, Dionysus is often depicted as a baby, perhaps to suggest the natural appeal and unfettered appetite of this great god.

Origins of Dionysus

Along with the story of his birth, there are many tales describing the homecoming of Dionysus back to Greece. Some interpretations suggest that his origins are ultimately in the northern part of Greece, in Thrace or Macedonia, or perhaps in the east in Phrygia. But as the story is told, after he grows to manhood, Dionysus returns home to Greece to spread the message of his worship. The myths tell how Dionysus freely gives the blessings of joy and prosperity to those who follow him, but those who reject the god are cursed with insanity and death. These tales of Dionysus' arrival in Greece do not necessarily mean he was a latecomer to the Olympian *pantheon*; rather they suggest the challenges inherent in understanding the Dionysian mystery.

God of Nature and Vegetation

Dionysus is essentially a god of fertility and the everlasting cycle of vegetation, and he symbolizes the fecundity and cultivation of the Earth. Dionysus is primarily charged with the cultivation of the grapevine and the making of wine, and so he is associated with all the emblems of these activities: grape clusters, grapevines, drinking cups, wine, and spirits in general. As a god who dies and comes back to life, Dionysus is also associated with those plants that retain their spark of life throughout the winter: ivy, evergreens, pine trees, and pinecones. Dionysus embodies the "sap of life," and is the god of all vital fluids: wine, sap, blood, sweat, and semen.

Thyrsos = **Magic Wand and Weapon**

The *thyrsos* is a staff topped with pinecone
and wrapped in grapevines or ivy
carried by followers of Dionysus.

Cult of Dionysus

The ritual celebrated by worshippers of Dionysus is a mystery religion that fundamentally reenacts his death and resurrection. In the myth, Dionysus is fatally born during his mother's burning, and then reborn from his father's thigh. During the rites of Dionysus, the celebrants seek to replay this divine cycle of death and rebirth by inviting the god Dionysus to be reborn inside themselves. As they worship Dionysus, the followers experience a compelling sense of release and freedom from the boundaries of society, yet they also come close to a dangerous edge of abandonment, violence, and excess. Dionysian worship involves several key elements:

Oreibasia = "Run for the hills"
Worshippers of Dionysus separate themselves from society and seek a natural setting out of doors. They often wear animal skins and garlands to signal that they are going "back to nature."

Thiasos = "Sacred band"
Group experience is essential to the worship of Dionysus: the god cannot be experienced alone. The sacred group, or *thiasos*, is usually made up of a male leader and group of followers. In Greek mythology, the nymphs who follow Dionysus are called *Maenads*; other female followers of Dionysus are called *Bacchae*, or *Bacchantes*.

Ekstasis = "Stand outside oneself; ecstasy"
The worshippers aim to stand outside of themselves to make room for Dionysus. They do this with drums, music, dancing, and intoxication. They loosen the boundaries of their personal selves so they can "break on through to the other side."

Enthousiasmos = "Having the God inside; enthusiasm"
After standing outside of themselves, the worshippers invite Dionysus to possess them. This is done by drinking spirits, and the sharing of the communal sacrifice.

Sparagmos = "Ripping apart"
The worshippers bless a small animal (or substitute) to represent Dionysus, and then tear it apart, symbolizing the ritual "death" of Dionysus.

Omophagia = "Raw-eating"
After tearing the animal apart, the worshippers eat its flesh in a communal sharing of the sacrifice. Since the animal represents Dionysus, the act of eating allows the god to be "reborn" inside his worshippers, who are now, like the god himself, immortal.

The Bacchic Ritual
Dionysus is reborn in the worshippers, delivering the promise of human immortality.

Satyrs

Satyrs are male nature spirits who are followers and frequent companions of Dionysus. Satyrs are mostly human, with some goat (horns, hooves) and sometimes some horse (ears, tail) attributes. The combination of human and animal attributes suggests that satyrs contain aspects of both in their natures. Satyrs are divine representations of the essential masculine sexual impulse, and they are often shown *ithyphallic*, meaning "with erect penis." Satyrs are creatures of appetite, and they love music, wine, and sex—they are always in pursuit of one or the other, or all three. They are depicted constantly trying to seduce Maenads, and sometimes they are successful. Satyrs are frequent participants at Dionysian celebrations.

Symposium in Greek means "drinking together."
What really goes on at those "academic meetings"?

Dionysian Animals

As a god of nature, Dionysus is associated with many animals. When worshipping Dionysus, his followers typically wear wild animal skins, usually the spotted variety, because wearing the skins brings you closer to nature and allows you to express your animal spirit. The animals primarily associated with Dionysian worship are the goat, deer, and fawn. But Dionysus the god is most closely identified with the leopard or the panther, both powerful, sleek, sensual, and ferocious feline creatures. The essential characteristic of the feline nature is that it is unpredictable, like Dionysus himself. Anyone who has ever shared space with a cat knows that Kitty can be the sweetest thing on earth, all purrs and cuddles; but when she is done with you, she can turn savage, clawing and biting for no reason! This sweetness followed by savagery embodies the fundamental dual quality of the Dionysian experience.

Dionysus' Sacred Attributes

- Wine, spirits, drinking cups
- Grape clusters, grapevines, ivy
- Pine trees, pinecones, evergreens
- *Thyrsos*
- Leopard, panther
- Goat, fawn

The Dual Nature of Dionysus

Dionysus is the god of communal ecstasy and the excitement of nature,

but also fanaticism, mob fury, and the irrational impulse.

Our journey through Greek mythology will take us to several places where we will have to negotiate the borders between the immortal and the mortal realms. Let's always watch out for the tricks of Hermes and the terrible punishment of too much Dionysus!

SOURCES FOR THIS CHAPTER

Clay, Jenny Strauss. (1989). *The Politics of Olympus: Form and Meaning in the Major Homeric Hymns*. Princeton: Princeton University Press.

Dodds, E. R. (1951). *The Greeks and the Irrational*. Berkeley: University of California Press.

Hyde, Lewis. (1998). *Trickster Makes This World: Mischief, Myth, & Art*. New York: Farrar, Straus & Giroux.

Kerényi, Karl. (1976). *Dionysos: Archetypal Image of Indestructible Life*. Translated by Ralph Mannheim. Princeton: Princeton University Press.

Kerényi, Karl. (1976). *Hermes Guide of Souls: The Mythologem of the Masculine Source of Life*. Translated by Murray Stein. Zurich: Spring Publications.

Leeming, David, and Page, Jake. (1997). *God: Myths of the Male Divine*. Oxford and New York: Oxford University Press.

Morford, Mark P. O., and Lenardon, Robert J. (2007). *Classical Mythology*, 8th ed. Oxford: Oxford University Press.

Otto, Walter F. (1965). *Dionysus: Myth and Cult*. Bloomington: Indiana University Press.

Ruden, Sarah. (Trans.). (2005). *Homeric Hymns*. Indianapolis: Hackett Publishing Company.

Seaford, Richard. (2006). *Dionysos*. In the series *Gods and Heroes of the Ancient World*. London and New York: Routledge.

POPULAR CULTURE REFERENCES

Film

The Crying Game (1992). Director: Neil Jordan.
Leaving Las Vegas (1995). Director: Mike Figgis.

Television

Xena: Warrior Princess (1996). Syndicated series.
Season 2, Episode 4: "Girls Just Wanna Have Fun."

Online

Greek Mythology Link (www.maicar.com/GML)

Self-Quiz for Chapter 7

1. What are Hermes' main titles?

_____

_____

_____

_____

2. What does Hermes do when he is born?

_____

_____

_____

_____

_____

3. What is the *caduceus*?

_____

_____

_____

4. What is meant by the title *Psychopompos*?

_____

_____

_____

_____

5. Who is Hermaphroditus?

_____

_____

_____

6. What are Dionysus' main titles?

_____

_____

_____

_____

7. What happens to Semele?

_____

_____

_____

_____

_____

_____

8. What are Dionysus' main attributes?

_____

_____

_____

_____

_____

9. What is a *thyrsos*?

_____

_____

_____

_____

_____

_____

10. Who are the satyrs?

_____

_____

_____

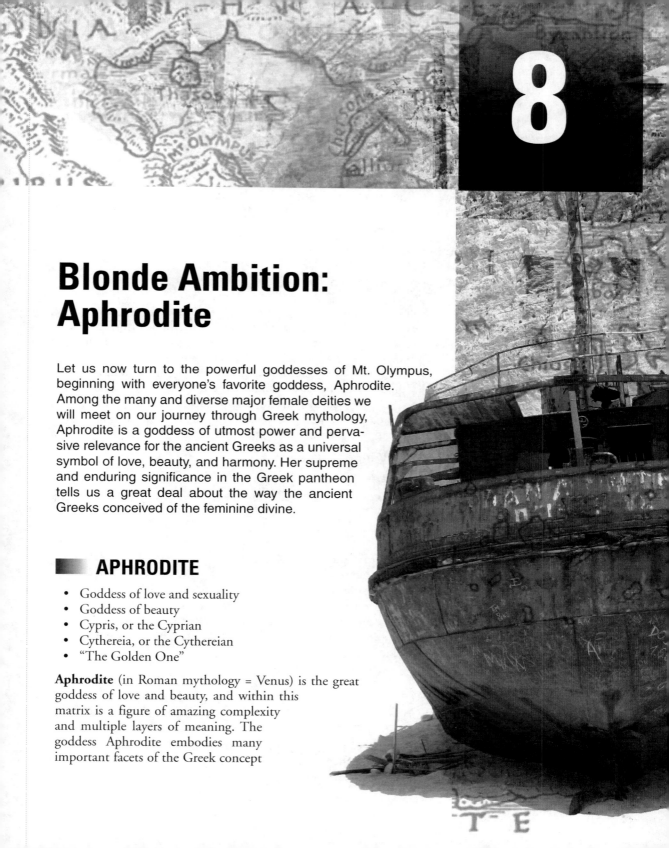

8

Blonde Ambition: Aphrodite

Let us now turn to the powerful goddesses of Mt. Olympus, beginning with everyone's favorite goddess, Aphrodite. Among the many and diverse major female deities we will meet on our journey through Greek mythology, Aphrodite is a goddess of utmost power and pervasive relevance for the ancient Greeks as a universal symbol of love, beauty, and harmony. Her supreme and enduring significance in the Greek pantheon tells us a great deal about the way the ancient Greeks conceived of the feminine divine.

APHRODITE

- Goddess of love and sexuality
- Goddess of beauty
- Cypris, or the Cyprian
- Cythereia, or the Cythereian
- "The Golden One"

Aphrodite (in Roman mythology = Venus) is the great goddess of love and beauty, and within this matrix is a figure of amazing complexity and multiple layers of meaning. The goddess Aphrodite embodies many important facets of the Greek concept of female divinity: love, desire, sexuality, fertility, and the power of creation. Aphrodite is depicted as a beautiful woman at the peak of her adult maturity, with flowing hair, flashing eyes, a curvy body, and full breasts, often nude but always wearing a smile. She was the most popular of all the Greek goddesses, as her many shrines and temples attest.

Aphrodite

Her name is synonymous with female sexuality.
A 1950s/1960s Aphrodite archetype is Marilyn Monroe.
A 1980s/1990s Aphrodite archetype is Madonna.

Who are our current Aphrodite archetypes in popular culture?

Goddess of Love and Sexuality

As a love goddess, Aphrodite symbolizes feminine sexuality, intimacy, tenderness, and playfulness, and the arts of seduction and attraction, including the adornment of the physical body as well as the intellectual skills of erotic persuasion, flattery, and deceit. As a goddess of sexuality, Aphrodite also represents aspects of fertility, procreation, and maternity. As we shall see, Aphrodite loves children and has many of them—though, unfortunately, none of them with her legitimate husband, Hephaestus, the blacksmith god. Aphrodite's immense power encompasses the instinctive urge of all humans to have sex: how to find it, how to get it, and how to do it. Aphrodite symbolizes that first flush of passionate love.

"Venereal" (= "from Venus") Disease

This is an old-fashioned name for sexually transmitted disease—
what you get if you're not careful in amorous pursuits!

Aphrodite's Origins

There are many different interpretations regarding the essential origins of and influences upon the Greek goddess Aphrodite. In terms of her sexuality, Aphrodite shares some similar features with the Near Eastern goddesses of love and war, especially the Sumerian goddess Inanna and the Babylonian goddess Ishtar. In terms of her fertility, Aphrodite shares similar features to the other great goddesses in the Greek system, such as Gaia. It is likely that the classical Greek figure of Aphrodite is the result of many complex layers of religious and mythological meaning.

Eos and Aphrodite

The goddess Aphrodite appears to share several significant features with the Greek goddess Eos, goddess of the dawn and sunrise (in Roman mythology = Aurora). Eos is a beautiful sky goddess, and she rises from the sea over the eastern horizon, bringing her golden morning light to the world. Eos is called by the poet Homer "Rosy-Fingered Dawn," suggesting the way she streaks the warm colorful sunrise on the canvas of the sky. In Greek mythology, Eos is a very promiscuous and erotic goddess, and there are many tales of how she seduces her lovers first thing in the morning. Like Eos, Aphrodite is born from water and returns to it often; she is associated with sunlight and the colors red and gold; and she is linked to sexuality and multiple male lovers. So Aphrodite may also be originally a sky goddess, and the two main stories of her birth both confirm her direct origin from male sky gods.

Aphrodite's Birth Story

In Hesiod's version of the story (*Theogony* 188–206), as we recall from an earlier chapter, Aphrodite is born after Ouranos is castrated by his son, the wily Cronos. The divine genitals are thrown upon the sea, where the god's semen mixes with the sea foam, or *aphros*, and from that mixture is born the goddess Aphrodite. The moment of her birth calms the surging seas, and when she comes ashore at her favorite islands, Cythera and Cyprus, grass springs up around her slender feet. As an allegory, Aphrodite's Hesiodic birth story indicates her direct origin from the sky god, her connection to water and islands, as well as her absolute relationship to sexuality.

Aphrodite

As the goddess of peaceful seas,
smooth sailing, and successful voyages, Aphrodite was worshipped by sailors.

A well-known artistic depiction of Aphrodite is *The Birth of Venus* (1485) by Sandro Botticelli, or "Venus on the Halfshell."

Olympian Aphrodite

In other versions of her birth, Aphrodite is said to be the daughter of the great god Zeus and the goddess Dione. The name Dione is a feminine form of the name Zeus, so there is some uncertainty about Dione's identity, although Hesiod says Dione is an Oceanid, a daughter of the Titans Oceanos and Tethys (*Theogony* 353). In this story of her birth, Aphrodite is securely part of the Olympian family as the direct offspring of the sky god Zeus, who then marries his sexy daughter off to Hephaestus, the blacksmith god (more on this in Chapter 11). Many Greek myths show how close Aphrodite is to her "father" Zeus, the lusty sky god.

Aphrodite's Sacred Places

Aphrodite is a Pan-Hellenic goddess, with the most cults, shrines, and temples throughout the Greek world. But her favorite places are islands, as they are associated with water and navigation, and mountain peaks, with their connection to the sky and their liminal position between the divine and mortal worlds. Aphrodite's favorite islands are Cythera and Cyprus, the scene of her first manifestation after her birth. She is also associated with Mt. Ida in Troy, where she seduces her lover Anchises; also, Mt. Eryx in Sicily and Acrocorinth in Corinth are sacred centers of her worship.

Acrocorinth

Acrocorinth is the site of a major temple to Aphrodite, home of her sacred prostitutes.

Flowers

Aphrodite loves flowers, and she is the most floral of all the major goddesses. Flowers can be used for adornment, and to enhance one's beauty. Flowers also represent the sexual organs of plants, as their bright colors and intense fragrances attract bees and birds to help in the process of pollination and the creation of fruit. Aphrodite's favorite flower is the rose, especially the red rose, which is still the most popular modern floral symbol of love—just ask any florist on Valentine's Day. Aphrodite also adores lilies and poppies, the latter perhaps because of their narcotic properties.

Fruit

Aphrodite is also associated with a number of fruits, as fruits are the natural "offspring" of flowers. Aphrodite is particularly associated with apples, which were considered special love tokens in ancient Greece, but also peaches and pomegranates. Fruits are considered Aphrodite's symbols because of their eye-catching colors, alluring smells, and delicious taste, all particular aspects of sexiness. Aphrodite also has a sacred tree, the myrtle, a small flowering tree with aromatic flowers and berries.

Birds

Many Greek gods and goddesses are linked with animals or birds, and Aphrodite also has several *ornithomorphs*, or bird emblems. Aphrodite is linked with the common sparrow and pigeon, because of these species' prodigious reproductive capabilities. Aphrodite is also associated with all nonpredatory water birds, such as geese, ducks, and swans, because of her connection to the water as the place of her birth. But Aphrodite's most important avian symbol is the dove, whose affectionate "lovey-dovey" behavior with its mate and soft, cooing sounds represent her connection to peace and harmony.

Aphrodite's Female Attendants

Minor Goddesses or Nymphs

The Three Graces = *Charites*

Also the Hours, Seasons, Fates, Nereids

The Golden One

Aphrodite is known as "The Golden One," or the golden goddess, an epithet that suggests several multifaceted and intertwined meanings. As the most precious metal, goldenness to the ancient Greeks symbolized the best and most beautiful quality anything could have. In terms of brilliance, Aphrodite is associated with sunlight, and in many of her myths she is depicted seducing her lovers in broad daylight with the sun shining. Her solarity can also be seen in physical descriptions of her wearing an abundance of bright, gold jewelry. Aphrodite is also linked to the warm, golden planet, Venus, which because of its brightness is called the "Morning Star" or "Evening Star." Other goddesses have golden attributes, but only Aphrodite is intrinsically golden.

Friends and Lovers

Like Hermes, Aphrodite is very friendly and intimate with humans. She has many favorites in the mortal world, and she helps and protects them in their time of need. The most famous of her favorite humans is Helen of Troy (*née* Sparta), the most beautiful woman in the world, whom the goddess encourages to elope with her lover, Paris, Prince of Troy (more on this story in a later unit). Aphrodite also enjoys cruising around the human world to check out the handsome men, and she has many erotic affairs with humans, including the beautiful youth Adonis and the Trojan cattleman Anchises. Her lovemaking with Anchises is described in the *Homeric Hymn to Aphrodite* (1–293): after this affair, Aphrodite gives birth to her favorite son, Aeneas, a great Trojan warrior who goes on to found the city of Rome.

Aphrodite as the Roman Goddess Venus

In Roman mythology, Venus is the mother of the Roman people through her son, Aeneas, as told in Vergil's great epic, the *Aeneid*.

Goddess of Beauty

All the Greek gods and goddesses are beautiful, but Aphrodite is always the most beautiful goddess. Aphrodite's physical beauty is often described in detail: she has flashing eyes, a bright smile, glittering gold jewelry, and a rosy glow radiates from her lovely neck and breasts. She is often depicted with one of her main attributes, a mirror, so she can check on her appearance. The most powerful way to extol the beauty of a mortal woman is to compare her to Aphrodite. The goddess embodies erotic beauty that is used to attract and seduce—you might call it "beauty enhanced for a purpose"—so she rules over bodily adornment, such as clothing, jewelry, make-up, and perfume. Aphrodite is also the goddess of shopping.

Aphrodite's Sacred Attributes

- Dove, sparrow, pigeon
- Goose, duck
- Rose, poppy, lily
- Myrtle tree
- Apple, peach, pomegranate
- Mirror

Aphrodite and Ares

Aphrodite joins her favorite lover, the handsome warrior god Ares, as the two sides of the opposition between love and war. While Aphrodite herself is usually peaceful and not a very good fighter, some of her functions can be seen as aggressive and warlike: sexual conquest can be seen as a kind of military campaign. Aphrodite's son by Ares is Eros, the force of sexual desire, who in other versions of Greek mythology is depicted as one of the primal elements present at the creation of the universe. When love and war join together, the result is passionate mutual attraction.

Aphrodite

Most Potent Olympian Goddess
Goddess on the Mountain Top
The Fire of Your Desire

SOURCES FOR THIS CHAPTER

Boedeker, Deborah Dickmann. (1974). *Aphrodite's Entry into Greek Epic*. Leiden: E.J. Brill.

Breitenberger, Barbara. (2006). *Aphrodite and Eros: The Development of Erotic Mythology in Early Greek Poetry and Culture*. New York and London: Routledge.

Budin, Stephanie. (2002). *The Origin of Aphrodite*. Baltimore: University of Maryland Press.

Friedrich, Paul. (1978). *The Meaning of Aphrodite*. Chicago: University of Chicago Press.

Havelock, Christine Mitchell. (1995). *The Aphrodite of Knidos and Her Successors: A Historical Review of the Female Nude in Greek Art*. Ann Arbor: University of Michigan Press.

Leeming, David, and Page, Jake (1994). *Goddess: Myths of the Female Divine*. Oxford and New York: Oxford University Press.

Lefkowitz, Mary R. (2007). *Women in Greek Myth*, 2nd ed. Baltimore: The Johns Hopkins University Press.

Lombardo, Stanley. (Trans.). (2005). *Virgil: Aeneid*. Indianapolis: Hackett Publishing Company.

Morford, Mark P. O., and Lenardon, Robert J. (2007). *Classical Mythology*, 8th ed. Oxford: Oxford University Press.

Rosenzweig, Rachel. (2004). *Worshipping Aphrodite: Art and Cult in Classical Athens*. Ann Arbor: University of Michigan Press.

Ruden, Sarah. (Trans.). (2005). *Homeric Hymns*. Indianapolis: Hackett Publishing Company.

POPULAR CULTURE REFERENCES

Film

Mighty Aphrodite (1995). Director: Woody Allen.

Television

Hercules: The Legendary Journeys (1995–2000). Syndicated series.
Xena: Warrior Princess (1995–2001). Syndicated series.

Online

Greek Mythology Link (www.maicar.com/GML)

Self-Quiz for Chapter 8

1. What are Aphrodite's main titles?

_____

_____

_____

_____

2. What is Aphrodite's relationship to Eos?

_____

_____

_____

_____

3. What is Aphrodite's birth story, according to Hesiod?

_____

_____

_____

_____

4. What are Aphrodite's sacred places?

_____

_____

_____

_____

5. What flowers are sacred to Aphrodite?

_____

_____

_____

_____

6. What fruits are sacred to Aphrodite?

_____

_____

_____

_____

7. What birds are sacred to Aphrodite?

_____

_____

_____

_____

8. Why is Aphrodite called "The Golden One"?

_____

_____

_____

_____

9. Who are Aphrodite's attendants and favorite mortals?

_____

_____

_____

_____

10. Why is Aphrodite associated with the mirror?

_____

_____

_____

_____

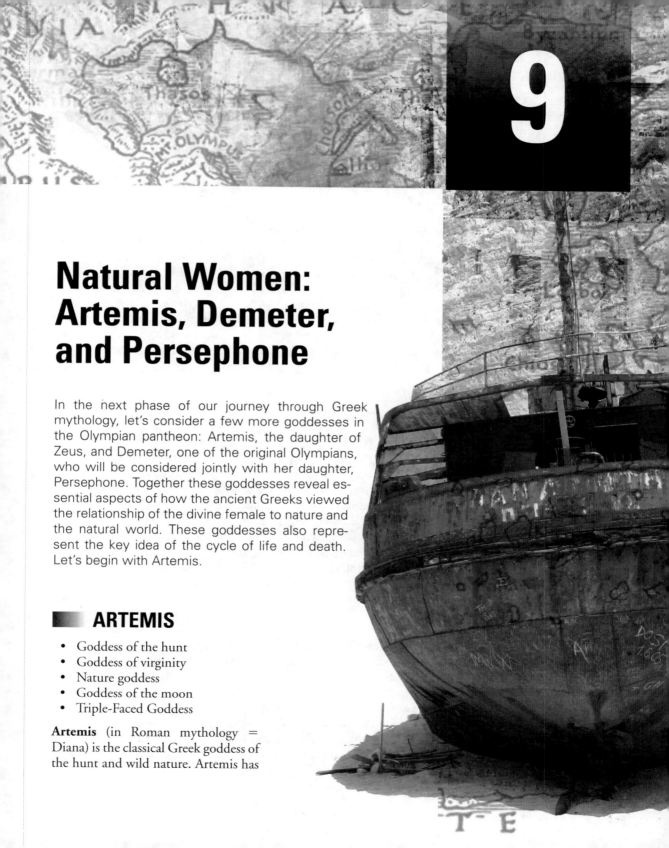

9

Natural Women: Artemis, Demeter, and Persephone

In the next phase of our journey through Greek mythology, let's consider a few more goddesses in the Olympian pantheon: Artemis, the daughter of Zeus, and Demeter, one of the original Olympians, who will be considered jointly with her daughter, Persephone. Together these goddesses reveal essential aspects of how the ancient Greeks viewed the relationship of the divine female to nature and the natural world. These goddesses also represent the key idea of the cycle of life and death. Let's begin with Artemis.

ARTEMIS

- Goddess of the hunt
- Goddess of virginity
- Nature goddess
- Goddess of the moon
- Triple-Faced Goddess

Artemis (in Roman mythology = Diana) is the classical Greek goddess of the hunt and wild nature. Artemis has many significant manifestations and spheres of influence that represent the idea of wildness and purity in the concept of divine femininity. Artemis is depicted as a beautiful but somewhat standoffish and unapproachable young woman wearing the short, belted dress of a huntress, with her long hair tied up to facilitate her quick, athletic movements. Artemis is said to be the tallest of all the Greek goddesses. She often has silver arrows and wears golden sandals.

Birth of Artemis

Artemis is the child of the great god Zeus and the goddess Leto, as well as the twin sister of the god Apollo. On our journey through Greek mythology, we have already encountered the story of Leto's pregnancy and her wandering to find a suitable place to give birth (Chapter 6). Leto arrives at the island of Delos, where she is allowed to give birth to her twins under a sacred palm tree. The goddess Artemis is born first, and then she assists her mother in giving birth to her younger brother, Apollo. This early feat is consistent with one of Artemis' functions as a goddess of childbirth. In other versions, Artemis is born first on the island of Ortygia, "Quail Island," which is near Sicily, and then goes with her mother to the island of Delos, where she helps Leto give birth to Apollo.

Sacred Places of Artemis

Delos and Ortygia
Hard, rocky islands

Artemis and Apollo, the Dynamic Duo

The Olympian twins, Artemis and Apollo, are associated with each other in numerous Greek myths where they are paired in various activities. Artemis and Apollo are both depicted as very vehement in their attitudes toward others, as well as protective of their mother, Leto. They are sometimes quite haughty and vindictive in their punishments of those who would challenge or defy them. On our journey through Greek mythology, we shall encounter many tales where Artemis and her brother Apollo are involved in the violent punishment and even death of others. Artemis and Apollo are known as the bringers of swift death to mortals.

Goddess of Virginity

The ancient Greeks believed that when Artemis was very young, she asked her father, the great god Zeus, that she be allowed to stay unmarried and thus a virgin. In a number of her myths, Artemis appears as a symbol of physical purity and chastity, and she keeps herself aloof from contact with the mortal realm. Artemis is remote, distant, inaccessible—always moving away from the company of others. She requires chastity not only for herself, but for those around her. Artemis insists that the few nymphs who accompany her also remain chaste and hold themselves detached from physical contact with other gods and mortals, especially males. Artemis is the divine symbol of the rejection of sexuality, and the urge toward personal asceticism.

> **Ursa Major**
>
> Artemis punishes Callisto
> for her erotic affair with Zeus
> by turning Callisto into a bear!
> The bear becomes the constellation *Ursa Major*,
> known to us as the "Big Dipper."

Goddess of the Hunt and Wild Nature

Artemis represents the divine symbol of the all-natural one. She is fierce, dangerous, harsh, and wild, like nature itself. She represents that part of nature that is untouched by human hands, such as the pristine meadows she loves to wander through, wild and pure, just like herself. Artemis is associated with wildflowers that grow without the benefit of cultivation. She is also symbolized by the wild animals that she loves to hunt, such as quail, hare, boar, and deer, and with the predators that she keeps with her as companions, such as wolves, bears, and lions. Artemis loves dogs and surrounds herself with hunting hounds. Artemis generally keeps away from people, and prefers isolated places.

Goddess of the Moon

Artemis is also identified with the moon and the monthly lunar phases as they change over the course of the month—the word "month" in English is related to the word "moon." Like the moon, Artemis is cool, distant, and pure as she moves through the night air. Artemis sometimes wears an image of the pointed crescent moon, a symbol of the changing lunar cycle. From her connection with the moon, Artemis is also associated with the female menstrual ("monthly" in Latin) cycle, and thus she is associated with pregnancy and childbirth. Though a virgin herself, Artemis was called upon for help by women in childbirth to assist with their labor pains, yet Artemis was also blamed for the death of women in childbirth. Artemis nurtures and protects human and animal babies from harm, though when they grow up, she hunts them. So Artemis can be seen as a symbol of the transitions in life, and especially the inexorable cycle of life and death, endlessly repeated.

> The origins of Artemis are ambiguous—
> she has both virginity and fertility aspects.
> Lunar Phases = Pregnancy = Cycle of Life

"Triple-Faced Goddess"

As a moon goddess, Artemis is also known as one aspect of a powerful tripartite divinity known as the Triple-Faced Goddess that also includes:

Selene: She is personification of the moon, as *selene* means "moon" in Greek. Selene drives her chariot drawn by pale white horses through the heavens at night.

Hekate: She is a goddess of the Underworld, a terrifying figure who oversees the punishment of sinners in the pit of Tartaros. Hekate carries a whip and blazing torches, and is accompanied by barking dogs. She is associated with crossroads and other haunted places. Hekate is the patroness of witches and those skilled in the dark arts.

Artemis is lunar and nocturnal, and is also linked with many star myths, such as the story of the Great Hunter, Orion.

Artemis' Sacred Attributes

- Silver bow and arrows
- Palm tree
- Wildflowers
- Wild animals, especially quail, deer, bear, wolf
- Hunting dogs

Artemis and Leto

Artemis is Zeus' daughter, but she is most protective of her mother, Leto, and the two share a powerful bond. In many myths, Artemis defends her mother from male sexual advances or predatory attacks from male giants and monsters. Leto experienced great distress in her relationship with Zeus and her ensuing troublesome pregnancy, and Artemis takes to heart her mother's difficulties. Together, Artemis and Leto represent female hostility toward the masculine sexual impulse, and female anxiety about human society in general. Artemis in particular is often depicted in her myths as wary, distrustful, vindictive, and unfriendly to mortals.

Actaeon

In many myths, Artemis is depicted as punishing anyone who invades her privacy or pollutes her purity. In one tale, the hunter Actaeon accidentally comes upon the goddess bathing in her private pool in the woods. When Artemis detects him there, she turns him into a stag, and then his own hounds attack him and tear him to pieces.

Artemis is the goddess of wild, pure nature untouched by humans.

But what about nature that is cultivated for human use and benefit?

Let us turn to Demeter and Persephone, and further explore the sacred cycle of all living things.

▮▮ DEMETER

- Goddess of agriculture, crops, and the harvest
- Great mother figure
- Joined in worship with her daughter, Persephone

Demeter (in Roman mythology = Ceres) is the great Olympian mother goddess, and especially the goddess of agriculture. She embodies the ripe grains in the fields cultivated by human hands, and the harvesting of crops to feed the people. Demeter is one of the original Olympians, born of the Titans Rhea and Cronos. Demeter represents the Olympian mother archetype, and her main attitude is one of powerful maternal love. She is depicted as a tall, majestic woman of a mature, motherly age, with thick golden hair, clothed in rich, heavy robes. Demeter is shown as strikingly beautiful with a kind expression on her face, and she often carries a golden stalk of grain.

Ceres

Demeter's Roman name is Ceres.
Demeter is the goddess of "cereal" grains.
Better eat your Wheaties!

cerevisia = "beer" or "ale" to the Romans
La Cerveza Mas Fina!

The Great Mother Archetype

On our journey through Greek mythology, we have already met Gaia, the primordial Earth mother. But among the Olympians, there are several splendid and important goddesses who manifest aspects of motherhood. The goddess Hera represents the social status of marriage and maternity, but not the emotion of motherly love. The virgin Artemis loves her mother Leto, and is associated with childbirth, but she is never a mother herself. Playful Aphrodite adores children, and has many of them, but her maternity is secondary to her sexuality. Only the great goddess Demeter embodies the pure mother archetype within the Olympian *pantheon*.

Demeter and Zeus

According to Hesiod, Demeter was an early wife of Zeus, before his last marriage to Hera (*Theogony* 917–919). The union of Zeus and Demeter is another manifestation of the sacred marriage motif, where the sky god and the Earth goddess join together in an ancient ritual of fertility. Demeter's daughter by Zeus is Persephone (in Roman mythology = Proserpina), and she is sometimes known simply as Kore, which means "girl" or "daughter" in Greek. The two goddesses together symbolize the growth of plants, especially grain—while Demeter represents the ripe, mature crops, Persephone represents the tender, immature buds.

Demeter and Persephone

These two goddesses are inseparable in myth and worship.
They represent two sides of the life cycle.
Mother and Daughter = The Female Continuum

Persephone is the growing shoot,
goddess of the spring bloom, the "little green sprout."

Demeter is the mature grain, goddess of the autumn harvest.

The Abduction of Persephone

The most famous myth of Demeter and Persephone presents an allegory of the death and rebirth of vegetation and the agricultural cycle of the seasons (as told in the *Homeric Hymn to Demeter*, 1–495). In this myth, Persephone is playing with her friends and gathering flowers in a meadow, and she wanders away from her mother's protection. Hades, lord of the Underworld, catches sight of the young girl and falls in love with her. He asks his brother, Zeus, for permission to take the girl, and Zeus assents. With a violent rush of his chariot, Hades seizes Persephone and carries her down to the land below to be his wife. Demeter is enraged and distraught at the loss of her beloved daughter, and her retaliation is great: she brings harsh winter to the world and doesn't allow anything to grow. Endless frost brings famine—as mortals are starving and the gods are deprived of their sacrifices, Zeus engineers a compromise with Demeter that allows Persephone to return to the upper world for a portion of each year in return for the restoration of the growing season. So Demeter is appeased, and the Earth blooms once again when Persephone returns.

Allegory of the Seasons

Persephone is "planted" in the ground like a seed during winter.
She reemerges in the spring
like a new budding plant.

The Cycle of Life and Death

The myth of Persephone in the Underworld also reflects allegorical meanings in the way the Greeks understood the important passages in the lives of human beings. Persephone's abduction by Hades can be interpreted as the event of death itself, and her passivity in her capture by the lord of the Underworld symbolizes our human helplessness in the face of death. As the survivor, Demeter represents the vengeful, grieving mother who takes forceful, destructive action in response to the loss of her daughter, while the sad daughter suffers her fate passively. But in negotiating the "shared custody deal" with Hades, and in bringing Persephone home for the spring and summer months, the goddess Demeter offers human beings the promise that we too may one day be allowed to reemerge into the Upper World.

It's not nice to fool Mother Nature!

Marriage to Hades

Persephone is also the symbol of the reluctant bride sent to a "new life" with her new husband and family, where the bride experiences the transition from her old life and the loss of her own family, and especially her father's love—remember, Zeus allowed the abduction, so Persephone must suffer what Artemis asked to avoid. While she is in the Underworld, Hades feeds Persephone a few seeds of the pomegranate, the fruit of

Aphrodite and a symbol of sexuality. By eating the fruit, Persephone "grows up" and gains sexual knowledge, so she can never again be the pure, innocent daughter figure. So Demeter is ultimately reconciled to her daughter's marriage to Hades, and Persephone becomes the queen of the Underworld, a melancholy figure who is constantly waiting for the moment when she can go visit her mother.

Eleusis

The sacred site of Demeter and Persephone was the town of Eleusis, fourteen miles west of Athens, where the myth tells us Demeter stayed while she was grieving the loss of her daughter. The cult of Demeter and Persephone celebrated here is called the *Eleusinian Mysteries*. Here worshippers celebrated their sacred ceremonies and secret rituals commemorating the death and rebirth of Persephone. By honoring and celebrating the experience of Persephone, worshippers hoped to participate in her miraculous cycle of death and rebirth. The myth of Persephone, as an allegory of the life-and-death cycle of vegetation, offers the promise of the soul's immortality.

Demeter's Sacred Attributes

- Stalk of grain
- Torch
- Basket of fruits and vegetables

Artemis
Goddess of Wild Nature

Demeter and Persephone
Goddesses of Cultivated Nature

■ SOURCES FOR THIS CHAPTER

Clay, Jenny Strauss. (1989). *The Politics of Olympus: Form and Meaning in the Major Homeric Hymns*. Princeton: Princeton University Press.

D'Este, Sorita. (2005). *Artemis: Virgin Goddess of the Sun & Moon*. London: Avalonia Books.

Foley, Helene P. (1994). *The Homeric Hymn to Demeter: Translation, Commentary, and Interpretive Essays*. Princeton: Princeton University Press.

Kerényi, Karl. (1967). *Eleusis: Archetypal Image of Mother and Daughter*. Translated by Ralph Mannheim. New York: Bollingen Foundation.

Leeming, David, and Page, Jake. (1994). *Goddess: Myths of the Female Divine*. Oxford and New York: Oxford University Press.

Lefkowitz, Mary R. (2007). *Women in Greek Myth*, 2nd ed. Baltimore: The Johns Hopkins University Press.

Marinatos, Nanno. (2000). *The Goddess and the Warrior: The Naked Goddess and Mistress of the Animals in Early Greek Religion*. New York: Routledge.

Morford, Mark P. O., and Lenardon, Robert J. (2007). *Classical Mythology*, 8th ed. Oxford: Oxford University Press.

Mylonas, George E. (1961). *Eleusis and the Eleusinian Mysteries*. Princeton: Princeton University Press.

Richardson, N. J. (1974). *The Homeric Hymn to Demeter*. Oxford: The Clarendon Press.

Ruden, Sarah. (Trans.). (2005). *Homeric Hymns*. Indianapolis: Hackett Publishing Company.

Suter, Ann. (2002). *The Narcissus and the Pomegranate: An Archaeology of the Homeric Hymn to Demeter*. Ann Arbor: University of Michigan Press.

■ POPULAR CULTURE REFERENCES

Film

Beauty and the Beast (1946). Director: Jean Cocteau.
The Matrix Reloaded (May 2003). Directors: Larry and Andy Wachowski.
The Matrix Revolutions (November 2003). Directors: Larry and Andy Wachowski.

Television

Hercules: The Legendary Journeys (1995–2000). Syndicated series.
Xena: Warrior Princess (1995–2001). Syndicated series.

Online

Greek Mythology Link (www.maicar.com/GML)

Self-Quiz for Chapter 9

1. What are Artemis' main titles?

   _____

   _____

   _____

   _____

2. Who is the mother of Artemis?

   _____

   _____

   _____

   _____

   _____

3. What are Artemis' sacred places?

   _____

   _____

   _____

4. Who is the Triple-Faced Goddess?

   _____

   _____

   _____

   _____

5. Who is Hekate?

   _____

   _____

   _____

6. What are Artemis' sacred attributes?

_____

_____

_____

_____

7. Who is the great Olympian mother archetype?

_____

_____

_____

_____

_____

_____

8. What happens to Persephone?

_____

_____

_____

_____

_____

9. How do Demeter and Persephone represent the cycle of life?

_____

_____

_____

_____

_____

_____

10. Why is Eleusis sacred?

_____

_____

_____

_____

Grrrl Power: Athena and the Amazons

As we continue on our journey through Greek mythology, let's consider a few more images of female power, both in terms of intellectual supremacy and physical strength. First let's take a look at the Olympian goddess Athena, daughter of the great god Zeus.

ATHENA

- Goddess of wisdom
- Virgin warrior
- Pallas Athena
- Patron of Athens
- Goddess of warcraft, strategy, and victory
- Goddess of human culture

Athena (in Roman mythology = Minerva) is the great goddess of wisdom, culture, statesmanship, and warcraft. Athena is a virgin goddess, and she is sometimes invoked by the epithet "Pallas," a name of unknown origin. Athena embodies the divine meaning of practical wisdom and righteous protection within human society. Athena is depicted as a tall, strong, imposing woman of striking beauty, with a fierce glare emanating from her grey eyes. She wears a long dress and military armor, including a helmet and shield, and she holds a spear in one of her bare, muscled arms. She is sometimes shown with a snake on her shield or coiled around her feet.

Athena's Birth Story

One of the most important and famous myths about Athena is the story of her birth from the head of the great god Zeus (as told by Hesiod in the *Theogony* 886–900, and in the *Homeric Hymn to Athena* 1–18). As the story goes, early in his reign Zeus was afraid that a child of his might overthrow him, as he did his own father, Cronos. So when Metis, whose name means "practical wisdom," who was one of Zeus' early consorts before Hera, became pregnant, Zeus swallowed her. As an allegory, then, the supreme ruler absorbs wisdom into himself forever. A few months later, Zeus gets a splitting headache, and asks Hephaestus (or in some versions, Prometheus or Hermes) to crack open his skull with a hammer. Out leaps Athena, fully grown and armed, shouting a thunderous war cry! This tale embodies several significant layers of meaning about the nature and functions of the goddess Athena.

Symbolic Birth

Athena is born adult and armed—a symbol of her physical power.
She is born from the head of Zeus—a symbol of her wisdom/knowledge.
That she is born from her father, the supreme male, suggests the basic masculinity of her nature.
Because she is born directly from the sky god, it is a symbol of her close bond with Zeus—Athena is Zeus' favorite child!

Goddess of Wisdom

Athena embodies a specific type of wisdom known to the Greeks as *metis*, after the goddess who was Athena's "mother." *Metis* encompasses the meaning of practical knowledge and constructive strategy, the type of working wisdom that helps human beings advance themselves and their culture. The Greeks contrasted *metis* with the more esoteric concept of *sophia*, the type of prophetic, divine wisdom associated with the god Apollo. *Metis* was often associated with women and was considered a feminine type of wisdom, though many famous males in Greek mythology exhibit crafty, resourceful *metis*, such as the god Hermes and the great hero Odysseus.

Patron Goddess of Athens

Athena is a Pan-Hellenic goddess; that is, she was worshipped all over the ancient Greek world. But she was specifically associated with the city of Athens that proudly bears her name. On our journey through Greek mythology, we have already encountered the story of the competition for patronage of the city, where Athena beat Poseidon by giving the citizens the gift of the olive tree (see Chapter 6). High above the city, on the tall rocky outcropping of the Acropolis, the Athenians dedicated a major temple to Athena, called the *Parthenon*, in honor of the goddess as maiden, as the word *parthenos* in Greek means "maiden" or "virgin." She was also sometimes called Athena *Polias*, meaning Athena "of the City."

> **Athena and the Olive Tree**
>
> The olive tree is a symbol of the economy and prosperity of Athens, as it gives fruit, oil, and wood.

"Mother" of the Athenians

A very clever Greek myth places Athena, the Virgin goddess, as the mother of the Athenian people. As the story goes, Athena was strolling around her city one day, when her half-brother, the god Hephaestus, caught sight of her and desired to make love to her. Athena rebuffed his advances, but an overly excited Hephaestus ejaculated all over the hem of her dress. Athena wiped off the offending substance with a tuft of wool, then buried it in the soil near her temple. Nine months later, a baby was born, whom grandmother Gaia handed up to a startled Athena. The goddess named him Erichthonius, meaning "Earth Born," and she placed him in a strong cradle guarded by her sacred snakes. Erichthonius becomes the first legendary king of Athens.

Athena's Sacred Animals

Athena is strongly associated with birds, mainly predatory birds such as hawks, vultures, and kites. This identifies her with her father, Zeus, whose ornithic symbol is the great eagle. But Athena's chief bird symbol is the owl, known to us as the "wise old owl." Most people assume the association here is that both the owl and Athena are associated with wisdom, and they both have a bright, sharp glance from their eyes. Yet it may also be a link due to location: all around the Acropolis near her temple, tiny owls called *glaukes* nested in the crevices of the overhanging rocks. However the connection came about, the owl is the primary symbol of Athena and the city of Athens: both the goddess and the owl adorn Athenian coins. Athena is also associated with snakes in many of her myths and in depictions of her in art. The snake is a universal symbol of wisdom, creativity, and protection.

> *Glaukopis*
>
> Athena is called *glaukopis* in Greek mythology, meaning "grey-eyed" or "owl-eyed."
> *glaukos* = "greyish green"
> *glaux, glaukes* = miniature owl/s

Goddess of Strategy and Warcraft

Athena is considered the goddess of the more noble aspects of warfare, such as military strategy and tactics, and she is also a goddess of diplomacy and negotiation. As a goddess of war, Athena is symbolized by armor and weapons, and she often leads troops into righteous battle with her thunderous war cry. Along with her helmet and spear, Athena carries the *aegis*, the magic goat-skin shield given to her as a gift from her doting father, Zeus (see Chapter 5). Later, Athena places on the *aegis* the snake-encrusted head of the Gorgon, Medusa, a gift from the hero Perseus after he conquered and beheaded the horrible monster. Thus the *aegis* becomes even more formidable as a protective device.

> Warrior Athena is accompanied by
> the goddess of winged victory, *Nike.*
> Nike = Goddess of Victory
> *Just Do It*!

Athena and Heroes

Like her half-brother, the god Hermes, the goddess Athena is very friendly and helpful to human beings, and is constantly active in the mortal realm. Athena is especially fond of the great Greek heroes, and she plays the role of the supportive, wise, sympathetic older sister—many of these heroes are her actual half-brothers and distant cousins, as they are often descended from the god Zeus. On our journey through Greek mythology, we will encounter several heroes who are helped and aided in their quests and labors by the goddess Athena. During and after the Trojan War, Athena guides many heroes, such as Achilles, Diomedes, and Odysseus. But by far her favorite hero is the great strongman Herakles, son of Zeus, who is supported throughout his exceptional career by the wisdom and protection of the goddess.

Goddess of Human Culture

Athena symbolizes the use of functional wisdom to create all of human culture. She is the divine Olympian symbol of progress and civilization. Athena is associated with the practical crafts, such as shipbuilding, carpentry, and horse training. In the story of the Trojan War, the goddess helps one of her favorite heroes, Odysseus, perform one of his most famous deeds: the building of the Trojan Horse. Athena is also the goddess of the more domestic, "female" arts, such as weaving, sewing, and cooking. She is especially identified with military and political expertise, and like her loquacious brother, Hermes, she is associated with the use of rhetorical skills in political debates and court speeches. Like her father, Zeus, Athena is considered a goddess of justice, and she holds sway over the social and political order of Greek civilization.

Athena's Sacred Attributes

- Owl
- Olive tree
- Snake
- *Aegis* = goat-skin shield
- Helmet, spear

Let us turn now
from the warrior goddess Athena
to the warrior women of Greek mythology,
the Amazons.

 AMAZONS

- Warrior women
- Daughters of Ares
- Horsewomen of the Caucasus

The **Amazons** are a mythical or legendary society of warrior women that captivated the imaginations of the ancient Greeks. There are many descriptions of the Amazons, but the basic aspects of the accounts are fairly constant. The Amazons are a fierce tribe of expert horsewomen who hunt and do battle on horseback. Because of their depiction as warriors, they are sometimes called the Daughters of Ares. The Amazons lived in the northern part of Asia Minor near the Caucasus Mountains, in an all-female society in which males were used for menial work and reproductive purposes only. Amazons are depicted as strong, healthy women wearing short leather tunics, leggings, and boots, as they sit astride magnificent horses.

The name *Amazon* is said to mean "without a breast,"
from the Greek *a* = "un-" or "no" + *mazos* = "breast."

It is believed that Amazon women removed their right breasts
to be able to pull back the bow and shoot with more strength and accuracy.

Amazons and Heroes

On our journey through Greek mythology, we will encounter many tales of heroes who must fight against Amazons as part of their heroic quest or as one of their labors, such as Bellerophon, Herakles, Theseus, and Achilles. Such a battle between heroes and Amazons is called an *amazonomachy*. This battle is an ultimate test of the hero's strength and skill against mighty opponents. Yet even with all their muscle and expertise, Amazons mostly lose these battles against Greek heroes. These stories of Amazon conflicts seem to suggest an anxiety about the possibility of female dominance and the loss of male potency, but this fear is always defeated in the end by the restitution of Greek male superiority.

Famous Amazons

- Hippolyte: Amazon queen whose belt is the goal of Herakles' ninth labor
- Antiope: Amazon won by Theseus
- Penthesilea: Amazon queen slain by Achilles in the Trojan War

Modern Amazons

In today's language, an "Amazon" refers to any tough, aggressive female, or one who is often of very tall stature. The name is also used to refer to female body-builders and professional wrestlers. The most well-known image of an Amazon was popularized by the character of Xena, the Warrior Princess, in the syndicated television series of the same name, starring Lucy Lawless as the title character (*Xena: Warrior Princess*, 1995–2001).

Athena = Warrior Goddess

Amazons = Warrior Icons

SOURCES FOR THIS CHAPTER

Hurwitt, Jeffrey M. (2000). *The Athenian Acropolis: History, Mythology, and Archaeology from the Neolithic Era to the Present.* Cambridge: Cambridge University Press.

Leeming, David, and Page, Jake. (1994). *Goddess: Myths of the Female Divine.* Oxford and New York: Oxford University Press.

Lefkowitz, Mary R. (2007). *Women in Greek Myth*, 2nd ed. Baltimore: The Johns Hopkins University Press.

Morford, Mark P. O., and Lenardon, Robert J. (2007). *Classical Mythology*, 8th ed. Oxford: Oxford University Press.

Neils, Jenifer. (Ed.) (1992). *Goddess and Polis: The Panathenaic Festival in Ancient Athens.* Princeton: Princeton University Press.

Neils, Jenifer. (1996). *Worshipping Athena: Panathenaia and Parthenon.* Madison: University of Wisconsin Press.

Ruden, Sarah. (Trans.). (2005). *Homeric Hymns.* Indianapolis: Hackett Publishing Company.

Wilde, Lyn Webster. (1999). *On the Trail of the Women Warriors: The Amazons in Myth and History.* New York: Thomas Dunne Books.

POPULAR CULTURE REFERENCES

Film

Amazons and Gladiators (2001). Director: Zachary Weintraub.

Television

Wonder Woman (1975–1979). ABC/CBS series.
Hercules and the Amazon Women (1994). TV movie, director: Bill L. Norton.
Hercules: The Legendary Journeys (1995–2000). Syndicated series.
Xena: Warrior Princess (1995–2001). Syndicated series.

Online

Greek Mythology Link (www.maicar.com/GML)
The Amazons (www.net4you.com/poellauerg/Amazons)
Whoosh (www.whoosh.org)

Self-Quiz for Chapter 10

1. What are Athena's main titles?

   _____

   _____

   _____

   _____

2. How is Athena born?

   _____

   _____

   _____

   _____

   _____

3. What is *metis*?

   _____

   _____

   _____

4. Why is Athena called the "mother" of the Athenians?

   _____

   _____

   _____

   _____

   _____

5. What are Athena's sacred animals?

   _____

   _____

   _____

6. What is on Athena's *aegis*?

_____

_____

_____

_____

7. Who is Nike?

_____

_____

_____

_____

_____

_____

8. Who are the Amazons?

_____

_____

_____

_____

_____

9. What is an *amazonomachy*?

_____

_____

_____

_____

_____

_____

10. What is the popular etymology of the name "Amazon"?

_____

_____

_____

_____

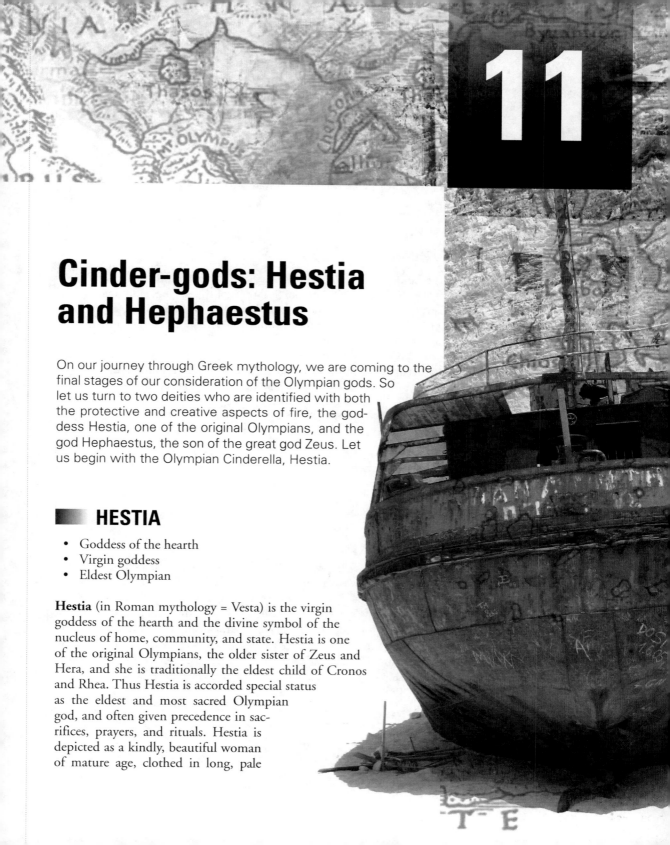

11

Cinder-gods: Hestia and Hephaestus

On our journey through Greek mythology, we are coming to the final stages of our consideration of the Olympian gods. So let us turn to two deities who are identified with both the protective and creative aspects of fire, the goddess Hestia, one of the original Olympians, and the god Hephaestus, the son of the great god Zeus. Let us begin with the Olympian Cinderella, Hestia.

HESTIA

- Goddess of the hearth
- Virgin goddess
- Eldest Olympian

Hestia (in Roman mythology = Vesta) is the virgin goddess of the hearth and the divine symbol of the nucleus of home, community, and state. Hestia is one of the original Olympians, the older sister of Zeus and Hera, and she is traditionally the eldest child of Cronos and Rhea. Thus Hestia is accorded special status as the eldest and most sacred Olympian god, and often given precedence in sacrifices, prayers, and rituals. Hestia is depicted as a kindly, beautiful woman of mature age, clothed in long, pale robes, often with a veil over her head. She is shown sitting at the central hearth, tending the sacred home fire in the great hall of Mt. Olympus.

Hestia's Roman name = Vesta

"Vestal Virgins" = her priestesses

The Vestal Virgins tended the sacred eternal flame of Rome
in her temple in the Roman Forum.

Goddess of the Hearth

Hestia represents the domestic and communal hearth fires that symbolize the continuing essence of the family, or the larger social and political units of tribes, cities, and states. Fire is a necessity for human culture and civilization to flourish, vital for the basic daily needs of work, living, and religious ritual, and so fire becomes a symbol of civilized society. In many cities and states, the sacred fire is kept alive in a central, communal "hearth" in an important and visible place as a symbol of society's "heart" or spirit. Oftentimes a spark from the communal fire is sent to ignite the hearths in new colonies as a symbolic and sentimental bond to the "Mother Country." Hestia personifies the warmth and kinship of the sacred home fire.

Hestia is the Greek word for "hearth."

As the sayings go:
Home is where the heart(h) is!

Keep the home fires burning!

Virgin Goddess

In Greek mythology, Hestia's appearances are few. The ancient Greeks believed she was courted by many gods, yet she vowed to remain a virgin. The virginity of Hestia, who feels neither the heat of passion nor the pall of coldness towards anyone, is an allegory for her dependability and steadiness as a symbol of protective fire. The fire neither blazes too hot and dangerously destructive, nor does it cool and go out, causing chill and darkness. So closely is Hestia identified with the sacred fire that we are told she gives up her Olympian throne to the god Dionysus and chooses instead to stay in the center of the great hall at the edge of the hearth. Hestia never leaves her place at the fire.

Hestia's Sacred Attributes:

- Hearth
- Fireplace
- Home

Three Olympian Virgins
Hestia
Athena
Artemis

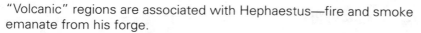 HEPHAESTUS

- God of the forge
- Divine blacksmith
- God of creative fire

Hephaestus (in Roman mythology = Vulcan) is the great god of the forge and the master artisan of Olympus. Hephaestus is the symbol of divine creative fire, technology, and metallurgy, and he produces extraordinary things from his workshop. Hephaestus is the only Olympian who is constantly at work, covered in grime and soot from laboring in the forge. He is depicted as a mature man, usually bearded, with powerfully muscled arms, chest, and shoulders. But Hephaestus is characterized as being lame from birth in his legs, which are weak and puny, and he often needs help walking or rides astride a donkey. Hephaestus is absolutely serious about everything he does.

Hephaestus' Roman name = Vulcan

His forge is located under Mt. Aetna in Sicily.

"Volcanic" regions are associated with Hephaestus—fire and smoke emanate from his forge.

Hephaestus' Birth Story

There are many different accounts of the birth of Hephaestus. In one version, Hera was angry at Zeus for giving birth to Athena on his own, so she gives birth to Hephaestus by *parthenogenesis*, or "maiden birth"—that is, without being impregnated by Zeus. Many myths show a special bond between Hephaestus and his mother, Hera. In other versions, Hephaestus is the son of the conjugal union of Zeus and Hera, and thus he is full brother to Ares, god of war. Some accounts say that Hephaestus was born with lame legs, and Hera was ashamed and disgusted by his deformity, an obvious symbol of her troubled marriage. So she cast baby Hephaestus off Mt. Olympus and he fell down into the sea, where he was rescued and nursed back to health by the sea goddess Thetis. In some versions, Hephaestus is crippled by the throw. Another account has Zeus casting Hephaestus out of heaven, and he lands on the island of Lemnos, where he is tended by some locals. Later, his half-brother Dionysus, god of wine, gets Hephaestus drunk and brings him home to Olympus.

Hephaestus' most sacred place is the island of Lemnos, where he fell to Earth.

Lemnos was an important center of his worship.

Divine Blacksmith

Hephaestus is known as the god of creative fire and the master craftsman. He is the divine symbol of the constructive use of fire in the forge, especially for metalworking, smelting, and welding. Like Athena, who is associated with the arts and crafts, Hephaestus was also revered by craftsmen, mainly blacksmiths and metalworkers. Hephaestus is identified by the tools of the trade: hammer, tongs, chisel, axe, anvil, and bellows (to deliver air to stoke the fire). The forge of Hephaestus is usually located under the Earth, often under a volcano, but sometimes he is at work in his workshop on Mt. Olympus. Hephaestus also has employees: the Cyclopes, who forged the thunder and lightening for Zeus, serve as his apprentices.

The mythological lameness of Hephaestus may come from the role of the blacksmith in ancient society.

Perhaps the blacksmith took up the trade because he couldn't hunt or plow; perhaps due to his trade, his upper body became more developed than his legs. Maybe the use of arsenic in hardening bronze was not very healthy, either!

The Craft of Hephaestus

On our journey through Greek mythology, we will encounter many extraordinary things created by Hephaestus to be used and enjoyed by gods and great heroes. These items, made of exquisitely wrought metalwork, are often imbued with magical powers and characteristics that set them apart from more ordinary items. Some of the exceptional masterpieces that are said to be fashioned by Hephaestus include:

- Hermes' winged hat and sandals
- Zeus' *Aegis*
- Aphrodite's magic sexy belt
- Achilles' armor and shield
- Eros' bow and arrows
- Golden robot attendants and magic wheelchair for himself

Hephaestus and Aphrodite

One of the most intriguing myths about Hephaestus is the story of his marriage to Aphrodite. As the tale goes, Zeus gives Aphrodite to Hephaestus to be his wife, in order to forestall any conflict among the other male gods over the beautiful goddess of love. But the couple does not have a very equitable marriage. Though Aphrodite is delighted to receive many ornately fashioned items of gold jewelry and trinkets from her hard-working husband's workshop, at the same time, while Hephaestus is at work, she is having erotic affairs with other gods and mortals, in particular with her favorite lover, Ares, her husband's brother. In one myth, Hephaestus traps the adulterous couple together in bed one day with finely wrought chains, invisible to the eye but absolutely unbreakable. All the other gods laugh at Hephaestus for having an unfaithful wife, except for Poseidon, who pays the fine for the sexual misconduct. Some scholars interpret the marriage of Hephaestus and Aphrodite as an inversion, or opposite, of the traditional sacred marriage motif, in that Aphrodite is a goddess associated with the sky and Hephaestus is a god identified with the Earth—where he falls after he is born and the location of his workshop. It does seem that Aphrodite has the upper hand in this unusual relationship, which at times appears to be a version of Beauty and the Beast. As in his marriage, Hephaestus is a figure of many contradictions. He is highly skilled, intelligent, and hard-working, but sometimes he is laughed at and disrespected by the other gods.

Divine Payback

Hephaestus creates Pandora:
"an evil men want to embrace."
He makes the first woman like his own wife: curious and dangerous.

Hephaestus' Sacred Attributes:

- Hammer, tongs, chisel, axe
- Anvil
- Bellows
- Fire, forge

Hestia = Protective Fire
Hephaestus = Creative Fire

The Olympian Pantheon

On our journey through Greek mythology, we have now met nearly all the major Olympian gods:

Zeus and Hera
Poseidon, Demeter, Hestia
Apollo, Artemis, Hermes, Aphrodite
Dionysus, Ares, Hephaestus, Athena

We will meet Hades when we go to the Underworld in Chapter14.

Nature Spirits

There exist many other categories of Greek mythological divinity beyond the Olympian gods. Among these are the numerous spirits of nature that inhabit the beaches, forests, mountains and woodlands of the Greek mythological landscape. These creatures of nature exist on a level below the Olympian gods in the divine hierarchy, but they are still considered supernatural beings who have magical powers and special characteristics.

Pan (in Roman mythology = Faunus) is the rustic god of shepherds and flocks, and he is especially worshipped in the pastoral societies of Arcadia in southern Greece. His father is Hermes (sometimes Apollo or Zeus) and his mother is usually a nymph from the local woodlands. Pan is not fully human in form: he has some goat attributes, such as the horns, ears, and legs of a goat. Like satyrs, Pan wanders the mountain forests in search of parties, music, wine, and sex, and he often joins in the revels of Dionysus. It is said that Pan invented a type of flute known as the *syrinx*, also called the "pan-pipe," in honor of a nymph he once loved. Pan embodies the animal and sexual nature in all humans.

Pan jumps out of his cave to scare people;
sudden impulse of terror = "panic."

Centaurs

These are creatures that also personify the joining of both human and animal natures, as they are half human and half horse. Centaurs generally have a human upper torso, arms, and head, set upon the lower body and four legs of a horse. In many myths, centaurs are depicted as starting fights or attempting other acts of a violent or sexual nature. In temperament, centaurs are lecherous and belligerent, and many Greek heroes must fight and conquer these rambunctious creatures. A battle against centaurs is called a *centauromachy*. On our journey through Greek mythology we will encounter many centaurs, mostly bad ones—such as Nessos—and only one good one, the kindly Chiron, tutor of Greek heroes.

Categories of Nymphs

- Naiads = Sexy fountain nymphs of freshwater springs
- Oreads = Mountain nymphs, shy pals of Artemis
- Dryads = Tree nymphs who live and die with their trees

■ SOURCES FOR THIS CHAPTER

Borgeaud, Philippe. (1988). *The Cult of Pan in Ancient Greece*. Chicago: University of Chicago Press.

Merivale, Patricia. (1969). *Pan the Goat God: His Myth in Modern Times*. Cambridge: Harvard University Press.

Morford, Mark P. O., and Lenardon, Robert J. (2007). *Classical Mythology*, 8th ed. Oxford: Oxford University Press.

Ruden, Sarah. (Trans.). (2005). *Homeric Hymns*. Indianapolis: Hackett Publishing Company.

Wildfang, Robin Lorsch. (2006). *Rome's Vestal Virgins*. New York: Routledge.

■ POPULAR CULTURE REFERENCES

Film

Pan's Labyrinth (*El Laberinto del Fauno*, 2006). Director: Guillermo del Toro.
Vulcan, Son of Jove (1961). Director: Emimmo Salvi.

Television

Hercules: The Legendary Journeys (1995–2000). Syndicated series.
   Season 3, Episode 3: "Love Takes a Holiday."
Xena: Warrior Princess (1995–2001). Syndicated series.
   Season 5, Episode 19: "Looking Death in the Eye."

Online

Greek Mythology Link (www.maicar.com/GML)

Self-Quiz for Chapter 11

1. What are Hestia's main titles?

   _____

   _____

   _____

   _____

2. Where does Hestia sit in the great hall of Olympus?

   _____

   _____

   _____

   _____

3. Who are the three Olympian virgins?

   _____

   _____

   _____

   _____

4. What are Hephaestus' main titles?

   _____

   _____

   _____

   _____

5. Why is Lemnos sacred to Hephaestus?

   _____

   _____

   _____

   _____

6. What are some of the extraordinary things created by Hephaestus?

_____

_____

_____

_____

7. What are Hephaestus' main attributes?

_____

_____

_____

_____

8. Who is Pan?

_____

_____

_____

_____

9. What are centaurs?

_____

_____

_____

_____

10. What are naiads? oreads? dryads?

_____

_____

_____

_____

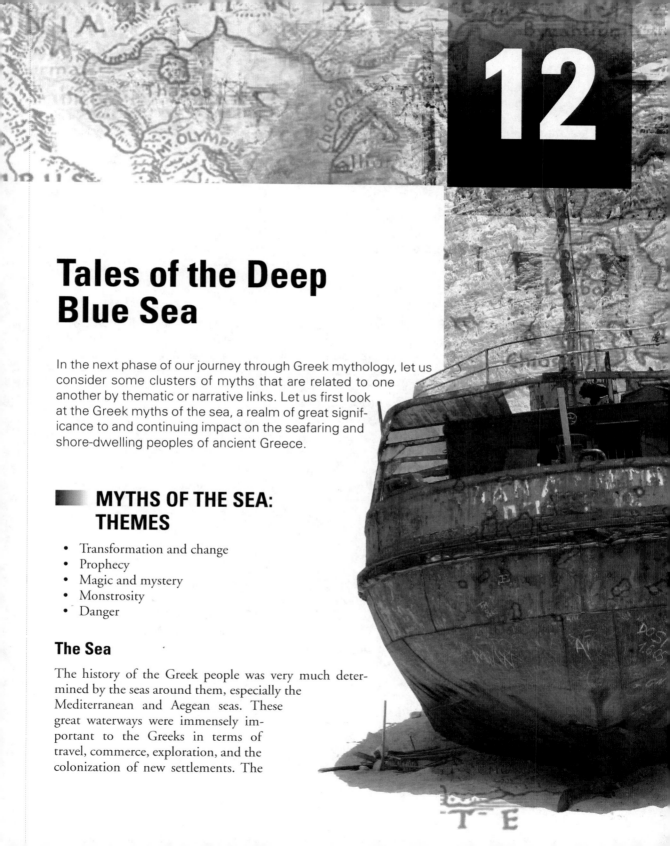

12

Tales of the Deep Blue Sea

In the next phase of our journey through Greek mythology, let us consider some clusters of myths that are related to one another by thematic or narrative links. Let us first look at the Greek myths of the sea, a realm of great significance to and continuing impact on the seafaring and shore-dwelling peoples of ancient Greece.

MYTHS OF THE SEA: THEMES

- Transformation and change
- Prophecy
- Magic and mystery
- Monstrosity
- Danger

The Sea

The history of the Greek people was very much determined by the seas around them, especially the Mediterranean and Aegean seas. These great waterways were immensely important to the Greeks in terms of travel, commerce, exploration, and the colonization of new settlements. The

Mediterranean and Aegean seas are dotted with many islands, and ancient Greek ships cruised from port to port on their way to Asia Minor, North Africa, and Sicily in search of trade and adventure. The character of the sea, as a fickle, ever-changing, exciting, and sometimes perilous realm influenced the nature of the Greek myths of the sea, where it is always a place of magic, change, and danger.

Dolphins in Greek Myth

Always lovable and intelligent
Helpful to humans

POSEIDON

On our journey through Greek mythology, we have already met Poseidon, the great Earth-shaker and the Olympian god of the sea (in Chapter 6). The ill-tempered Poseidon rules over the waters of the sea with ferocious control, and he causes tidal waves, tsunamis, and earthquakes with a stroke of his trident. We shall encounter many myths where Poseidon's wrath is unleashed against mortals who anger him, as in the tale of the attempted home-coming of Odysseus (in Chapter 20).

Many Sea Gods

Since the sea was a place of such significance for the ancient Greeks, it is no surprise that they had a multiplicity of sea deities, almost too many to recount. Sea gods tend to occur in bunches, like big schools of fishes! Many of the Greek gods and monsters of the sea are described and named by the poet Hesiod (*Theogony* 233–370).

Oceanos and Tethys

On our journey through Greek mythology, we have already encountered the two Titans, Oceanos and Tethys, children of Gaia and Ouranos (Chapter 2). Oceanos was believed to be the stream of water surrounding the flat disc of the Earth, and is thus an early and im-portant sea deity. The Titans Oceanos and Tethys lived in the Far West, and produced thousands of offspring, including gods and goddesses of rivers, springs, and waterfalls (Hesiod, *Theogony* 337–370).

Oceanos and Tethys

Their daughters are called *Oceanids*,
nymphs of rivers and waterfalls.

Old Men of the Sea

Another very important category of Greek sea deities are the Old Men of the Sea, in Greek known as *Halioi Gerontes*, literally meaning "salty old men." All of the Old Men of the Sea share the following characteristics:

- Old age
- Wisdom
- Power of prophecy
- Shape-shifting

Nereus

The most famous and oldest Old Man of the Sea is Nereus, son of Gaia and Pontos (Hesiod, *Theogony* 233–236). Nereus is depicted as a gentle old man, with a long beard and hair, and he is extremely wise. Like many other sea deities, Nereus has the gift of prophecy, and he is often consulted for information about the future. Nereus can also change his shape whenever he wishes, and he often changes into a fish or a dolphin when he wants to elude captivity. Many Greek heroes seek information from Nereus.

> Nereus marries Doris, an Oceanid.
> Their fifty daughters are called *Nereids*,
> salt-water nymphs.

Nereids

The daughters of Nereus are salt-water nymphs who dwell in the sea and often accompany Poseidon as he journeys through his realm. The Nereids are beautiful, playful young girls, often pictured as mermaids, half-female and half-fish, who sing, dance, play musical instruments, and ride the waves on the backs of dolphins, sea horses, and other sea creatures. Like their father, Nereus, they can change shape whenever they wish. Nereids are kind and helpful to humans who cross the sea, such as sailors, heroes, and other travelers, and assist them whenever they are in distress. Nereids are worshipped on islands, beaches, and at the mouths of rivers. In his poem, Hesiod proudly names all fifty of the Nereids (*Theogony* 240–264).

Famous Nereids

Thetis

The beautiful Nereid Thetis was loved by both Zeus and Poseidon, but because she was fated to have a son greater than his father, the gods married her off to a mortal king, Peleus. Thetis was very unhappy to be forced to marry a mortal, and she angrily changed her shape to try to avoid him. But eventually they are married in a grand, elaborate ceremony, and Thetis does indeed have a son greater than his father: Achilles, the greatest warrior ever and hero of the Trojan War. Later on our journey through Greek mythology, we shall see how Thetis calls in a favor by asking Zeus to help her son, Achilles (in Chapter 19).

The Wedding of Thetis and Peleus

This was the most important social event in the Greek mythological world.

Amphitrite

Another famous Nereid is the lovely Amphitrite, who was desired by the great god of the sea, Poseidon. Like her sister, Thetis, Amphitrite was an unwilling bride, but finally Poseidon was able to win her as his wife. Amphitrite is always trying to keep her husband in line, since Poseidon likes to play around with sea nymphs. As a couple, they mirror the roles of Zeus and Hera, with Poseidon as the adulterous husband and Amphitrite as the jealous wife. Amphitrite punishes many of Poseidon's lovers, such as the sea nymph Scylla, whom she turns into a monster by poisoning her tide-pool!

Amphitrite and Poseidon = First Couple of the Sea

Their Son = Triton, the Merman

Triton

The son of Amphitrite and Poseidon is Triton, a merman who is half human above the waist and has a fish tail below, who spends his days enjoying the sea. Like other sea deities, Triton can change his shape at will. Triton is called the Trumpeter of the Sea, because he plays on a conch shell, calling the herds of sea creatures together, or stirring up the waves as he likes. Sometimes Triton is considered in the generic plural, Tritons, as mermen who accompany the Nereids as they frolic through the sea.

Proteus

Another Old Man of the Sea is Proteus, who is sometimes considered part of the older, pre-Olympian generation of the gods. Like the god Nereus, with whom he is often confused, Proteus has the gift of prophecy and he can change his shape at will. Proteus is considered ornery: he demands that anyone who wants information from him must wrestle him for it, as he changes shape in order to outwit his competition.

Proteus = A Very Slippery Character!

Protean in English means

"easily changeable, variable, unpredictable."

Phorcys

Another Old Man of the Sea is Phorcys, who is important mainly for his powerful and notable offspring. Phorcys married his sister, the sea goddess Ceto (note that "cetacean" refers to the family of marine mammals), and they produced three sets of sea nymph daughters.

- **The Graiae:** These three sisters are the Spirits of Old Age, and their name means "The Old Ones." The Graiae are depicted as beautiful, swan-like ladies with long white hair. The sisters share one eye and one tooth among them. The Graiae are often visited by heroes who need information about their heroic quests.
- **The Gorgons:** These three sisters live at the Far Western Ocean and are usually named Stheno, Euryale, and Medusa, the most famous of the three Gorgons. The Gorgons were terrible monsters with snakes in their hair, huge staring eyes, and gaping mouths with dripping tongues. One look at the horrible face of a Gorgon would turn a human to stone.

    Medusa: The most famous Gorgon was Medusa, whose lover was the great god of the sea, Poseidon. When Medusa was pregnant by Poseidon, the Greek hero Perseus cut off her head—which he gave to his patron goddess, Athena, to adorn her shield, the *aegis*. Out of Medusa's severed neck were born two offspring:
    Pegasus = The Winged Horse
    Chrysaor = He of the "Golden Sword"
- **The Sirens:** These sisters (sometimes two or more in a group) are beautiful sea nymphs who are half woman and half bird in shape. As the story goes, the Sirens asked Zeus for wings so they could help in the search for their lost companion, the goddess Persephone, when she was captured by Hades. The Sirens sit on their rocky island and lure sailors to their deaths on the rocks with their beautiful singing. One famous sailor, the hero Odysseus, gets by them alive!

Siren in modern English:

A sound that signals alarm or danger,
such as on an ambulance or fire engine.

A woman who is sexy and dangerous,
such as a "screen siren."

Ladon

Phorcys and Ceto also produce a son, the dragon Ladon. This dragon helps the graceful nymphs, the Hesperides, Daughters of Evening, as he guards the sacred apples on the tree in the Garden of the Hesperides near the Far Western Ocean. We will encounter Ladon again on our journey through Greek mythology when we go along with Herakles on his eleventh labor (in Chapter 17).

Thaumas

Another Old Man of the Sea is Thaumas, brother of Phorcys, who is also significant mainly for his notable offspring. Thaumas married Electra, an Oceanid, and produced these daughters:

- **Iris**: The lovely goddess of the rainbow is Iris, whose name in Greek means "rainbow." Swift-footed Iris serves as a divine messenger, primarily for the great goddess Hera.
- **The Harpies**: These sisters (usually three or more) are vicious, swift, winged, and sharp-taloned female bird-monsters, whose name means "the Snatchers." The Harpies are always hungry and filthy. Like gusts of wind, the Harpies will snatch away anything they can: your food, your hat, even your soul! We will encounter them as foes for the Greek hero Jason (in Chapter 18).

The Generations of Monsters

The monsters of Greek mythology all originate from the sea, or from sea deities. Like the sea, monsters are dangerous and unpredictable, taking many grotesque shapes with strange, multiple forms. Many famous monsters are the offspring of Chrysaor, he of the "Golden Sword," who is born from the severed neck of the Gorgon, Medusa, after her affair with the great sea god Poseidon. The monsters of Greek myth serve as foes for many Greek heroes, such as the most famous hero of them all, Herakles (as we shall see in Chapter 17).

Chrysaor mates with an Oceanid, Callirhoë, whose name means "Beautiful Stream," and they produce:

- Geryon: the triple-bodied giant
- Echidna: half snake, half woman

Echidna mates with the dragon Typhon, and produces a litter of puppies and other fantastical creatures:

- Orthus: two-headed hound of Geryon
- Cerberus: three-headed hound of Hades
- Hydra: nine-headed water snake with dog body
- Chimaera: triple monster with lion front, goat middle, and snake tail

Chimerical in modern English means

"wildly fanciful, or highly improbable."

Echidna mates with her son, the dog Orthus, and they produce:

- Sphinx: winged monster with woman's head and lion's body
- Nemean Lion: monstrous, invincible lion

Myths of the Sea

These myths resemble the tall tales
told by fisherman and sailors.

"You should've seen the one that got away!"

On our journey through Greek mythology, let's keep in mind these important
themes and motifs that appear in myths of the sea and stories of heroes trav-
eling across the sea:

- Magic and fantasy
- Monsters and the grotesque
- Transformation and change
- Prophecy

SOURCES FOR THIS CHAPTER

Barringer, Judith M. (1995). *Divine Escorts: Nereids in Archaic and Classical Art*. Ann
    Arbor: University of Michigan.
Casson, Lionel. (1991). *The Ancient Mariners: Seafarers and Sea Fighters of the
    Mediterranean in Ancient Times*, 2nd ed. Princeton: Princeton University Press.
Haven, Kendall F. (2005). *Wonders of the Sea*. Westport, CT: Libraries Unlimited.
Lombardo, Stanley. (Trans.). (1993). *Hesiod: Works & Days, Theogony*. Indianapolis:
    Hackett Publishing Company.
Mills, Donald H. (2002). *The Hero and the Sea: Patterns of Chaos in Ancient Myth*.
    Wauconda, IL: Bolchazy-Carducci Publishers.
Morford, Mark P. O., and Lenardon, Robert J. (2007). *Classical Mythology*, 8th ed.
    Oxford: Oxford University Press.

POPULAR CULTURE REFERENCES

Film

20,000 Leagues Under the Sea (1954). Director: Richard Fleischer.
Clash of the Titans (1981). Director: Desmond Davis.
The Abyss (1989). Director: James Cameron.

Television

History's Mysteries: Monsters of the Sea (2001). The History Channel.

Online

Greek Mythology Link (www.maicar.com/GML)

Self-Quiz for Chapter 12

1. Who are the four Old Men of the Sea?

_____

_____

_____

_____

2. Who are the Nereids?

_____

_____

_____

_____

3. Who is Thetis? Amphitrite?

_____

_____

_____

_____

4. Who is Triton?   ,

_____

_____

_____

_____

5. Who are the Graiae? the Sirens?

_____

_____

_____

_____

6. Who are the Gorgons?

_____

_____

_____

_____

7. Who are the Harpies?

_____

_____

_____

_____

8. Who is Echidna?

_____

_____

_____

_____

9. Who is Orthus? Cerberus?

_____

_____

_____

_____

10. What are some common themes in myths of the sea?

_____

_____

_____

_____

13

Acts of *Hubris*: Punishment Myths

Let's continue on our journey through Greek mythology with a consideration of another set of mythological tales linked by narrative content and theme. These are the Greek myths of punishment.

▰ PUNISHMENT MYTHS: THE UNBREAKABLE CHAIN

- *Hubris*
- *Atē*
- *Nemesis*

▰ PUNISHMENT MYTHS

The punishment myth pattern is a universal and ubiquitous story motif in Greek mythology that serves the function of a narrative warning to human beings about the necessity for correct behavior. While the Greek gods can be very close to humans, and many myths draw attention to the unique bond between gods and mortals, punishment myths accomplish the opposite: these myths emphasize the distance that exists between gods and mere humans, underscoring the gap between their blissful divine existence and the troublesome mortality of humans. When humans overstep the boundaries between mortal and immortal, myths of punishment remind them of the dire consequences of unacceptable actions.

Punishment Myths = Warnings

When someone is made to say:

"Oops, my bad!"

Hubris

The vicious cycle of punishment begins with an act of *hubris*, which means an act or deed of thoughtless presumption, impudence, or arrogance. Whenever a mortal dares to challenge, offend, or deny a god, or if a mortal attempts to do a super-human feat, this is seen as an act of *hubris*. Such *hubris* draws the attention and displeasure of the gods, and initiates the next stage of the punishment cycle.

Atē

In the next stage of the vicious cycle of punishment, those guilty of *hubris* are afflicted with *atē*, which means madness and moral blindness, a type of dangerous cluelessness sent by the gods. *Atē* makes people act stupidly and rashly, and causes them to say or do stupid things that will bring on the final stage of divine retribution.

Nemesis

The final stage of the vicious cycle is the punishment itself, called *nemesis* by the ancient Greeks, meaning retribution, reprisal, the ultimate penalty. The inevitable outcome of *hubris* is always divine *nemesis*, or total ruin. It is only the fear of *nemesis* that causes people to try to avoid *hubris*—this is a strong deterrent.

Nemesis is also the name of the goddess of retribution.

The Furies are the *Erinyes*,
special divine agents of vengeance

The Furies chase down criminals,
especially murderers of family members.

Blood demands blood!

 ## "CELEBRITY SINNERS"

Now let's take a look at a few of the most famous offenders in Greek mythology and their punishments. As we review these punishment myths, note how many of the punishments seem to "fit the crime"—that is, there is a strong element of balance between the nature of the offense and the nature of the penalty imposed.

Salmoneus

One of the worst offenses that mortals could commit was to pretend to be one of the gods. King Salmoneus committed great *hubris* when he decided to pretend to be the great god Zeus. Salmoneus dressed up as Zeus, drove around in a chariot with clanging bronze pots to imitate the sound of thunder, and hurled lighted torches to copy Zeus' lightning bolts. Worst of all, Salmoneus demanded the divine honors reserved solely for Zeus. For the *hubris* of impersonation, Zeus zapped Salmoneus with a real thunderbolt down to Tartaros, the deep pit of Hades, to spend the rest of eternity.

Tartaros

Maximum-Security Lock-up in Hades

Holds all the "Celebrity Sinners"

Daedalus

The story of Daedalus demonstrates the *hubris* of going beyond human ability, when humans express greater-than-mortal powers. Daedalus was a master craftsman and a skilled inventor who served Minos, the King of Crete. One day Minos prayed to the god of the sea, Poseidon, to send him a bull to sacrifice, but the bull Poseidon sent was so beautiful that Minos decided not to sacrifice him, and sacrificed a less good-looking bull instead. This angered the sea god, and so as punishment, Poseidon caused Minos' wife, Queen Pasiphaë, to fall in love with the bull from the sea. Pasiphaë commanded Daedalus to help her satisfy her lust for the bull, so the master craftsman created a life-like hollow cow costume for Pasiphaë, who then had sex with the bull and became pregnant. The offspring of Pasiphaë and the bull is the monstrous Minotaur, half man and half bull, which terrorized all of Crete. The Minotaur was then locked up in an elaborate prison constructed by Daedalus, called the *Labyrinth*. Later, the Minotaur was killed by Theseus, hero of Athens.

Labyrinth in modern English = a maze
an intricate, complex structure
of interconnecting passageways.

Daedalus and Icarus

Soon Daedalus had enough of the strange happenings on the island of Crete, and decided to make his escape together with son, Icarus. To flee the island without detection, Daedalus fashioned two pairs of feathered wings held together with wax. Daedalus warned his son to stay away from the sun during his flight, as the heat of the sun would melt the wax. But young Icarus, enchanted by the light of the sun, ignored his father's warnings: Icarus flew too close and the wax of his wings melted, sending him plummeting into the sea to his death. For the *hubris* of attempting the super-human feat of flight, Daedalus is punished by the loss of his son.

Phaëthon

Another cautionary tale about the *hubris* of trying to go beyond mortal powers is the story of Phaëthon, the son of Apollo. Rash Phaëthon presumed to do a god's work when he asked his father to drive the sun chariot across the sky. The inexperienced boy could not control the divine steeds, and the Earth was alternately frozen and scorched as Phaëthon careened wildly through the heavens, dragged by the sun-horses. Zeus finally heeds the pleas of Gaia, and he hurls a thunderbolt at Phaëthon, shattering the chariot and sending the boy crashing to the ground. For the *hubris* of trying to do a god's job, Phaëthon failed miserably and is punished with death.

Icarus and Phaëthon

These stories carry a warning: Fly too close to the sun, and come crashing down.

They are stories of boys who fail to become men.

Asklepios

On our journey through Greek mythology, we have already met Asklepios, the great physician and son of Apollo (in Chapter 6). Trained as a young man by the wise centaur Chiron, Asklepios grew to be skilled in the arts of healing. Asklepios is so good at medicine that he can even restore the dead to life. This angered Zeus and Hades for the disruption of the natural order of life and death, so Zeus zapped Asklepios with a thunderbolt. For the *hubris* of going beyond human powers, Asklepios is punished with death.

Tantalus

One of the most famous, or rather notorious, malefactors in all of Greek mythology is King Tantalus, the son of Zeus. There are various versions of the crime of Tantalus, but whatever its specific details, it is an abuse of the hospitality and trust of the Olympian gods. One version of the story recounts that Tantalus invited the gods over to his palace for dinner. As a trick, he decided to test the gods' omniscience by cutting up his own son, Pelops, and serving him as the main course. All the gods immediately recognized the grisly nature of the dish—except Demeter, who, it is said, was still grief-stricken over the loss of her daughter, Persephone, so she absent-mindedly gnawed on poor Pelops' shoulder. Hermes brought Pelops back from the Underworld, and Hephaestus fashioned a new shoulder for him out of ivory. For the *hubris* of offending the gods at table, Tantalus is sent down to the deep pit of Tartaros. There he is surrounded by delicious food and sparkling water, but is never allowed to eat or drink. His punishment is to be forever starved and parched, provoked but never satisfied.

> *Tantalize* in modern English means
> to excite someone by offering something desirable,
> while keeping it out of reach.

Sisyphus

Another (in)famous offender in Greek mythology is King Sisyphus, who was well known for his cunning and smarts, which he even used to outwit the gods. As the story goes, Zeus became angry at Sisyphus for divulging one of his sexual escapades, so Zeus sent Death down to take Sisyphus away. But Sisyphus used all his cunning to trick Death, and even put him in chains! As long as Death was bound up, no one could die, so the gods were upset by this inversion of the natural order of things. Zeus sent Ares to free Death, and to make certain Sisyphus is sent to the Underworld. But the wily Sisyphus left explicit instructions to his wife, Merope, not to give him any burial rites. Hades is so disturbed by Merope's apparent neglect that he sends Sisyphus back to the Upper World to chastise his wife. When he got home, Sisyphus lived a long, happy life with his family, and then finally died at an advanced age. The gods were waiting for him in the Underworld, and they confined him to the pit of Tartaros, where Sisyphus faces his penalty: he is forced to push a huge boulder up a hill, but when it gets to the top, the stone rolls down again. For the *hubris* of outwitting the gods, and denying the power of Death, Sisyphus is punished with an eternally frustrating task.

Pentheus

Many myths of punishment involve Dionysus, the god of wine and ecstasy, and the resistance to his worship. One such story is the tale of Pentheus, King of Thebes, home of Dionysus' mother, Semele. When Dionysus arrived to introduce the mystery of his worship, Pentheus refused to allow the Theban people to worship Dionysus, whom he considered to be dangerous to social order. After the *hubris* of denying a god, Dionysus forced Pentheus to suffer from *atē*—he believes he is immune to the god's power. But Pentheus is torn up in a ritual *sparagmos* by maenads, led by Agave, Pentheus' own mother. For denying the power of a god, Pentheus is punished with total destruction of self.

Arachne

A number of punishment myths center upon the tale of someone who challenges a god to a competition, and for the *hubris* of issuing such a challenge, eventually loses that contest. These stories include the tale of Arachne, an expert weaver of tapestries, who boasted that she could beat Athena herself in a contest of weaving. Always a fair goddess, Athena went to Arachne disguised as an old woman and warned her not to be so presumptuous. But Arachne ignored the warning, so Athena resumed her form and took up the challenge. Arachne weaves a tapestry showing the scandalous doings of the gods, while Athena weaves a tapestry showing the fates of presumptuous mortals. Since Arachne's work rivaled her own, Athena angrily tore the girl's work to shreds. In shame, Arachne hanged herself, but Athena felt pity for her and turned her into the first spider, which keeps all of Arachne's skill at weaving.

Arachne in Greek = "Spider"

Arachnid in English = Class of spiders and scorpions

What is *arachnophobia*?

Marsyas

Another case of a competition gone bad is the story of the satyr Marsyas, who one day found a flute and started playing it. Marsyas became so proficient at playing the flute that he decided to challenge Apollo to a music contest: Apollo would play his lyre, and the Muses would judge the competition. Apollo agreed, with the stipulation that the winner would get to inflict any punishment on the loser. Both Apollo and Marsyas played very well, but then Apollo challenged Marsyas to play his instrument upside down, something that can be done with a lyre but not with a flute. So Marsyas lost the contest, and Apollo skinned him alive: the satyr's blood flowed down to form the River Marsyas. For the *hubris* of thinking he could rival the god of music, Marsyas paid the ultimate penalty.

Ixion

In some instances, an offense against a great goddess initiates the cycle of retribution. One of the more fascinating tales of punishment involves King Ixion, who murdered his father-in-law and had to be purified. As the story goes, Zeus offered to perform the purification himself and so invited Ixion to Mt. Olympus. There Ixion tried to seduce Hera, the wife of Zeus. When Hera complained of the offense, the great god didn't believe her version of events, and so Zeus decided to test Ixion with a *faux* Hera that he fashioned out of a cloud. But Ixion failed the test: as he is making love to the "Cloud-Hera," Zeus catches him in the act and zaps him down to Tartaros. There Ixion is bound to a wheel of fire that rolls through the Underworld forever and ever.

Offspring of Ixion and "Cloud-Hera" = The Lusty Centaurs

Tityos

Another sexual offense against a goddess involves the Giant Tityos, son of Gaia, Mother Earth. Tityos tried to ravish the goddess Leto, mother of Apollo and Artemis, as she was on her way to Delphi. The Twin Gods shot Tityos with arrows, and Zeus hurled a thunderbolt at him, sending him down to Tartaros. There the huge body of Tityos is stretched out along the ground and tied down, and vultures peck out his liver every day. For his *hubris*, Tityos is punished with never-ending torment.

Celebrity Sinners in Tartaros:

- Tantalus
- Sisyphus
- Tityos
- Salmoneus
- Ixion
- Titans

Punishment Myths

These myths offer warnings to humans
about what is unacceptable behavior.

They emphasize the distance between gods and mortals.

▮ SOURCES FOR THIS CHAPTER

Camus, Albert (1955). *The Myth of Sisyphus and Other Essays*. Translated by Justin
O'Brien. New York: Alfred A. Knopf, Inc.

Hart, Gerald D. (2000). *Asclepius: The God of Medicine*. London: The Royal Society of
Medicine Press Ltd.

Lombardo, Stanley. (Trans.). (1993). *Hesiod: Works & Days, Theogony*. Indianapolis:
Hackett Publishing Company.

Lyons, Lewis. (2003). *The History of Punishment*. Guilford, CT: Lyons Press.

Morford, Mark P. O., and Lenardon, Robert J. (2007). *Classical Mythology*, 8th ed.
Oxford: Oxford University Press.

▮ POPULAR CULTURE REFERENCES

Film

Labyrinth (1986). Director: Jim Henson.
Arachnophobia (1990). Director: Frank Marshall.

Television

Tantalus: Behind the Mask (2001). PBS documentary, directed by Dirk Olson.

Online

Greek Mythology Link (www.maicar.com/GML)
The Labyrinth Society (www.labyrinthsociety.org)

Self-Quiz for Chapter 13

1. What is *hubris*?

   _____

   _____

   _____

   _____

2. What is *nemesis*?

   _____

   _____

   _____

   _____

3. Where are the "Celebrity Sinners" confined?

   _____

   _____

   _____

   _____

4. What happens to Salmoneus?

   _____

   _____

   _____

   _____

5. What happens to Phaëthon?

   _____

   _____

   _____

   _____

6. What happens to Tantalus?

_____

_____

_____

_____

7. What happens to Sisyphus?

_____

_____

_____

_____

8. What happens to Arachne?

_____

_____

_____

_____

9. What happens to Ixion?

_____

_____

_____

_____

10. What happens to Tityos?

_____

_____

_____

_____

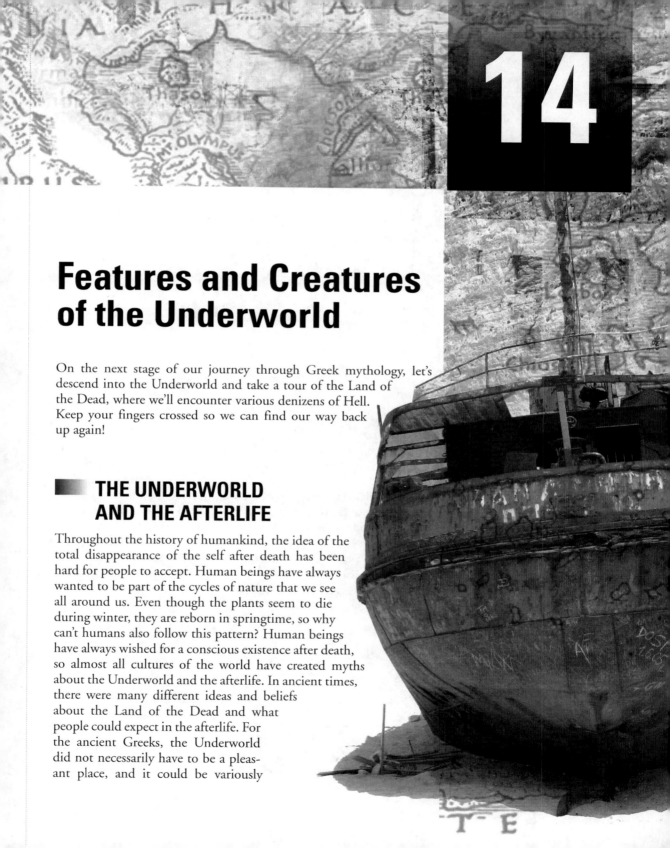

14

Features and Creatures of the Underworld

On the next stage of our journey through Greek mythology, let's descend into the Underworld and take a tour of the Land of the Dead, where we'll encounter various denizens of Hell. Keep your fingers crossed so we can find our way back up again!

▰ THE UNDERWORLD AND THE AFTERLIFE

Throughout the history of humankind, the idea of the total disappearance of the self after death has been hard for people to accept. Human beings have always wanted to be part of the cycles of nature that we see all around us. Even though the plants seem to die during winter, they are reborn in springtime, so why can't humans also follow this pattern? Human beings have always wished for a conscious existence after death, so almost all cultures of the world have created myths about the Underworld and the afterlife. In ancient times, there were many different ideas and beliefs about the Land of the Dead and what people could expect in the afterlife. For the ancient Greeks, the Underworld did not necessarily have to be a pleasant place, and it could be variously depicted as a place of both punishment and purification. But the idea that there was another stage of life after death seemed to help people cope with the inevitability of their mortality.

As the Sibyl says to the hero Aeneas:

"Goddess-born son
Of Trojan Anchises, the road down
To Avernus is easy. Day and night
The door to black Dis stands open.
But to retrace your steps and come out
To the upper air, this is the task,
The labor."

—Virgil, *Aeneid* 6.124–129, translated by Stanley Lombardo

HADES

- Lord of the Dead
- King of the Underworld
- "The Unseen One"
- "The Wealthy One"

Hades (in Roman mythology = Pluto or Dis) is the lord of the Underworld. Hades is one of the original Olympians, the son of the Titans Cronos and Rhea and the brother of Zeus and Poseidon, from whom he received the Underworld as his share of the universe. In Greek mythology, Hades is depicted as a mature, bearded man wearing dark robes, and his nature is violent, unpredictable, and easily aroused. Hades is also known as Pluto, meaning the "Wealthy One," which may refer to his role in agriculture, or to his access to the gems and metal ores underground, or to his possession of all the souls that ever lived on Earth. His wife is his abducted niece, Persephone, the gloomy Queen of the Dead, who spends her time moping until she can return to the Upper World in springtime to join her mother, Demeter. Together, Hades and Persephone rule over the Underworld.

Hades

Place for the Dead = The Underworld

God = Lord of the Dead

"Map" of Hades

The ancients had many names for the realm of the Underworld: Hades, Erebus, Tartaros, Avernus, or Dis. The geographical description of the Underworld comes mainly from surviving ancient literary accounts, primarily from Homer's *Odyssey* (Book 11) and Virgil's *Aeneid* (Book 6). On our journey to the mythological Underworld, we will be considering the main universal features and creatures of Hades that occur most commonly in these ancient accounts. These various ancient myths of the Underworld have had a huge influence on modern culture, in literature, art, music, and film.

Shades

Ghosts/spirits in the Underworld are called "shades"—shadowy, smoky images of their former selves.

They keep the same emotions and memories—hurt, anger, love.

Homer's *Odyssey*

The earliest Greek description of the Underworld occurs in Book 11 of Homer's epic poem the *Odyssey*. In this episode, Odysseus goes to the gate of Hades to find the shade of the old prophet Teiresias, in order to seek information about how to get home to Ithaka after the Trojan War. The shade of Teiresias must drink the warm blood of a sacrificial animal, a black ram, so he can foretell the future to Odysseus. All around are the sad, shrieking spirits of his slain comrades and deceased relatives, too insubstantial for him to touch or embrace. In this Homeric account of the Underworld, Hades is a place of darkness, hopelessness, and despair.

Odysseus even meets the unhappy shade of the great hero Achilles, and congratulates him for being a big shot among the dead in the Underworld.

But the shade of Achilles tells Odysseus:

> "Don't try to sell me on death, Odysseus.
> I'd rather be a hired hand back up on earth,
> Slaving away for some poor dirt farmer,
> Than lord it over all these withered dead."
> —Homer, *Odyssey* 11.488–491, translated by Stanley Lombardo

---

The unburied cannot enter Hades.
The shades of men lost at sea wander until given funeral rites.

A *cenotaph* is an empty grave, a memorial for the lost.

▰ NOW, LET'S ENTER HADES!
Gate of Hades

Just inside the entryway to Hades, waiting to exit to assault humankind, are the causes of death: old age, diseases, grief, toil, hunger, poverty, fear, and anxiety, along with strife and war. Near the gate is a huge elm tree, whose branches are hung with empty dreams that torment and mislead humans. There, too, are the twin brothers *Thanatos*, Death, and *Hypnos*, Sleep, who fly from Hades to capture human souls. Various monsters, such as Gorgons and Harpies, dwell near the doorway of Hades.

Hypnos and Thanatos = Twin Brothers

Morpheus = God of Dreams
Morpheus is the son of Hypnos, and
can take any shape.

Morphine is a strong pain-killing narcotic made from the opium poppy.

The River Styx

Through the gate of Hades is the main river of Hell, usually identified as the River Styx, the "River of Hate," but in some versions this first river is identified as one of the other rivers of Hell. To enter Hades fully, the souls of the dead must cross the River Styx, which is marshy, muddy, slimy, and disgusting. The grimy banks of the river are crowded with miserable shades shrieking, begging, and jostling one another, trying to get in line to go across. It is a noisy scene of confusion and anguish. Hermes *Psychopompos*, the "Guide of Souls," makes his appearance as he leads the newly dead souls from the Upper World down to the riverbank.

The Rivers of Hades

Styx = The River of Hate
The gods swore solemn oaths by the River Styx.

Pyriphlegethon = The River of Fire

Acheron = The River of Woe

Cocytus = The River of Wailing

Lethe = The River of Forgetfulness

Charon

At the riverbank is Charon, the grim boatman, who ferries the souls of the dead across the river, for a steep fee. Charon is a horrible figure with dirty clothes and a matted white beard: he is old, mean, greedy, nasty, and rude as he propels the rusty vessel with his pole. The sad shades beg and scream to be let across, but only those souls who have enough cash money to pay the fare, and those who have received a proper burial, are allowed to cross the river, and Charon violently pushes back all the rest. Only a few shades make it onto his boat and across the River Styx into the main part of Hades.

> ### Charon's Crossing Fee
> The Greeks had an ancient custom of burying the dead with coins "for the boatman."

Cerberus

Across the River Styx, there is another slimy bank, and beyond that is a huge cavern guarded by Cerberus, the hound of Hell. Cerberus is a ferocious, monstrous guard dog with three heads that bristle with snakes. Cerberus was Hades' own beloved pet! In order to get through the cave without being bitten, the souls must throw some honey-cakes to the hungry dog to distract him.

The Fields of Mourning

Through the cave is another gate leading into a neutral zone, where the sounds of continuous weeping and lamentation can be heard. This zone was called the Fields of Mourning, a type of waiting area, where souls of the untimely dead waited to be admitted into Hades. Here were the souls of those who had died too soon—babies, suicides, murder victims, and those condemned to die by false accusation—all who did not have a chance to fulfill their allotted time of life. Here too were the heroic souls of those who recently died in battle, still wandering, shell-shocked from the clamor and turmoil of war. All these souls had to wait until their appointed time of admission into the Underworld.

> ### Ancient Greek Gestures of Mourning
> - Beat the head and chest with the hands
> - Tear out the hair

Crossroads now lead to two different paths: one way leads to Tartaros, and the other way leads to the Elysian Fields.

Tartaros

Also called Erebus, Tartaros is the deep pit of Hades, used primarily as a place of punishment, the maximum-security lock-up of the Underworld. Tartaros is bordered by a huge gate of solid iron and massive fortification walls, and surrounded by Pyriphlegethon, the "River of Fire," seething with flames and lava rocks. Locked up in Tartaros are murderers, tyrants, misers, traitors, bribe-accepters, and those who committed *hubris* against the gods, suffering their everlasting punishments. Here too are all the most infamous "celebrity sinners," such as Tantalus and Sisyphus, performing their various penalties of vain, frustrating effort. Tartaros is guarded by the Furies, those spirits of vengeance who make certain that the inmates carry out their sentences properly. The pit is also patrolled by

Hekate, goddess of black magic, who uses her whips and burning torches to enforce order and control over the prisoners.

Judges of the Underworld

Minos
Rhadamanthus
Aeacus = a.k.a. the Gatekeeper

The Elysian Fields

Down the other path are the Elysian Fields, also called *Elysium*, or the Isles of the Blessed, the paradise of the Underworld, with pleasant green meadows and lots of sunlight and air. Here dwell all those souls who led good lives: heroes, poets, teachers, inventors—those who fought for their countries, honored the gods, and made the world a better place to live. These souls dance, sing, feast, exercise, and play sports to their heart's content. When they are ready, they drink of the pure waters of the River Lethe, the "River of Forgetfulness," to purify their souls of all their old hurts and bad memories, and to forget the trauma of living. Then these purified souls wait for new bodies to be reborn again to the Upper World.

General Maximus to his troops before the battle in Germania:

"Three weeks from now, I will be harvesting my crops.
Imagine where you will be, and it will be so.
Hold the line! Stay with me!
And if you find yourself alone, riding in green fields with the sun on your face...
Do not be troubled!
For you are in *Elysium*, and you are already dead!
Brothers: what we do in Life... echoes in Eternity."
—*Gladiator* (2000)

▦ DENIZENS OF THE UNDERWORLD

- Hades and Persephone, King and Queen of the Dead
- Hermes *Psychopompos*
- Charon, the boatman
- Cerberus, the guard dog
- The Furies = *Erinyes*: Alecto, Megaera, Tisiphone
- Hekate, goddess of black magic
- The judges: Minos, Rhadamanthus, Aeacus
- *Thanatos* = Death, and *Hypnos* = Sleep

> **Hades**
>
> Hades is not evil; he is not like "Satan."
>
> Hades doesn't have to compete for souls.
>
> Everyone ends up in Hades' realm,
>
> where everyone finds their own heaven or hell.

SOURCES FOR THIS CHAPTER

Bernstein, Alan E. (1993). *The Formation of Hell, Death and Retribution in the Ancient and Early Christian Worlds*. Ithaca: Cornell University Press.

Bremmer, Jan (1983). *The Early Greek Concept of the Soul*. Princeton: Princeton University Press.

Garland, Robert (1985). *The Greek Way of Death*. London: Duckworth.

Lombardo, Stanley. (Trans.). (2000). *Homer: Odyssey*. Indianapolis: Hackett Publishing Company.

Lombardo, Stanley. (Trans.). (2005). *Virgil: Aeneid*. Indianapolis: Hackett Publishing Company.

Morford, Mark P. O., and Lenardon, Robert J. (2007). *Classical Mythology*, 8th ed. Oxford: Oxford University Press.

Russell, Jeffrey Burton. (1997). *A History of Heaven*. Princeton: Princeton University Press.

Terpening, R. H. (1985). *Charon and the Crossing: Ancient, Medieval and Renaissance Transformations of a Myth*. Lewisburg: Bucknell University Press.

Turner, Alice K. (1993). *The History of Hell*. Orlando: Harcourt Brace.

Vermeule, Emily. (1979). *Aspects of Death in Early Greek Art and Poetry*. Berkeley: University of California Press.

POPULAR CULTURE REFERENCES

Film

Field of Dreams (1989). Director: Phil Alden Robinson.
Groundhog Day (1993). Director: Harold Ramis.
What Dreams May Come (1998). Director: Vincent Ward.
Gladiator (2000). Director: Ridley Scott.

Television

Hercules in the Underworld (1994). Director: Bill L. Norton
Cerberus (2005). The Sci-Fi Channel, directed by John Terlesky.

Online

Greek Mythology Link (www.maicar.com/GML)
The River Styx (www.theriverstyx.net)

Self-Quiz for Chapter 14

1. Who or what is Hades?

   _____

   _____

   _____

   _____

2. Who is Teiresias?

   _____

   _____

   _____

   _____

3. Who is Hypnos? Thanatos?

   _____

   _____

   _____

   _____

4. Who is Charon?

   _____

   _____

   _____

   _____

5. Who is Cerberus?

   _____

   _____

   _____

   _____

6. Which souls dwell in the Fields of Mourning?

_____

_____

_____

_____

7. Which souls dwell in Tartaros?

_____

_____

_____

_____

8. Who are the Furies?

_____

_____

_____

_____

9. Which souls dwell in Elysium?

_____

_____

_____

_____

10. What is the River Lethe?

_____

_____

_____

_____

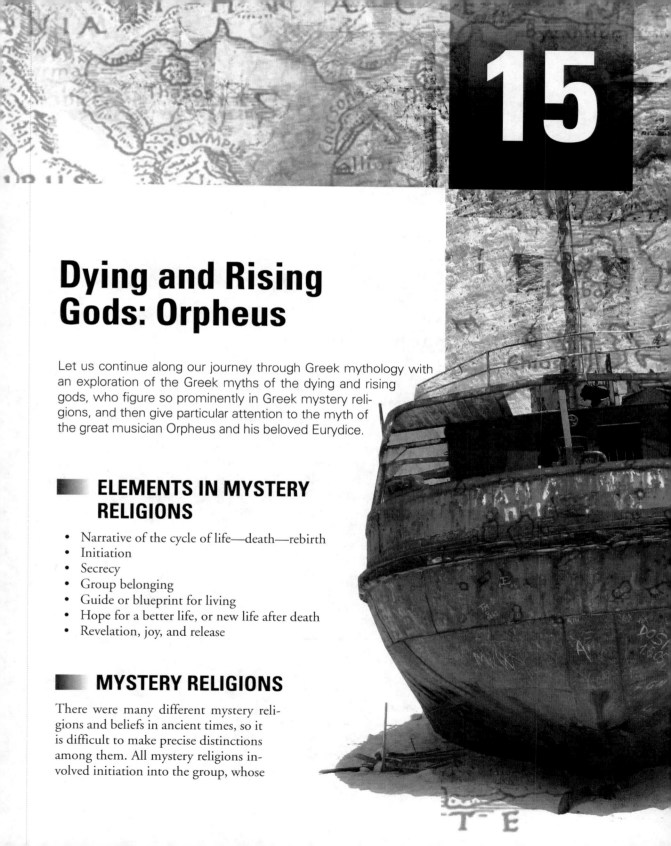

15

Dying and Rising Gods: Orpheus

Let us continue along our journey through Greek mythology with an exploration of the Greek myths of the dying and rising gods, who figure so prominently in Greek mystery religions, and then give particular attention to the myth of the great musician Orpheus and his beloved Eurydice.

ELEMENTS IN MYSTERY RELIGIONS

- Narrative of the cycle of life—death—rebirth
- Initiation
- Secrecy
- Group belonging
- Guide or blueprint for living
- Hope for a better life, or new life after death
- Revelation, joy, and release

MYSTERY RELIGIONS

There were many different mystery religions and beliefs in ancient times, so it is difficult to make precise distinctions among them. All mystery religions involved initiation into the group, whose members had access to secret knowledge, signs, and practices. The initiate is said to be "reborn" into the mystery religion. Since those initiated into mystery religions often kept silent about their cult practices, many aspects of the rituals in these religions remain shrouded in secrecy. Yet mystery religions have as their core belief the narrative of the cycle of life, death and rebirth, and this cycle is represented by the story of a dying and rising god. Thus, the figure of the resurrected god, a deity, hero, or supernatural figure who lives, dies, and comes back to life, is of major significance to an understanding of how the ancient mystery religions worked.

Modern-day secret societies,

such as Skull & Bones at Yale University,

stoke popular interest in conspiracy theories.

DYING AND RISING GOD

The figure of the dying and rising god provides a divine analogy for human worshippers, or, in other words, a model or guide for human initiates to follow. The mystery of the god who dies and comes back to life follows a very ancient pattern, devised long before the classical tales of Greek mythology. The dying and rising god can be either male or female, and is universally linked to the natural cycle of vegetation. Thus, he or she is often associated with trees, seeds, plants, vines, and flowers. He or she is commonly linked to a great mother goddess, either as her offspring or consort, and the narrative often involves the god being born or hidden somewhere in nature—in a cave, rock, or tree, as if a seed planted in Mother Earth. When the god dies, the great mother is often depicted as mourning the loss, and when the god rises again, in either a real or symbolic rebirth, the mother is shown rejoicing as she witnesses the rebirth.

Mystery religions offer initiates
hope of rebirth after death.

This is an analogy to the cycle of nature—
birth, death, and rebirth of soul

"Scapegoat"

There is very often a social aspect to the story of the dying and rising god, wherein the god assumes the characteristics of a communal "scapegoat." In many incarnations of the narrative, the dying and rising god takes on the burdens, problems, or sins of a society, and thus with the god's death, those burdens are removed, and the sins are cleansed. The dying and rising god dies for the benefit of society. So, belief in the god's resurrection would offer hope to mortal worshippers that a new beginning is possible, and a new life is even promised, with the rebirth of the god.

Scapegoat in modern English refers to a person, group, or thing blamed for the mistakes or crimes of others.

Let's review some of the major mystery religions practiced by the Greeks and the dying and rising gods associated with each religion.

Adonis

One of the most important Greek myths of a dying and rising god involves the handsome youth Adonis, the mortal lover of the goddess Aphrodite. There are many versions of the tale, but the most common account says that Adonis was born when his mother, Myrrha, tricked her father into an incestuous union. When her father discovered the horrible deed, Myrrha fled and Aphrodite turned her into a tree. A few months later, Adonis emerged from the trunk of the tree, and grew into the most handsome young man on the face of the Earth, so Aphrodite made him her lover. One day while hunting, Adonis was fatally gored in the groin by the tusk of a wild boar. As he lay dying, Aphrodite rushed to his side, and wept as she cradled him in her arms. Adonis bled out his mortal life onto the grass, and the goddess turned him into a red flower, the *anemone* or "windflower," a beautiful but fragile bloom that enjoys a brief life then wilts and dies. Thus, the mortal Adonis dies but is resurrected as a flower, suggesting his link to plant fertility. Adonis became the central figure in the mystery religion called the *Adonia*, celebrated by women in the heat of mid-summer. Women would plant tiny gardens and leave them up on the hot rooftops to wilt and die, and then they would weep and mourn for the untimely death of the beautiful god.

Adonis in modern English refers to an exceptionally good-looking young man—sometimes vain, but deservedly so!

Demeter and Persephone

On our journey through Greek mythology, we have already encountered the story of Demeter, the great Olympian mother, and her daughter, Persephone, who is abducted by the Lord of the Dead, Hades (in Chapter 9). This is the best-known Greek myth of a dying and rising god, or in this case, goddess. In this tale, Demeter, Grain Mother, mourns the loss of her daughter and causes winter to scourge the Earth with cold and famine. After the great god Zeus rules that Hades and Demeter must share Persephone, Demeter rejoices and causes the dead plants to spring back to life. Persephone is a symbolic representation of the Earth's fertility: she is a figure for the seasonal cycle of vegetation, as the goddess "dies" in winter and returns to her mother in springtime, mirroring the natural cycle of the crops. As an analogy, the perpetual return of Persephone in the springtime also provides a parallel for the rebirth of the human soul. To express her thanks to the town of Eleusis that sheltered her during her period of mourning, Demeter established their cult sanctuary and temple there. The mystery religion associated with Demeter and Persephone was called the *Eleusinian Mysteries*, a popular religion celebrating the two goddesses in secret rituals that promised initiates a happier life after death.

Dionysus

One of the most popular mystery religions in ancient times was the cult of Dionysus, god of wine, intoxication, and ecstasy. As we have already seen on our journey through Greek mythology (in Chapter 7), Dionysus was known as the "Twice-Born God" because of his miraculous double birth: first from the ashes of his incinerated mother, the mortal princess Semele, and then from the thigh of his father, the great god Zeus. The tale of Dionysus' birth indicates he "dies" with his mother, and is "reborn" from his father. So, the essence of the worship of Dionysus involves acts and symbols of the God's rebirth inside his followers. The devotees of Dionysus would stand outside of themselves in the process of *ekstasis*, using wine, dancing, and music, and then invite the God inside them in *enthousiasmos*. The climax of the ritual was the sacrifice of an animal representing the god, and partaking of the god's flesh and blood.

Universal World Myth Pattern

In the Egyptian story of the great god Osiris, he is

cut apart and reborn to Isis, the great mother goddess.

ORPHEUS AND EURYDICE
Music, Love, and Death

One of the most famous myths from ancient times is a narrative of music, love, death, and the wish for the soul's immortality. This is the story of Orpheus and his beloved, Eurydice, where the power of love and the enchantment of music nearly triumph over the inevitability of death. Because of the myth's universal significance, there are many different versions of the tale. But the classical account says that Orpheus was the son of one of the Muses, usually Calliope, and the god Apollo; other versions say he is the son of Oeagrus, a river god. Orpheus was an expert musician, a lyre player, from the northern Greek land of Thrace, who wooed and won the love of Eurydice, a Dryad, or tree nymph. On their wedding day, or shortly afterward, Eurydice is bitten by a snake and dies immediately. Orpheus is devastated by grief and vows to reclaim her.

Orpheus in the Underworld

Orpheus goes to find Eurydice in Hades. There he charms the deities of the dead with his beautiful music, and argues that Eurydice's life was unfairly cut off too soon. Persephone, the sad queen of the Underworld, is persuaded by Orpheus' words and his lovely lyre playing, so she allows Orpheus to rescue his wife. But the wife of Hades issues a stern condition: Orpheus is not to look back on their way out of the Underworld! As Orpheus made his way back to the Upper World, a silent Eurydice followed behind him, guided by Hermes *Psychopompos*. But Orpheus was overcome with curiosity and doubt, so he turned and looked at her, and she immediately faded back into Hades. It was like dying a second time!

Fairytale Motif of the "Impossible Condition"

The "impossible condition" occurs when someone is told *not* to do something,

but invariably does that very thing:

"Don't look back!"

"Don't eat that apple!"

"Don't open that box!"

Aftermath

Because he failed the test and lost his wife, Eurydice, when he could have had her back, Orpheus sinks into despair. Heartbroken, Orpheus wanders over the hills of Thrace, drowning his sorrows as he plays melancholy music, wanting only to be alone. His gloomy attitude offended the local maenads, followers of Dionysus, who become enraged when Orpheus refused to join their festivities. In a fit of jealousy and frustration, the maenads attacked Orpheus and tore him to pieces in the ritual *sparagmos*, scattering his flesh all over the land. They hurled his head, still singing sadly for Eurydice, and his lyre into the river and they floated out to sea. The shade of Orpheus goes down to Hades and is joyfully reunited with his beloved Eurydice in the Elysian Fields.

Themes in the Myth of Orpheus and Eurydice:

- The power of love
- The enchantment of music
- Human frustration about death
- Idea of soul's immortality

Orphism

In ancient times, Orpheus was considered a hero, teacher, and prophet who founded a mystery religion called *Orphism*. As a mystery religion, *Orphism* was concerned with a set of sacred texts that prescribed certain rules of correct behavior to its followers. *Orphism*, and the myth of Orpheus at its core, suggests a curious mixture of elements that seem to come from the worship of both Apollo (music, prophecy) and Dionysus (mystery, resurrection). But whatever its precise nature, *Orphism* offered the initiates a promise of ritual purification through living a good life, after which the soul could be reborn. Like other mystery religions, *Orphism* provided a paradigm for the soul's immortality.

Modern Adaptations

The myth of Orpheus and Eurydice has been extraordinarily influential upon the Western tradition in art, literature, music, and film. There have been numerous modern adaptations of the Orpheus theme in plays, opera, novels, and our favorite contemporary medium, film. Two very influential films from the 1950s are French director Jean Cocteau's *Orphée* (1950), and a film from Brazil, Marcel Camus' *Black Orpheus* (1959). Both of these films adapt the Orpheus myth of love and loss in unique and brilliant ways, as they respond to their respective audiences and times.

Moulin Rouge (2001)

The Orpheus myth takes shape in a more recent film, Australian director Baz Luhrmann's *Moulin Rouge* (2001). In this film, the Moulin Rouge, a famous gentleman's club in turn-of-the-century Paris, takes the place of the Underworld, full of spooky, strange characters. The fateful lovers are Christian and Satine, who are joined, separated, and ultimately re-united. Christian is a sensitive poet, like the Greek musician Orpheus, while Satine plays the role of the doomed Eurydice, marked for death by tuberculosis. The nasty Duke (Death) wants to keep Satine, but Christian comes to claim her. In the final scene of the film, the "Look Back Scene," the essence of the Orpheus myth is presented as a reflection on the power of love and music.

▌▌ DYING AND RISING GODS AND THEIR MYSTERY RELIGIONS:

- Adonis = the *Adonia*
- Demeter and Persephone = the *Eleusinian Mysteries*
- Dionysus = the Dionysian *ekstasis*
- Orpheus = *Orphism*

▌▌ SOURCES FOR THIS CHAPTER

Bremmer, Jan. (1983). *The Early Greek Concept of the Soul*. Princeton: Princeton University Press.

Burkert, Walter. (1987). *Ancient Mystery Cults*. Cambridge: Harvard University Press.

Detienne, Marcel. (2002). *The Writing of Orpheus: Greek Myth in Cultural Context*. Translated by Janet Lloyd. Baltimore: The Johns Hopkins University Press.

Graf, Fritz, and Johnston, Sarah Iles. (2007). *Ritual Texts for the Afterlife: Orpheus and the Bacchic Gold Tablets.* New York and London: Routledge.

Guthrie, W. K. C. (1993). *Orpheus and Greek Religion.* Princeton: Princeton University Press. Originally published by Methuen & Co., London, 1952.

Morford, Mark P. O., and Lenardon, Robert J. (2007). *Classical Mythology*, 8th ed. Oxford: Oxford University Press.

Witt, R. E. (1997). *Isis in the Greek and Roman World.* Baltimore: The Johns Hopkins University Press.

POPULAR CULTURE REFERENCES

Film

Orphée (1950). Director: Jean Cocteau.
Orfeu Negro (Black Orpheus) (1959). Director: Marcel Camus.
Moulin Rouge (2001). Director: Baz Luhrmann.
The Good Shepherd (2006). Director: Robert De Niro.

Television

Orpheus Descending (1990). Film of Tennessee Williams' play, directed by Peter Hall.

Online

Greek Mythology Link (www.maicar.com/GML)
Orpheus Music Library (www.orpheusmusiclibrary.com)

Self-Quiz for Chapter 15

1. What are some elements of the Greek mystery religions?

   _____

   _____

   _____

   _____

2. What is a dying and rising god?

   _____

   _____

   _____

   _____

3. What is a "scapegoat"?

   _____

   _____

   _____

   _____

4. Who is Adonis?

   _____

   _____

   _____

   _____

5. What mystery religion is associated with Demeter and Persephone?

   _____

   _____

   _____

6. Who is Orpheus?

_____

_____

_____

_____

7. What happens to Eurydice in the Underworld?

_____

_____

_____

_____

8. How does Orpheus die?

_____

_____

_____

_____

9. What is *Orphism*?

_____

_____

_____

_____

10. Who are the two main characters of the film *Moulin Rouge* (2001)?

_____

_____

_____

_____

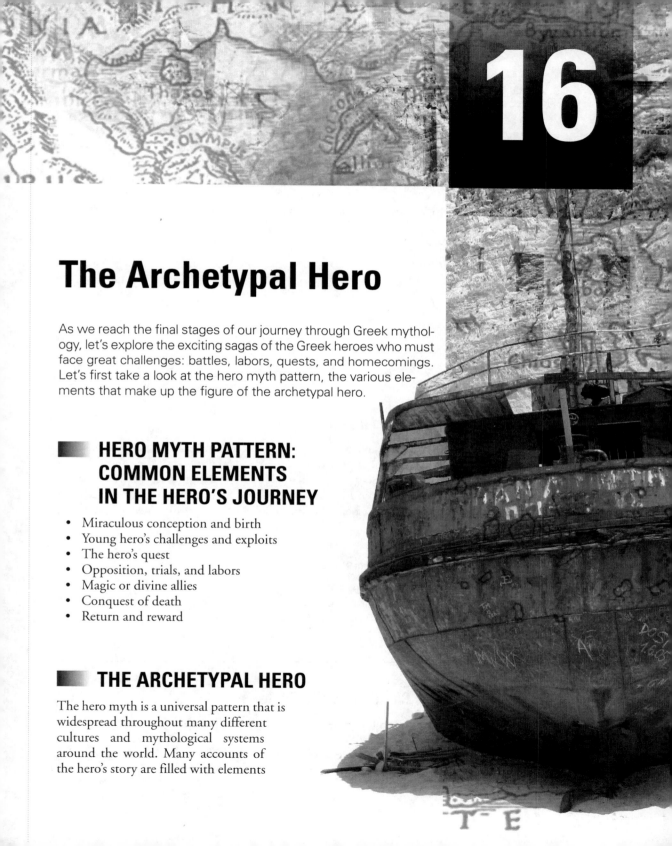

16

The Archetypal Hero

As we reach the final stages of our journey through Greek mythology, let's explore the exciting sagas of the Greek heroes who must face great challenges: battles, labors, quests, and homecomings. Let's first take a look at the hero myth pattern, the various elements that make up the figure of the archetypal hero.

HERO MYTH PATTERN: COMMON ELEMENTS IN THE HERO'S JOURNEY

- Miraculous conception and birth
- Young hero's challenges and exploits
- The hero's quest
- Opposition, trials, and labors
- Magic or divine allies
- Conquest of death
- Return and reward

THE ARCHETYPAL HERO

The hero myth is a universal pattern that is widespread throughout many different cultures and mythological systems around the world. Many accounts of the hero's story are filled with elements of miracle, mystery, violence, and redemption, and the hero myth shares some narrative aspects with the myth of the dying and rising god. As an archetype, the hero myth emerges from several versions of the essential core narrative of the hero's quest. The hero's quest can be interpreted as a universal metaphor for the individual human search for self-knowledge, that is, the desire to understand both the limits and the capabilities of the human experience. Societies have always imagined heroes in their distant or legendary pasts, human beings with special skills and endowments who by their contributions leave the world a better place than when they found it. Although not every hero goes through every element of the pattern, every hero shares a common identity in the shared experience of these rites of passage.

The Hero's Journey: A Rite of Passage

Leaves the ordinary world

Enters a dark world

Overcomes destructive forces

Returns with new wisdom

Miraculous Conception and Birth

The hero is born under unusual or extraordinary circumstances. These conditions may vary according to the nature of the hero and his particular culture, but the context always serves to highlight the special status of the hero's birth. The hero is born when needed, often represented by the "winter solstice" or some other dark or deficient hour of need in a society, which confirms that the hero's birth symbolizes the hope for a new beginning in springtime.

Hero's Parents Have Special Status

Father = Supreme Being figure
Hero often loses/searches for Father

Mother = Great Goddess figure
Hero's birth in hidden spot = Mother Earth

The Young Hero's Challenges and Exploits

If the birth of the hero stands for the hope for a new beginning, the forces of the *status quo* naturally resist the change and fight against what the hero represents. These forces—evil kings, jealous kinsmen, nasty demons and monsters—pose threats to the young hero's life and try to get rid of him. But the young hero immediately reveals his special status, and he faces this resistance by performing great exploits, miraculous deeds, and special inventions. This part of the hero myth pattern corresponds in many ways to the "divine child" motif we have already encountered on our journey through Greek mythology (in Chapter 3).

Call to Adventure

The Hero leaves his family

to proceed on his quest.

The Hero's Quest

After hearing the call to adventure, the young hero separates himself from his family to start on his quest, the predominant aspect of the hero myth pattern. The quest or journey is often initiated by a crossing over into a world of dark forces, inhabited by supernatural creatures such as monsters, demons, ogres, wizards, and other fiendish enemies of the hero.

Opposition, Trials, and Labors

The quest is marked by trials, ordeals, tests, labors, and confrontations with hostile, evil forces. The hero faces grave challenges and threats from monsters, demons, and ogres. In many versions, the male hero is threatened or tempted by a female supernatural force, such as a sorceress, witch, or some other *femme fatale*.

Famous *Femme Fatales* in Hero Tales

Circe

The Sirens

Morgan le Fay

Delilah

Magic or Divine Allies

To offset the threats, perils, and risks of the quest, the hero is given great resources of strength, power, and skill. The hero is protected from danger by divine powers and guided on his path by magical helpers, such as patron gods and goddesses, wise old men, fairy godmothers, fools, and trickster buddies. With such wonderful supernatural aid, the hero is able to face all challenges, and succeeds in beating back all attacks. The hero is tested and ultimately wins!

Conquest of Death

The most extreme test or trial faced by the hero is the conquest of death. At some point on the quest, the hero must face his ultimate foe, death itself, in either a real or metaphorical form. The hero may wrestle with Death or the god of the dead, or he may undertake a trip to the Underworld. During this element of the quest, the hero confronts the essence of what it means to be human and learns the meaning of human mortality. By demonstrating his courage in the face of death, the hero robs death of its power to manipulate, coerce, and frighten human beings. The hero meets death head-on, conquers it, and returns to share this new wisdom of the human existence with his people: these are the great benefits the hero brings to his culture or society. The hero is "reborn" to the world of humans as an almost divine being—now he is a true hero.

Conquest of Death

This ultimate act of courage and wisdom—conquest of death—

defines a true hero.

Return and Reward

Finally, the hero returns to the world that sent him forth and reunites with the family that produced him, or starts his own family. In the motif of the return, the hero often reunites with his parents: he may experience a "rebirth" symbolized by an encounter with feminine energy, through either his mother or wife. The hero may also be reconciled and rejoined with the supreme father figure, often through the symbolism of fire, in an ascension or divine *apotheosis*. After the quest, the hero is rewarded for the trials and tribulations suffered during the journey. These rewards may include marriage, wealth, sovereignty, or even immortality. The significance of the pattern is that the hero symbolizes the continuing life of the eternal human experience.

"The individual hero mask must die like all of us...
But the hero behind the mask lives forever."

—Joseph Campbell

■ SOME RECENT POPULAR CULTURE HEROES

- Luke Skywalker
- Indiana Jones
- Simba
- Ariel
- Mulan
- Neo
- Frodo Baggins
- Xena
- Buffy Summers
- Hiro Nakamura

Concept of the Hero

The hero concept is widespread in all myth systems.

The hero is always better
than ordinary humans.

SOURCES FOR THIS CHAPTER

Campbell, Joseph. (1959–1968). *The Masks of God.* Four volumes. New York:
  Viking Press.
Campbell, Joseph. (1972). *The Hero with a Thousand Faces.* Princeton: Princeton
  University Press. First published in 1949.
Kerényi, Karl. (1960). *The Heroes of the Greeks.* New York: Grove Press.
Larson, Jennifer. (1995). *Greek Heroine Cults.* Madison: University of Wisconsin Press.
Lyons, Deborah. (1997). *Gender and Immortality: Heroines in Ancient Greek Myth and
  Cult.* Princeton: Princeton University Press.
Mackey-Kallis, Susan. (2001). *The Hero and the Perennial Journey Home in American
  Film.* Philadelphia: University of Pennsylvania Press.
Morford, Mark P. O., and Lenardon, Robert J. (2007). *Classical Mythology,* 8th ed.
  Oxford: Oxford University Press.
Propp, Vladimir. (1968). *Morphology of the Folktale.* Translated by Lawrence Scott.
  Austin: University of Texas Press. First published in 1928.
Segal Robert A. (Ed.). (1990). *In Quest of the Hero.* Essays by Otto Rank, Lord Raglan,
  and Alan Dundes. Princeton: Princeton University Press.
Segal, Robert A. (Ed.). (2000). *Hero Myths: A Reader.* Oxford: Blackwell.

POPULAR CULTURE REFERENCES

Film

Star Wars (1977). Director: George Lucas.
Raiders of the Lost Ark (1981). Director: Steven Spielberg.
The Little Mermaid (1989). Directors: Ron Clements and John Musker.
The Lion King (1994). Directors: Roger Allers and Rob Minkoff.
Mulan (1998). Directors: Tony Bancroft and Barry Cook.
The Matrix (1999). Directors: Andy and Larry Wachowski.
The Lord of the Rings: The Fellowship of the Ring (2001). Director: Peter Jackson.
The Lord of the Rings: The Two Towers (2002). Director: Peter Jackson.
The Lord of the Rings: The Return of the King (2003). Director: Peter Jackson.

Television

Joseph Campbell and the Power of Myth (1988). Documentary interview with Bill
  Moyers. PBS.

Hercules: The Legendary Journeys (1995–2000). Syndicated series.

Xena: Warrior Princess (1995–2001). Syndicated series.

Buffy the Vampire Slayer (1997–2003). The WB, UPN series. Creator: Josh Whedon.

Heroes (2006–2008). NBC series. Creator: Tim Kring.

Online

Greek Mythology Link (www.maicar.com/GML)

Rescue Me: the Fanlisting for Disney Heroes (long-ago.net/hero)

Ultimate Disney Top Heroes & Heroines (www.ultimatedisney.com/countdown5)

Self-Quiz for Chapter 16

1. What is the hero myth pattern?

   _____

   _____

   _____

   _____

2. What is the element of miraculous conception and birth?

   _____

   _____

   _____

3. What is the element of young hero's challenges and exploits?

   _____

   _____

   _____

   _____

4. What is the call to adventure?

   _____

   _____

   _____

5. What is the element of the hero's quest?

   _____

   _____

   _____

   _____

6. What is the element of opposition, trials, and labors?

_____

_____

_____

_____

7. What is the element of magic or divine allies?

_____

_____

_____

_____

8. What is the element of conquest of death?

_____

_____

_____

_____

9. What is the element of return and reward?

_____

_____

_____

_____

10. Who are some recent heroes in popular culture?

_____

_____

_____

_____

17

Herakles

The first hero we will encounter on our journey through Greek mythology is Herakles, the greatest Greek hero of them all, and the last mortal son of the great god Zeus. The story of Herakles is the most important, most famous, and most popular of all the sagas of the Greek heroes.

HERAKLES: MAN, HERO, GOD

- Warrior prince
- Pan-Hellenic hero
- God on Mt. Olympus

Herakles (in Roman mythology = Hercules) is the greatest Greek hero, whose fame reached throughout the ancient Mediterranean world and who was worshipped more than any other Greek hero. Herakles is *pan-Hellenic* (= "all of Greece"), which means he is significant through the entire Greek world and beyond. As a hero, Herakles displays all the most extreme aspects of human nature: he is strong, good-humored, charismatic, and generous, but he is also violent, hot-tempered, lustful, and greedy. Herakles' saga takes place in the generation before the Trojan War, and is contemporary with Jason and the voyage of the *Argo* (discussed in Chapter 18). The most vital part of Herakles' story is that he experiences three stages in his career: first as a man, then as a hero, and finally as a bona fide god on Mt. Olympus. After his long and eventful life, full of trials, challenges, and labors, Herakles marries Hebe, goddess of eternal youth, and thereby attains his immortality as a god who is forever young. The figure of Herakles remains popular today, and his hero myth influences many aspects of modern popular culture, such as books, plays, cartoons, television shows, and films.

Herakles

His name means "Glory of Hera."

Hera's jealousy is a major theme

in the saga of Herakles.

Birth of Herakles

Like all heroes, Herakles is born under special circumstances. Zeus looked all over the world to find a woman smart and beautiful enough to be the mother of his last mortal son, who was destined to be a great hero. Zeus chose a mortal woman, Alkmene, and one night he came to her bed disguised as her own husband, Amphitryon. It is said that Zeus made the night last three times its normal length because he was determined to beget a son powerful enough to save the world. Later, Amphitryon also had sex with his wife and so begat his own son as well. When Hera found out that Alkmene was about to give birth, she was furious, and commanded her daughter Eileithyia, the goddess of childbirth, to prolong the poor woman's labor. One of Alkmene's maids, Galanthis, tricked Eileithyia into ending Alkmene's labor, and so Alkmene gave birth to twin boys: the half-immortal Herakles, son of Zeus, the elder by a single night, and an all-mortal baby, Iphikles.

Early Danger

Baby Herakles wasted no time in proving which of the twin boys was the half-divine son of Zeus. One night when they were about eight months old, the goddess Hera, still angry over Zeus' new child, sent two serpents to attack the twin babies while they were asleep together in their crib. Iphikles was the lighter sleeper, so he woke first and screamed, which awakened his older brother. Standing up in the crib, Baby Herakles grabbed the snakes, one in each of his little fists, and strangled them to death. Their frightened parents came running in, and immediately realized that Herakles was the son of Zeus. This early exploit of Herakles reflects the "divine child" motif we have already encountered on our journey through Greek mythology (in Chapter 3). It is also what is known as a *parergon*, or a "side-deed" (plural = *parerga*), one of the many feats of daring and strength performed by Herakles "alongside" his main twelve labors.

Parergon = "Side Deed"

Any exploit of Herakles

outside of the main twelve labors is called a *parergon*.

Young Herakles

As a young boy, like many heroes, Herakles received special training and education in several areas, including chariot driving, archery, boxing, fencing, and wrestling. It is said that Herakles' favorite weapon was the bow and arrow, but that he was also a strong wrestler and an accurate spear thrower. One area in which Herakles did not excel was music. His music teacher Linus, son of Apollo, often complained that Herakles was an inattentive student and a poor lyre player. One day Herakles became so frustrated with his lessons that he whacked Linus on the head with his lyre, killing him instantly. For this manslaughter, Herakles had to pay a price: he was exiled to the countryside to tend the flocks in the pastures, and there he grew to his full manhood.

Herakles' Next *Parergon*

Young Herakles kills the Thespian Lion, then

sleeps with the fifty daughters of King Thespius and has fifty sons!

Hera's Wrath

After a few years, Herakles marries a local princess named Megara and starts a family with her. But the resentment of Hera was aroused, so the goddess sent a "fit of madness" to attack Herakles. In a rage, Herakles aimed his bow and killed his wife and his three young sons. When he finally regained his senses, Herakles went to the Oracle at Delphi to seek advice about how to expiate the blood guilt he incurred by slaying his family. To purify himself, the Oracle told him, Herakles must perform this sentence: he must submit to Eurystheus, the weakling King of Argos, and perform a series of labors for him, a type of "community service" sentence. The usual number of labors is fixed at twelve, although in some versions, Herakles is assigned ten labors, but then has to do two extra to make up for two that are not accepted. But the total sum is always twelve.

Origin of the Twelve Labors

Herakles performs twelve labors in service to King Eurystheus to cleanse himself of the blood guilt of killing his family. But these labors are also assigned to him with the promise of a great reward: if he successfully completes all the labors, Herakles will win immortality, the greatest prize of all. This reward for completion of the labors is promised up front. That is why the Greek name for "labors" is *athloi*, meaning "contests undertaken for a prize." The order of the labors varies, but the official order of the list is set by the depiction of the labors in the sculptural decoration of the Temple of Zeus at Olympia completed in the fifth century BC.

Labor = *Athlos* = "Contest for a Prize"

Athlos in modern English: "athlete" = competitor in a physical contest.

The Twelve Labors = *Athloi*

- Peloponnesian Group (1–6)
- International Group (7–12)
- Eastern Group (7, 8, 9)
- Western Group (10, 11, 12)

In performing his labors,

Herakles goes from local hero

to pan-Hellenic hero

to international hero

to global superstar!

Divine Aid

Like all heroes, Herakles is supported by special helpers to balance the challenges he must face. Herakles is assisted throughout all the labors by his patron goddess, Athena, the goddess of wisdom and strategy. Herakles is also accompanied by Iolaus, his nephew, the son of his mortal brother, Iphikles. Iolaus is sometimes called the "Squire of Herakles." With their help, Herakles accomplishes all these difficult tasks.

THE TWELVE LABORS

1. The Nemean Lion

For his first task, Eurystheus told Herakles to slay the Nemean Lion and bring back the lion's skin. This monstrous lion ranged throughout Nemea, and it was invulnerable, in that its skin could not be pierced by weapons. So, with the help of an olive-wood club given to him by Athena, Herakles wrestles and pounds the beast with the club, strangles it, then uses its own claws to remove the impenetrable hide. Eurystheus was so frightened by the terrifying appearance of the lion skin upon Herakles' return that he hid in a storage jar!

After his first labor,
Herakles always wears the lion skin and
always carries the wooden club.

In art, Herakles is always depicted with the lion skin over his head.

2. The Lernaean Hydra

On his second labor, Herakles is ordered to slay the venomous Hydra, a nine-headed water snake who lived in the swamps of Lerna. But every time Herakles tried to club off one of the Hydra's heads, two more heads grew in its place! So Herakles gets help from Iolaus, who cauterized each stump with a burning brand as Herakles clubbed it off. Here Herakles also took the opportunity to dip his arrows in the Hydra's poisonous blood, thus starting a chain of events that will lead to his own death.

3. The Cerynitian Hind

This labor is a confused tale with many versions, but basically Herakles captures a female deer, sometimes known as the Cerynean Hind. The most common account tells of a magic doe with golden horns that lived near the River Cerynites and was sacred to the goddess Artemis. Herakles did not want to offend the goddess, so he captured the doe in a net, showed it to Eurystheus, and then released her unharmed back into the wild.

4. The Erymanthian Boar

For his fourth labor, Herakles was ordered to bring back—alive—a ferocious boar that was ravaging the countryside around Erymanthia. Herakles chased the boar into some deep snow, and there trapped it with a net. Once again, the weak Eurystheus was terrified of the beast and jumped into a storage jar.

> ### *Parergon*
>
> In another side mission, Herakles kills some drunk, rowdy centaurs.
>
> One centaur, Nessos, escapes and
>
> vows to take revenge on Herakles.

5. The Augean Stables

For his next task, Herakles was commanded to clean, all in one day, the stables of Augeas, who owned vast herds of cattle but never cleaned out his stables. Herakles bargained with Augeas to give him a percentage of the herds as a fee, and Augeas agreed. For this task, Herakles uses both his brain and his brawn: he diverts the River Alpheius and points it through the stables, so that the water washes all the cow dung clean away. But Augeas reneged on the payment he promised, so many years later Herakles returned and killed Augeas in revenge.

> ### *Parergon*
>
> Herakles starts the Olympic Games in Olympia, near the River Alpheius, to honor his father, Zeus.
>
> At the first Olympic Games, Herakles wins every event!

6. The Stymphalian Birds

For the sixth labor, Herakles was told to kill the vicious birds that infested the wooded shores of Lake Stymphalus. These disgusting birds shot people with their steel-tipped feathers and defiled the local crops with their pestilent droppings. Herakles flushed the birds out of the trees with a bronze rattle given to him by the god Hephaestus, and then he picked them off one by one with his bow and arrows.

7. The Cretan Bull

At the start of his international labors, Herakles is directed to the Island of Crete, where he is sent to fetch the beautiful bull who fathered the monstrous Minotaur. King Minos was only too happy to get rid of the bull who had caused him so much domestic trouble. So Herakles brought the bull back alive to Eurystheus, and then released it into the wild.

8. The Mares of Diomedes

For his next task, Herakles is sent to Thrace in northern Greece to fetch the man-eating mares owned by King Diomedes, the brutal son of Ares. As Herakles was capturing the horses, Diomedes attacked him, so Herakles killed Diomedes and fed his flesh to the mares, who then became miraculously tame. Herakles took the mares to Eurystheus, who dedicated them to Hera and set them free.

9. The Belt of Hippolyte

The ninth labor sets Herakles against the Amazons, a legendary tribe of warrior women who lived on the north coast of Asia Minor. In Greek mythology, many heroes must do battle against the Amazons to prove their skill and worth as heroes. Eurystheus sent Herakles to fetch the magic belt of the Amazon queen, Hippolyte, given to her by her father, Ares, god of war, for protection in battle. The queen was impressed by the hero, so she simply gave the belt to Herakles. But the goddess Hera was so angry at this easy victory that she disguised herself as an Amazon and roused the other warriors, saying that Herakles had carried off their queen. When the Amazons attacked, Herakles believed Hippolyte had tricked him, so he killed the queen and many other Amazons, and took the magic belt back to Eurystheus.

Last Three Labors: "Western Group"

The last three labors contain the conquest of death motif.

Herakles travels west to the ends of the Earth.

West to the Land of Sunset = Death

10. The Cattle of Geryon

As Herakles travels west to perform his last three labors, he is sent to fetch a herd of cattle owned by Geryon, the monstrous triple-bodied giant. Geryon lived on the Island of

Erythia, meaning "Red Place," with his two-headed dog, Orthus, litter-mate of Cerberus. In fact, Geryon may have been an earlier Underworld god, a figure like Hades, who lived in the far west and had his own hell hound. After Herakles killed Geryon and Orthus, he drove the herd of cattle into the Golden Bowl lent to him by Helios, god of the sun, and sailed back home along the ocean stream.

Parerga

Among the many *parerga* on his way back through Europe, Herakles stops in Italy and sets up his cult at Rome as *Hercules*.

11. The Golden Apples of the Hesperides

For his eleventh labor, Herakles is again sent to the west. This time he is sent to the secret Garden of the Hesperides to fetch the Golden Apples, which Gaia had given to her granddaughter, Hera, on her wedding day. The Golden Apples, hanging from the sacred Tree of Life, symbolize the prize of immortality sought by the hero: golden objects never rust, and thus represent eternal vitality. The Hesperides are the three daughters of Evening, or more commonly, of the Titan Atlas, who supported the world on his shoulders near the Garden of the Hesperides. The Golden Apples are guarded by a fierce dragon, Ladon, who coils around the Tree of Life. Since the garden was well hidden, Herakles had to wrestle the sea god Nereus for information on its location. Once he found the garden, Herakles asked Atlas for help in getting the apples from his daughters, and Atlas agreed, but only if Herakles would hold up the world for him, which he did, with Athena's help. But when Atlas returned with the apples, he refused to take the world back on his shoulders, so Herakles tricked Atlas by asking him to hold the world for a minute while he padded his back. The dim Titan complied, and Herakles snatched the apples and took off. Later, Athena restored the holy apples to their rightful place in the garden.

Herakles is involved in many *Parerga* while searching for the Garden of the Hesperides:

- Herakles stops in Egypt and kills King Busiris, who tried to sacrifice him.
- Herakles frees Prometheus from his bonds in the Caucasus Mountains.
- Herakles stops in Libya and wrestles the Giant Antaeus, son of Gaia.

12. Cerberus

The final labor of Herakles most clearly reflects the conquest of death motif, the ultimate challenge faced by any hero. Herakles is sent to Hades to fetch Cerberus, the three-headed hound of hell, who belongs to Hades, the Lord of the Dead. Guided by Hermes and aided by Athena, Herakles entered the Underworld, where he frightened Charon, the boatman, and fought with Hades for the hound. After taking the beast to Eurystheus, who hid in his jar, Herakles returns Cerberus to Hades as agreed. By completing this labor, Herakles successfully faces death, and so justifies his claim to immortality.

While in Hades, Herakles met the Shade of the dead hero Meleager and promised to marry his sister, Deianira.

In so doing, Herakles sets in motion another link in the chain of events leading to his own death.

After the Labors

So many tales and legends are attached to the name of Herakles that it would be impossible to go through them all. But after the completion of his labors, it is said Herakles entered an archery contest held by King Eurytus of Euboea for the hand of his daughter, the Princess Iole. Although Herakles easily won the competition, he was denied the prize, because Eurytus feared for his daughter to be married to such a violent man. Herakles was enraged, either in madness sent by Hera or by his own wounded pride, so he killed Prince Iphitus, the son of Eurytus. Once again, Herakles went to the Oracle at Delphi to be purified of a blood crime, but this time the priestess refused to help him, so a furious Herakles started trashing the temple. Apollo arrived, and the two began to fight, when Zeus appeared and ordered that an expiation sentence be given to Herakles.

Sentence

Herakles must be a slave in Lydia
to Queen Omphale (meaning "Belly Button").

There he performs many deeds, and is finally purified.

The Story of Deianira

Herakles remembered his promise to the Shade of the hero Meleager, and so he went to find Deianira. To win her hand in marriage, Herakles had to fight her suitor, the river god Achelous. During the wrestling match, Herakles broke off the river god's horn, which became the *cornucopia*, or "Horn of Plenty." At their wedding party, Herakles accidentally killed a noble boy for spilling wine on him, so once again, Herakles had to go into exile, this time taking his new bride, Deianira. On their journey to the city of Trachis, they came to the edge of a swiftly flowing river, where the centaur Nessos appeared and offered to carry Deianira across. Once they were on the far bank, Nessos tried to rape Deianira, so Herakles shot one of his poisoned arrows at him. As he lay dying, Nessos told Deianira to save some drops of his blood in a flask as a love charm, should Herakles ever turn his affections to another woman. Unknown to Herakles, the naïve Deianira did as the wily centaur suggested, but she didn't realize that his blood was now steeped in the Hydra's venom. Even dead, Nessos would get his revenge upon Herakles.

Herakles' Final Days

Many years passed, and Deianira bore Herakles two children, a son, Hyllus, and a daughter, Macaria. But Herakles still fumed with anger at the insult done to him by Eurytus, so he attacked his kingdom, killing the king and capturing his daughter, Iole. When Deianira discovered that Herakles had taken the young princess to be his concubine, in despair and jealousy she sprinkled drops of the centaur's blood on her husband's tunic, thinking it would rekindle his love for her. Herakles put on the tunic and stood before the sacred fire to give thanks for his successful campaign, but the fire ignited the Hydra's poison and the garment melted into his flesh, burning him. In fierce agony, Herakles tried to rip off the tunic, but he tore off chunks of his own charred flesh. When poor Deianira realized she had been tricked by the centaur, she killed herself in remorse. Herakles ordered that a funeral pyre be built for him on the mountain, and he climbed upon it, commanding his son Hyllus to marry Iole and to light the pyre. When Hyllus could not bring himself to do the job, Herakles asked a passing shepherd, Poeas, to light the pyre, and gave him his bow as a reward. As the flames burned away the mortal part of Herakles, there was a flash of lighting, and the hero disappeared: it is said Athena came down from Mt. Olympus in her chariot to lift the immortal Herakles with her up to Heaven.

Herakles the God

After the end of his mortal life, Herakles becomes a fully fledged god on Mt. Olympus. Herakles is reconciled with the goddess Hera by marrying her daughter, Hebe, goddess of eternal youth, and thus he attains everlasting youth and vitality. Herakles is the only human being in Greek mythology ever deified for his heroism. The great pan-Hellenic hero Herakles performed deeds all over Greek world, including his famous twelve labors as well as many *parerga*, too many to tell them all. On his arduous and challenging path from man to hero to god, Herakles gains the ultimate prize of immortality.

Herakles

Great Provider * Civilizing Force * "Beast Master"

The Nature of Herakles

On our journey through Greek mythology, we will meet many more heroes who are tested in their tales of great effort and glory. But we'll see that Herakles is different from those other heroes. In Herakles' saga, we notice a distinctly "primitive" aspect to him. Herakles wears an animal skin, the skin of the Nemean Lion, not armor; he carries a wooden club, not sophisticated weapons such as spears and shields. In the violent tales of his labors, Herakles is closely linked to animals, especially cattle, an important source of food for ancient peoples. Herakles tames the savage beasts and monsters that threaten human society. Herakles is clearly seen as a great provider, a hero who tames the wild and brings civilization to his people.

Recap of the Twelve Labors:

1. The Nemean Lion

2. The Lernaean Hydra

3. The Cerynitian Hind

4. The Erymanthian Boar

5. The Augean Stables

6. The Stymphalian Birds

7. The Cretan Bull

8. The Mares of Diomedes

9. The Belt of Hippolyte

10. The Cattle of Geryon

11. The Golden Apples of the Hesperides

12. Cerberus

Herakles

Man, Hero, God

Last Mortal Son of Zeus

Most Famous Greek Hero

■ SOURCES FOR THIS CHAPTER

Campbell, Joseph. (1972). *The Hero with a Thousand Faces*. Princeton: Princeton University Press. First published in 1949.

Galinsky, Karl. (1972). *The Herakles Theme: The Adaptations of the Hero in Literature from Homer to the Twentieth Century*. Oxford: Blackwell.

Morford, Mark P. O., and Lenardon, Robert J. (2007). *Classical Mythology*, 8th ed. Oxford: Oxford University Press.

Padilla, Mark W. (1998). *The Myths of Herakles in Ancient Greece*. Lanham: University Press of America.

Roller, Duane W. (2006). *Through the Pillars of Herakles: Greco-Roman Exploration of the Atlantic*. New York: Routledge.

▨ POPULAR CULTURE REFERENCES

Film

Hercules (1959). Director: Pietro Francisci (with Steve Reeves).
Hercules in New York (1970). Director: Arthur Allan Seidelman (with Arnold Schwarzenegger).
Hercules (1983). Director: Luigi Cozzi (with Lou Ferrigno).
Hercules (1997). Directors: Ron Clements and John Musker (Disney version).

Television

The series of pilot films (with Kevin Sorbo):
  Hercules and the Lost Kingdom (1994). Director: Harley Cokeliss.
  Hercules and the Amazon Women (1994). Director: Bill L. Norton.
  Hercules and the Circle of Fire (1994). Director: Doug Lefler.
  Hercules in the Underworld (1994). Director: Bill L. Norton.
  Hercules and the Maze of the Minotaur (1994). Director: Josh Becker.
Hercules: The Legendary Journeys (1995–2000). Syndicated series.
Xena: Warrior Princess (1995–2001). Syndicated series.
Young Hercules (1998–1999). Fox Kids Network series.

Online

Greek Mythology Link (www.maicar.com/GML)
Legendary Heroes (www.legendaryheroes.com)

Self-Quiz for Chapter 17

1. Who are Herakles' parents?

   _____

   _____

   _____

   _____

2. What is a *parergon*?

   _____

   _____

   _____

   _____

3. What happens to Herakles in his crib?

   _____

   _____

   _____

   _____

4. Why must Herakles perform the twelve labors?

   _____

   _____

   _____

   _____

5. What is an *athlos*?

   _____

   _____

   _____

   _____

6. Who helps Herakles on his labors?

_____

_____

_____

_____

7. Who is Omphale?

_____

_____

_____

_____

8. Who is Deianira?

_____

_____

_____

_____

9. Who is Hyllus?

_____

_____

_____

_____

10. Whom does Herakles marry on Mt. Olympus?

_____

_____

_____

_____

Students: You should also be able to
- Name all twelve labors
- Distinguish them from the *parerga* described in this chapter

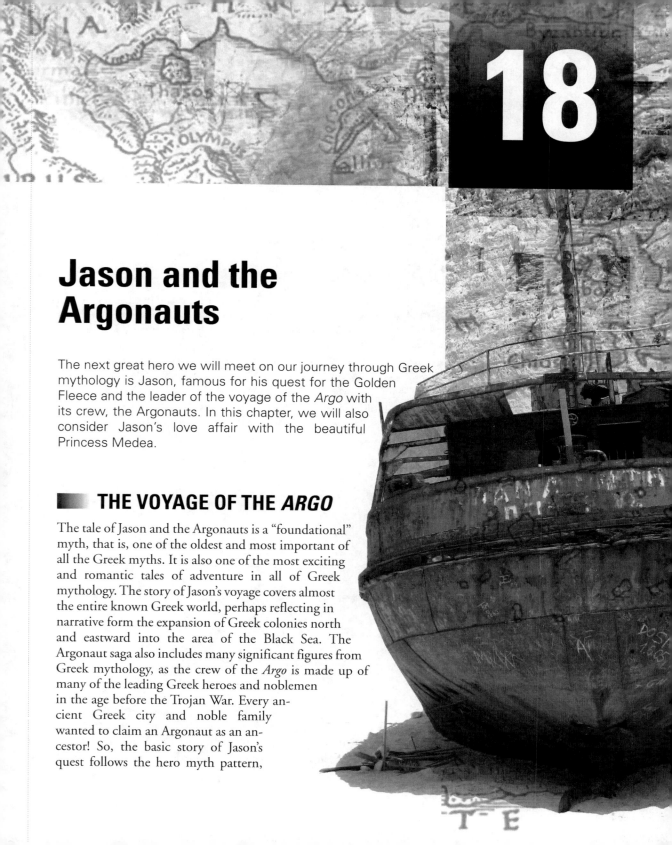

18

Jason and the Argonauts

The next great hero we will meet on our journey through Greek mythology is Jason, famous for his quest for the Golden Fleece and the leader of the voyage of the *Argo* with its crew, the Argonauts. In this chapter, we will also consider Jason's love affair with the beautiful Princess Medea.

THE VOYAGE OF THE *ARGO*

The tale of Jason and the Argonauts is a "foundational" myth, that is, one of the oldest and most important of all the Greek myths. It is also one of the most exciting and romantic tales of adventure in all of Greek mythology. The story of Jason's voyage covers almost the entire known Greek world, perhaps reflecting in narrative form the expansion of Greek colonies north and eastward into the area of the Black Sea. The Argonaut saga also includes many significant figures from Greek mythology, as the crew of the *Argo* is made up of many of the leading Greek heroes and noblemen in the age before the Trojan War. Every ancient Greek city and noble family wanted to claim an Argonaut as an ancestor! So, the basic story of Jason's quest follows the hero myth pattern, where a hero sets off to accomplish some incredible goal, but the story also reflects some historical elements as well. And as we will see, many folktale aspects of the supernatural have been added to this story to make it so thrilling, truly the "Magical Mystery Tour" of Greek mythology.

Argonaut = "Argo sailor"

Nautes in ancient Greek = "Sailor"

Astronaut = "Star sailor"

■ THE GOLDEN FLEECE

Since the goal of Jason's quest is the Golden Fleece, let's consider the back story of this miraculous object. A Greek prince, Phrixus, was the victim of a palace intrigue, and thus was almost sacrificed by his father, but at the last moment he was saved by a magical golden-fleeced ram sent from the heavens. Phrixus rode the golden ram from Greece toward the East to the city of Colchis at the eastern end of the Black Sea. There he was received by King Aeëtes, who generously gave him his eldest daughter, Chalciope, as his wife. Phrixus sacrificed the golden ram to Zeus as an offering for his escape from death, and gave the extraordinary Golden Fleece to Aeëtes, who hung it upon a tree in a grove sacred to the god of war, Ares. There the Golden Fleece was guarded by a dragon that never slept.

The Golden Fleece

Like the Golden Apples of the Hesperides,

the Golden Fleece is a symbol of immortality,

the object of the hero's quest.

■ JASON

- Son of Aeson, King of Iolcus
- Leader of the Argonauts
- Hero of the Golden Fleece

Jason's Story

Jason is the son of Aeson, who was the rightful heir to the kingdom of Iolcus, but the throne was seized by Aeson's evil brother, Pelias. The name of Jason's mother is usually given as Polymede. Because of all the trouble in the royal household, Polymede sent Jason away when he was a little boy to be raised in safety by the wise centaur Chiron. Young Jason's education reflects those elements of the hero myth pattern where the young hero faces danger, must be separated from his family for his protection, and also receives special training. As a young man, Jason returned to Iolcus to claim his birthright. On his way home, Jason came to the banks of the River Anauros, where he met the goddess Hera disguised as an old woman. The goddess asked Jason to help her cross the raging river, and Jason complied, losing one of his sandals in the deep muddy river bottom as he carried her across. In exchange for this kindness, Hera ever after favored and protected Jason on his travels.

King Pelias heard a prophecy:

"Beware of the man with one sandal!"

Quest for the Golden Fleece

There are many different variations in the story at this point, but the most common account goes as follows. When Jason arrived in Iolcus, wearing only one sandal, Pelias did not directly refuse to give him the throne, but he promised to yield the throne only if Jason would first bring him the Golden Fleece. So Jason vowed to Pelias that he would get the Golden Fleece and bring it to Iolcus, both to prove his worth as a hero and to reclaim the kingdom for himself and his family. Thus Jason responded to the call to adventure with a rousing affirmative.

Building the *Argo*

To prepare for the expedition to attain the Golden Fleece, the *Argo* was built, the best and fastest ship ever constructed. The *Argo*'s name means "Swift," to indicate the unsurpassed velocity of the vessel. The ship may also have been named for its carpenter, Argos, who designed and crafted the miraculous *Argo* with the help of Athena, the patron goddess of carpentry and ship-building. In the prow of the ship, Athena inserted a piece of magic wood that gave the *Argo* the power of speech.

The Argonauts

This is the name given to the crew of the *Argo*—the Argonauts, the finest heroes of their generation. It is said that the goddess Hera roused in the hearts of the noblest and bravest men all over Greece the desire to join Jason on his great quest. The list of Argonauts is usually set at fifty, which is the number of oars on a standard Greek rowing ship, but the names on the list vary considerably with the different versions of the myth. Throughout Greek history, cities and families were eager to have an ancestor represented on the list of Argonauts, so it was common practice simply to add the names they wanted to see onto the catalogue of crew members. Still, it is clear that some names rightfully belong on the original "cast list" as the names of famous heroes who sailed with Jason. Note too that some of the Argonauts had special skills or talents that allowed them to perform particular feats to help Jason while on the expedition.

Some Famous Argonauts

- Jason, the leader of the expedition
- Argos, the shipwright
- Tiphys, the helmsman
- Mopsus, the seer
- Peleus, father of Achilles
- Telamon, father of Ajax
- Meleager, hero of the Calydonian boar hunt
- Castor and Polydeuces, the *Dioscuri*, or twin sons of Zeus
- Zetes and Calais, the *Boreads*, sons of Boreas, the North Wind

Two "Celebrity" Argonauts

Orpheus
Herakles

Island of Lemnos

After leaving Iolcus, the *Argo* sailed across the open waters of the Aegean Sea and stopped first at the Island of Lemnos. There the Argonauts found only women, who had killed all their menfolk for neglecting them sexually. The queen of Lemnos was Hypsipyle, granddaughter of the god of wine, Dionysus. The women of Lemnos gladly received the Argonauts, and the men stayed on the island for over a year, fathering many children. Jason had a love affair with Queen Hypsipyle, who bore him twin boys before the Argonauts departed to continue on their voyage.

Phineus and the Harpies

After the Argonauts encountered several more adventures on their voyage, the next stop they made was at Salmydessus. There they are received by the old blind prophet Phineus—it is said he had been blinded as punishment for revealing the secrets of the gods. Phineus was also tormented by ferocious flying monsters, the Harpies, who stole his food and polluted his surroundings with their foul stench. Aided by the winged Boreads, Zetes and Calais, Jason got rid of the Harpies. In exchange for this service, Phineus gave Jason valuable information about how to proceed into the Black Sea to Colchis and how to avoid the dangers that awaited him on his journey.

Symplegades = Clashing Rocks

The Clashing Rocks destroy ships as they are passing through.
The Argonauts send a dove through first, and then the *Argo* crosses into the Black Sea.

After the *Argo*'s passage, the rocks remain stuck together forever!

Arrival at Colchis

As the Argonauts sailed through the Black Sea, they experienced a few more adventures, then finally reached the shores of Colchis. There King Aeëtes did not give them a hospitable welcome, angered that they had come to rob him of his prized possession, the Golden Fleece. But Aeëtes told Jason he would give him the fleece, if he could accomplish a series of impossible tasks (note the presence here of the folktale motif where tasks are imposed upon the hero). Jason had to yoke a pair of bronze, fire-breathing bulls and use them to plow furrows into a huge field, which he would then sow with the teeth of a dragon. From the sown dragon's teeth, armed demon warriors would sprout, whom Jason would have to fight and defeat. Clearly, Aeëtes did not expect Jason to live through these tasks, and he planned to kill the other Argonauts after Jason's failure.

 **MEDEA**

- Daughter of Aeëtes, granddaughter of Helios
- Princess of Colchis
- Priestess of Hekate

Medea's Story

At this point, the saga takes a romantic turn with the introduction of Medea, the younger daughter of Aeëtes. The goddess Hera was eager to protect Jason, so she commanded the help of Eros, god of desire, to cause Medea to fall in love with Jason, so the princess would help the hero succeed. In this part of the tale, Medea plays the role of the fairy princess who helps the hero accomplish his impossible tasks. But Medea is much more than just that: she is also a priestess of Hekate, goddess of black magic, and an expert sorceress in her own right. Medea is especially skilled in the use of *pharmaka*, "drugs" and special potions. Struck by the sharp arrow of Eros, she is filled with love for Jason, so she helps him prepare for the trials by giving him some magic oil to make his body invulnerable. Thus protected, Jason conquered the fire-breathing bulls and killed the demon warriors unscathed. In gratitude, Jason also fell in love with Medea.

Medea protects Jason with magic oil

made from the blood of Prometheus

chained in the nearby Caucasus Mountains.

Escape with the Fleece

After Medea helped Jason perform the allotted tasks unharmed, next she guided him to the sacred grove to find the Golden Fleece. There Medea drugged the eyes of the dragon guarding the fleece, allowing Jason to seize his prize. With her father, King Aeëtes, in hot pursuit, Medea threw her lot in with Jason, joining him and the Argonauts as they headed for the ship. Thus did Medea betray her father and her homeland: not only did she help Jason capture the fleece, but she also ran away with him. It is said that Medea killed her brother, Apsyrtus, during her escape from Colchis. One version says Medea murdered Apsyrtus, still a boy, to delay her father's pursuit: by throwing bits of her brother's body overboard, her father had to slow down and collect them for burial. Another account says Apsyrtus was a grown man and led the pursuers: Medea set up an ambush where she pretended to negotiate with him, but Jason jumped out and killed him. Either way, Medea and Jason successfully escaped with the fleece.

Return of the *Argo*

Many different narratives describe the return route of the *Argo* as Jason and his crew made their way back across land and sea to Iolcus. The simplest version takes the *Argo* back the same way it came, but other versions are much more complicated and take the *Argo* much farther afield, across Europe or Africa, even having the Argonauts carry their ship over land for several days at a time. It may be that the great variety of these tales reflects the various commercial routes for actual trade and colonization that were in use in early times in ancient Greece. In these various accounts, the *Argo* also made several stops along the way back home and the crew had various adventures. When the talking prow of the *Argo* informed Medea and Jason that they had to be purified of the murder of Apsyrtus, the lovers stopped on the southwestern coast of Italy to visit Medea's aunt, Circe, the famous sorceress. Circe immediately recognized her niece, and purified the couple of the pollution.

Now Jason and Medea celebrate their wedding:

they consummate their union upon the Golden Fleece.

Back in Iolcus

Finally the Argonauts reached Iolcus, where Jason handed over the fleece to Pelias and expected to take the throne. But Pelias reneged on the deal and refused to hand over the throne to Jason. So once again, Medea came up with a strategy to help Jason using her magic arts. Medea made a show of rejuvenating an old ram by cutting it up and putting it into a boiling cauldron filled with magic herbs, and so she tricked the daughters of Pelias into believing they could rejuvenate their elderly father in the same way. But when they cut up their father and put him in the cauldron, without the magic herbs the experiment only led to the death of Pelias. Thus Jason had his revenge on Pelias, but he did not attain the throne. Now polluted with murder, Jason and Medea were exiled from Iolcus by Acastus, the son of Pelias, and the couple fled to Corinth.

Jason dedicates the *Argo* to Poseidon at Corinth.

Years later, Jason is killed
when a rotting timber from the *Argo*
falls and hits him on the head.

The Tragedy of *Medea*

In the final stage of their story, Jason and Medea go to Corinth in exile, where they live quietly for a few years and have two young sons. Corinth is the setting of the great tragic play, the *Medea*, written by the Greek tragedian Euripides (it was first performed in Athens in 431 BC). This magnificent and powerful play describes what happens when Jason decided to divorce Medea and make a new political marriage to the daughter of Creon, the King of Corinth. The tragedy focuses on the response of Medea to this insult, and how she gets her revenge on Jason.

Medea and Jason: Game Over

The summary of the drama is as follows. When Medea discovers that Jason plans to divorce her and marry the Princess of Corinth, she is furious that Jason would treat her so poorly after everything she has done for him. She believes their marriage bond is for life and cannot be broken. But Medea is in a quandary: as an exile with no family and a foreign woman in Greece, her options are limited. Soon she learns that Creon, the King of Corinth, also plans to deport her and her two young sons by Jason out of the city, so she is even further strained by the idea of wandering destitute through a strange country. So Medea decides on two courses of action: first, she must locate a suitable safe haven for herself in exile, and then she will be able to get revenge on the faithless Jason and his new Corinthian relations. A stroke of luck occurs when Medea's old friend, Aegeus, King of Athens, happens through Corinth, so she arranges for his protection if she were to show up in Athens. Then Medea sends her two boys with wedding gifts for Jason's new bride: but the gifts are smeared with deadly poison, so when the princess touches them, she burns up and dies horribly. Creon also dies as he tries in vain to save his only child. Next Medea plans the best way to exact vengeance on her husband: she decides to kill their two sons. Her reasoning is that while their deaths will hurt her as their mother, it will hurt him even more, and therefore it will achieve her goal of revenge. Medea also reasons that the Corinthians will now be after them for their part in the murder of the royal family, so it is better for them to die at their mother's hand. Just as she finishes stabbing the two boys to death, Jason comes running to save them, but he is much too late. In the final tableau of the tragedy, Medea appears high above the stage in a divine chariot drawn by fiery dragons, and as she holds the bodies of her slain children, she doesn't even let Jason touch them. Medea's supernatural chariot is a symbol of her transformation, as she has now become like a goddess looking down on Jason's mortal suffering and gloating. She tells him she will dedicate the boys' bodies in the sanctuary of Hera, goddess of marriage, and informs Jason of his own miserable death in the future. Then Medea herself flies off to Athens.

Jason and Medea: a fairytale love story
gone terribly wrong!

◼◼ SOURCES FOR THIS CHAPTER

Anderson, Graham. (2000). *Fairytale in the Ancient World*. London and New York: Routledge.

Claus, James J., and Johnston, Sarah Iles. (Eds.). (1997). *Medea: Essays on Medea in Myth, Literature, Philosophy and Art*. Princeton: Princeton University Press.

Griffiths, Emma. (2006). *Medea*. In the series *Gods and Heroes of the Ancient World*. London and New York: Routledge.

Hunter, Richard L. (1993). *The Argonautica of Apollonius*. Cambridge: Cambridge University Press.

Hunter, Richard L. (Trans.). (1998). *Jason and the Golden Fleece (The Argonautica)*. Oxford: Oxford University Press.

Morford, Mark P. O., and Lenardon, Robert J. (2007). *Classical Mythology*, 8th ed. Oxford: Oxford University Press.

Severin, Timothy. (1986). *The Jason Voyage: The Quest for the Golden Fleece*. New York: Simon & Schuster.

Svarlien, Diane Arnson. (Trans.). (2007). *Euripides: Alcestis, Medea, Hippolytus*. Indianapolis: Hackett Publishing Company.

◼◼ POPULAR CULTURE REFERENCES

Film

Jason and the Argonauts (1963). Director: Don Chaffey. Special effects by Ray Harryhausen.
Medea (1970). Director: Pier Paolo Pasolini.
A Dream of Passion (1978). Director: Jules Dassin.
Ocean's Eleven (2001). Director: Steven Soderbergh.

Television

Medea (1983). Film of Euripides' play, directed by Mark Cullingham for PBS.
Jason and the Argonauts (2000). Directed by Nick Willing for Hallmark Entertainment.
Hercules: The Legendary Journeys (1995–2000). Syndicated series.

Online

Greek Mythology Link (www.maicar.com/GML)

Self-Quiz for Chapter 18

1. What is the origin of the Golden Fleece?

   _____

   _____

   _____

   _____

2. Where is Jason from and who are his parents?

   _____

   _____

   _____

   _____

3. Who is Pelias?

   _____

   _____

   _____

   _____

4. Who are Zetes and Calais?

   _____

   _____

   _____

   _____

5. Who is Hypsipyle? Who is Phineus?

   _____

   _____

   _____

   _____

6. What are the Symplegades?

_____

_____

_____

_____

7. Who is Aeëtes and what tasks does he set for Jason?

_____

_____

_____

_____

8. How does Medea help Jason?

_____

_____

_____

_____

9. Why and how does Medea get revenge on Jason?

_____

_____

_____

_____

10. Who is Aegeus?

_____

_____

_____

_____

19

The Trojan Saga

As we continue to explore the tales of the great heroes on our journey through Greek mythology, let us turn now to the Trojan saga, sometimes called the Trojan cycle, and consider the stories that led up to the Greek expedition to Troy, the events of the Trojan War itself, and the fall of Troy.

▰▰ THE TROJAN CYCLE

- Back story: the judgment of Paris
- The expedition to Troy
- The Trojan War
- The fall of Troy

▰▰ ARCHAEOLOGICAL EVIDENCE

Before we begin our examination of the Trojan saga, let us consider the question: Did the Trojan War really happen? As we have seen, the tales of Greek mythology often contain a significant historical element, so we are justified in asking this question. The site of ancient Troy, called *Troia*, *Ilios*, and *Ilion* in ancient times, was located on the north coast of Asia Minor (in modern Turkey) and situated on the hill of Hisarlik, about five miles (eight kilometers) from the sea shore. Archaeologists have shown that the site of Troy was inhabited since the Early Bronze Age (ca. 3000 BC), and there were seven successive settlements evident on the site down into the Late Bronze Age/Early Iron Age (ca. 1150 BC). The different settlements are assigned consecutive numbers based on their archaeological levels.

Troy I to V (ca. 3000–1700 BC)

These Early to Middle Bronze Age sites experienced periods of considerable wealth, with evidence of trade in timber, wool, and pottery.

Troy VI (ca. 1700–1250 BC)

This was an exceptionally prosperous and impressive city, with huge fortification walls surrounding the site. Some archaeologists believe this site was the city of Priam, which Homer calls "well-walled Troy." Excavations show that this city was destroyed by an earthquake sometime around 1250 BC.

Troy VII (ca. 1250—1040 BC)

The inhabitants immediately rebuilt another fine city on the site. Some archaeologists believe that the first city in this phase, Troy VIIa, was the city of Priam, as it shows signs of being devastated around 1150 BC by a violent military siege and fire, with evidence of weapons, burnt debris, and human skeletal remains.

The most famous account of the Trojan War

is Homer's great epic poem, the *Iliad,* which

tells one part of the tenth year of the war.

The traditional Greek date for the Trojan War is 1184 BC.

City of Priam

Either Troy VI or Troy VIIa could be the Trojan city that fell to Greek invaders, since they show evidence of destruction in the period 1250 to 1150 BC, which is close to the traditional date the Greeks later assigned to the Trojan War, 1184 BC. In fact, the two sites together may represent the city of Priam in two different stages. Some have suggested that the earthquake that ruined Troy VI may be the actual historical event remembered in the legend as the interference of Poseidon, god of earthquakes: did the god perhaps allow the Trojan Horse—one of Poseidon's symbols—to enter and weaken the walls of Troy so that the invaders could finally take the city? Was the city of Priam first damaged by a historical earthquake, and then easily conquered by invading Greeks? This may be the element of history that proves the romantic legend of the Trojan War.

Element of History in Trojan Saga

Was there really a beautiful Helen?

The Greeks believed Helen was the cause of the war.

HELEN'S STORY

The ancients believed Helen was the cause of the conflict that led to the Trojan War, so let's consider her background story. Helen was the daughter of Leda, the beautiful Queen of Sparta, wife of King Tyndareus. Zeus desired Leda and made love to her in the form of a swan. Soon Leda laid two eggs, one immortal and the other mortal, and two children (one male and one female) were born from each egg: the lovely Helen and Polydeuces were born from the immortal egg sired by Zeus, and Clytemnestra and Castor were born from the mortal egg fathered by Tyndareus.

Castor and Polydeuces (in Roman mythology = Pollux) were known as the *Dioscuri*, the "Zeus Boys," or the "Divine Twins," the *Gemini*. Castor, a skilled horseman, was the mortal son of Tyndareus, while Polydeuces, an expert boxer, was the immortal son of Zeus. The *Dioscuri* shared many exploits as twin heroes: they sailed together with Jason on the *Argo*, and were involved in many other adventures. In one battle, Castor was mortally wounded, so Polydeuces prayed to his father, Zeus, to let him share his immortality with his brother. The twins were worshipped as gods especially at Sparta and later in Rome as protectors of sailors and soldiers.

The *Dioscuri*

The ancients believed the *Dioscuri* appeared

as lights/sparks around the masts of ships,

known today as *St. Elmo's Fire,* or

electrical charge during a thunderstorm.

Clytemnestra

One of Leda's daughters was the mortal Clytemnestra, sister of Helen. Clytemnestra married Agamemnon, King of Mycenae, the leader of the Greek expedition to Troy, and bore him several children, including their eldest daughter, Iphigeneia. When a victorious Agamemnon returned home to Mycenae after the Trojan War, Clytemnestra murdered him and seized the throne.

Helen's Early Life

The daughter of Zeus and Leda was marked by a strong destiny from her very earliest years. Helen was favored by the goddess Aphrodite, who showered her with the gifts of beauty, charm, and intelligence. Soon Helen of Sparta became famous as the "Most Beautiful Woman in the World." Suitors came from all over Greece hoping to seek her hand in marriage. On the advice of Odysseus, one of the suitors, Helen's earthly father, Tyndareus, had them all swear a great oath to protect the rights of whatever man won Helen as a bride, in case Helen should be "lost or stolen." Helen chose Menelaus, who married her and assumed the kingship of Sparta. There the couple lived uneventfully together for some years, and Helen bore a daughter, Hermione. One day, Paris, a handsome young Trojan prince, arrived in Sparta, and he and Helen fall madly in love. So Paris and Helen ran away from Sparta, taking a great deal of Spartan treasure, and made their way across the sea to Troy. How and why did this happen?

Paris' Early Life

The Trojan prince, Paris, also called Alexander, was the son of King Priam and Queen Hekabe of Troy. When Hekabe was pregnant with Paris, she dreamed she gave birth to a torch that burned down the city of Troy. So when Paris was born, his fearful parents abandoned him in the mountains to die. But Paris was miraculously suckled by a she-bear, and then he was found and raised by shepherds (note the "divine child" motif). When he had grown to manhood as a very handsome young man, Paris was reconciled with his royal family, but decided to stay in the mountains pasturing his father's flocks. There he married Oenone, a mountain nymph, and spent his days playing his lyre and enjoying the good life.

Meanwhile, Back on Mt. Olympus...

The biggest social event of Greek mythology was taking place,
the wedding of Peleus and Thetis.

All of the gods were invited to the party, except one:
Eris, goddess of discord.

The uninvited Eris crashes the party,
tossing a golden apple inscribed "for the fairest."

The Judgment of Paris

A major brawl erupted among the goddesses at the wedding party over who should be awarded the golden apple that had been designated "for the fairest" (it is a feminine superlative in Greek, "*Kallistē*"). Finally the argument came down to three claimants: Hera, Athena, and Aphrodite. Zeus wisely decided not to have anything to do with this touchy competition between his wife and two of his daughters, so he sent his son Hermes down to Earth with the contestants to find a suitable human judge to break the three-way tie. Hermes escorted the three goddesses to the wooded mountains above Troy, where he persuaded a surprised Paris to render his famous judgment.

Divine Beauty Contest

Each goddess offers Paris a bribe:
* Hera = Greatest Royal Power in the World
* Athena = Guaranteed Victory in War
* Aphrodite = Most Beautiful Woman in the World

And the Apple Goes to...

After this display of divine persuasion, no doubt part of the talent segment of the competition, Paris realized that he was "a lover, not a fighter." So he awarded the golden apple to Aphrodite, who thereafter favored Paris in all his endeavors. Hera and Athena, however, were furious at the insult to their divine persons, and so they were forever hostile to Paris and the Trojans. It is at this point that Paris went to Sparta to claim his prize, and found that Helen was already married. So Helen ran away with Paris to Troy, where they were welcomed into the royal family.

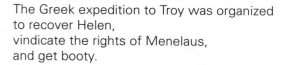

Loss of Helen = Cause of War

The Greek expedition to Troy was organized
to recover Helen,
vindicate the rights of Menelaus,
and get booty.

Preparations for War

A huge army was now gathered from all over Greece and its neighboring allies. The combined forces of the *Achaeans* (Homer's name for the Greeks) were to be led by Menelaus' brother, Agamemnon, King of Mycenae. Heroes, princes, and chiefs were summoned from all over Greece and reminded of the oath they swore to protect the rights of Menelaus—they were also lured with the promise of great martial glory and rich booty. They brought their contingents together under Agamemnon's leadership, but retained their independence and control over their own men.

Two Famous "Draft-Dodgers"

- Odysseus = tried to avoid going to war by pretending to be crazy
- Achilles = his mother tried to hide him dressed as a girl

ACHILLES

- Greatest Greek warrior ever
- Son of Peleus and the sea goddess Thetis
- Leader of the Myrmidons = "Ant Men"
- Fastest = "Achilles, Swift of Foot"
- Best-looking = "Godlike Achilles"

Birth of Achilles

The great warrior Achilles was the son of the mortal Peleus, King of Phthia, and the sea goddess Thetis, a Nereid. Remember that Thetis was married off to a mortal because the gods feared a prophecy that said her son would be stronger than his father. The wedding of Peleus and Thetis, and the judgment of Paris that followed, set into motion the events that led to the Trojan War. After Thetis gave birth to Achilles—a son who was indeed greater than his father—she left her human husband for good. Thetis tried to make her half-mortal son all immortal by submerging him into the waters of the River Styx: all the parts of his body were made invulnerable to attack, except his heel, where she held him while she was dipping him. Thus, the heel was Achilles' only vulnerable spot.

> Achilles tendon = Tendon that connects the heel to the calf muscles
>
> *"Achilles' heel"* = One fatal weakness among overall strength

Achilles' Early Life

Like many young heroes, Achilles was sent off to receive special training from Chiron, the wise old centaur. But Thetis continued to worry about her son, since she had heard a prophecy that said Achilles had a choice between two destinies: he could either live a long inglorious life, or die young but gloriously at Troy. Thetis knew her son would choose the more glorious fate. So when she heard that preparations were being made for the campaign against the Trojans, Thetis tried to prevent him from going to war: she dressed her son as a girl and hid him among a group of girls on the island of Scyros. But when the Greek envoys arrived, Odysseus tricked Achilles into revealing himself by tempting him with a display of brilliant armor and weapons. So over his mother's objections, Achilles happily joined the expedition to Troy.

> On Scyros, Achilles loved a girl, Deidamia.
>
> After he left for Troy, she gave birth to a son:
>
> Neoptolemos = "New War."
>
> Neoptolemos later takes part in the capture of Troy.

Aulis

The Achaean contingents, with over 1200 ships, now gathered on the east coast of Greece at the port of Aulis, waiting to set sail for Troy. But the winds were unfavorable, and the ships could not set sail. Calchas, the seer, informed Agamemnon that the goddess Artemis was angry because the king had offended her by defiling her sacred grove. So Artemis demanded that Agamemnon sacrifice his eldest daughter, Iphigeneia, to appease her divine wrath. The king was in a bind: he didn't want to sacrifice his daughter, but the Achaean armies were amassed on the beach waiting for his leadership. So he tricked his wife, Clytemnestra, telling her to bring Iphigeneia to Aulis for a wedding to Achilles. But when they arrived, Agamemnon sacrificed the girl instead, thus incurring the enmity of both Achilles and Clytemnestra. Some say that Artemis saved Iphigeneia at the last minute by exchanging a deer for the girl on the altar. Nevertheless, after the Trojan War, Clytemnestra avenges her favorite daughter's death by slaying Agamemnon.

Arrival at Troy

Finally the Achaean fleet crossed the sea and arrived at the beaches of Troy. The various squadrons set up their camps along the sands, and each contingent kept their ships together as a group—it is said Odysseus and his men established their camp in the center, while Achilles and the Myrmidons were at the far end. The Achaeans settled in for what would turn out to be ten long years of besieging the city of Troy, and they spent much of their time raiding local villages to feed their vast armies and collect booty: weapons, precious metals, and slaves. Under the stable rule of King Priam, Troy was well fortified, strong, and prosperous, and Troy had many powerful allies from the surrounding areas of Asia Minor. It would not be an easy task to take the city of Troy.

The Gods Took Sides in the Trojan War:

Greek side
- Hera, Athena
- Poseidon
- Hephaestus
- Hermes
- Zeus (at the end)

Trojan side
- Aphrodite
- Ares
- Apollo, Artemis
- Leto

▬ HOMER'S *ILIAD*

The *Iliad*, the great epic poem of Homer, tells the story of the quarrel that took place between Agamemnon and Achilles in the tenth and final year of the Trojan War. The Achaeans spent nine years raiding the local villages for booty, and after each skirmish, the booty would be divided up by rank and prestige: Agamemnon, as the expedition leader, would receive the best prize, and Achilles, as the greatest warrior, would receive the next best, and so on down the line of warriors and chiefs. The prize each hero received was a visual marker of his rank, glory, and honor in the eyes of his peers. In the tenth year of the war, the Achaeans raided the nearby town of Chryse, and Agamemnon received the best girl, Chryseis, daughter of the Priest of Apollo, while Achilles received the second most prestigious girl, Briseis. When Agamemnon was forced to return his girl to her father, he was left with nothing to indicate his rank as leader, so he yanked Briseis, Achilles' prize of honor and symbol of his status.

> **Anger of Achilles over Insult = Main Theme of Epic Story**
>
> Achilles' romance is built up in the film *Troy*,
>
> but the *Iliad* is really about Achilles' honor.

The Wrath of Achilles

After this humiliating insult, Achilles dropped out of the Trojan War. He refused to fight, and sat sulking in his tent, crying to his mother, Thetis, about the dishonor he endured at the hands of Agamemnon. The hero is not a team player; rather, he is obsessed with his own honor and how he is viewed by his peers. Achilles wanted the Achaeans to suffer badly in his absence, so that they would realize what a valuable warrior he is, and give him the honor he deserves. And indeed, without Achilles in the field, the Achaeans started to suffer great losses, and many Achaeans died. Achilles began to question the whole reason they were in Troy, and whether the acquisition of glory was really worth all the trouble.

CAST OF LEADING CHARACTERS IN THE TROJAN WAR

The Trojans

Priam and Hekabe (in Roman mythology = Hecuba) are the king and queen of Troy. Together they have nineteen legitimate offspring, while Priam has several illegitimate children as well. The royal couple greatly loved their doomed city.

Paris (also called Alexander) is the younger prince of Troy, son of Priam and Hekabe, whose actions caused the Trojan War. The favorite of Aphrodite, and husband of the stolen Helen, Paris is vain, sensual, and handsome. Though not a powerful warrior, Paris is skilled with the bow. His big moment comes when he shoots Achilles fatally in his vulnerable heel with an arrow guided by the god Apollo.

Hector is the crown prince, son of Priam and Hekabe, the heir to the throne of Troy, and the great champion of Troy. In contrast to his little brother, Hector is brave, honorable, and dutiful. Hector fights courageously, but he has a grave sense of awareness that Troy is doomed to fall. As a warrior, Hector is second only to Achilles. The climax of the *Iliad* comes when Hector meets Achilles one-on-one on the field of battle.

Andromache is the wife of Hector, the daughter of King Eëtion, a local ally of the Trojans, who was killed by Achilles. Their young son is Astyanax, whose name means "Lord of the City." Andromache supported her husband's sense of duty, but she also knew Troy was doomed. On the night the city fell, Andromache and Astyanax fought for their lives before they were captured. The Achaeans threw Astyanax from the walls—they could not let Hector's heir live—and Andromache was allocated to Neoptolemos, Achilles' son.

Cassandra is the princess of Troy, the daughter of Priam and Hekabe, and the Priestess of Apollo. Apollo gave her the gift of prophecy to win her love, but when she rejected him, Apollo cursed Cassandra so that nobody would ever believe her prophecies. When she foretold the fall of Troy and warned against the Trojan Horse, nobody listened. On Troy's final night, Cassandra was seized by Ajax in Athena's temple and allotted to Agamemnon.

Polyxena is a younger princess of Troy, the virgin daughter of Priam and Hekabe. After the fall of Troy, the greedy ghost of Achilles, still obsessed with his honor, claimed her as his share of the spoils, so Polyxena was sacrificed upon his tomb.

Aeneas is a leading warrior, the son of the goddess Aphrodite and her mortal Trojan lover, Anchises. Aeneas was related by marriage to the Trojan royal house, as he was married to one of Priam's daughters, Creusa. After Troy fell, Aeneas escaped the burning city with a few refugees and went on to found the city of Rome (as told in Virgil's *Aeneid*).

Penthesilea is the queen of the Amazons, who came to fight alongside the Trojans as their allies. An exceedingly brave warrior, Penthesilea fought Achilles one-on-one: it is said that the moment Achilles drove his sword into her breast, he looked into her eyes and fell in love with her.

The Achaeans (Greeks)

Agamemnon is the king of Mycenae, and the principal leader of the expedition against Troy, thus he held the greatest prestige and rank. Agamemnon was also very wealthy, and brought the biggest fleet. Though Agamemnon was the leader of the assembled forces, the Achaean coalition was made up of individual units led independently by their chiefs.

Menelaus is the king of Sparta, and Helen's legal husband, cuckolded by her and Paris. Menelaus was a wealthy king and a strong warrior. His signal moment comes when he fights a duel with Paris and holds him at his mercy, but he is tricked by Aphrodite, who rescued Paris from the battlefield.

Odysseus is the king of Ithaka, famous for being the smartest of all the Achaeans. Though he has only a small contingent, Odysseus is a powerful leader and brave warrior. His homecoming after the war is told in Homer's *Odyssey* (see Chapter 20).

Ajax (his Greek name is **Aias**) is the king of Salamis, and the son of Telamon. Ajax is the second-best warrior on the Achaean side after Achilles, and he was particularly good on defense. After the war, Ajax was cheated out of the armor of Achilles, a prize he felt was his due. The shame of losing made him crazy, and when he regained his senses, he committed suicide rather than suffer the disgrace to his injured honor.

Diomedes is the king of Argos, and the second-ranked Achaean after Agamemnon in wealth, power, and prestige. Diomedes is also a great warrior, the third best on the Achaean side after Achilles and Ajax. As a hero, Diomedes was favored by Athena, who helped him in battle.

Achilles is the prince of Phthia, the leader of the Myrmidons, greatest of the warriors on both sides. After he was dishonored by Agamemnon, Achilles dropped out of the war. But without Achilles, the Trojans started winning, and the Achaeans suffered terrible losses.

Patroklos is the beloved best friend of Achilles, and one of the Myrmidons. Patroklos felt bad that the Achaeans were losing without Achilles. So Patroklos put on Achilles' armor, and tricked the Trojans into believing that Achilles had returned. For a while Patroklos helped the Achaeans beat back the Trojans, and he killed many of them, but then he is slain by Hector in single combat. A fierce battle ensued over the corpse of Patroklos, where Hector stripped his body and took the armor of Achilles as a prize.

*Turning Point of the *Iliad**

Achilles now driven by rage and guilt over the death of Patroklos.

Achilles' one goal is to kill Hector.

He returns to the battle and massacres countless Trojans.

Achilles vs. Hector

The climax of the epic poem comes with the one-on-one battle between Achilles and Hector, the two greatest heroes of the Trojan War. Hector fought bravely, but Achilles, the better warrior, killed Hector. But Achilles' wrath was not appeased: still furious over the death of Patroklos, Achilles refused to show any mercy. He tied the corpse of Hector to the back of his chariot, and for twelve days he dragged the body around the walls of the city before the stunned eyes of the Trojans. The gods were appalled at this outrage! So Zeus ordered Achilles to ransom the body of Hector back to Priam. The *Iliad* ends with the funeral of Hector.

Death of Achilles

Soon afterward, Achilles was battling Trojans near the city, and he was killed by an arrow—shot by Paris, but guided by Apollo into his vulnerable heel. Achilles was given a splendid funeral and buried at Sigeum, the promontory near Troy.

Death of Paris

Not long after, Paris is killed by an arrow shot by Philoctetes, the son of Poeas, from the magic bow of Herakles, who had given it to Poeas on his funeral pyre. As Paris lay dying, he begged his first wife, Oenone, to heal his wound, but she refused, still angry over being abandoned for Helen. After he died, Oenone killed herself in remorse.

The Trojan Horse

The Achaeans finally conquered the city of Troy with a ruse devised by Odysseus. They built a huge wooden horse and filled it with their best warriors, and then the rest of the Achaeans sailed off to hide at a nearby island. Though Cassandra warned them not to accept the horse, the Trojans were tricked into receiving the gift from the Achaeans to be dedicated to the gods, and they pulled down their great walls to wheel the horse inside the city. All night long, the Trojans celebrated the end of the war, till they all fell into an exhausted sleep. At the appointed moment, the warriors emerged from the belly of the horse and opened the city gates to the rest of the Achaean army.

As the Trojan seer tells Priam and the Trojans:

"Do not trust the Horse, Trojans! Whatever it is,
I fear the Greeks, even when they bring gifts."

—Virgil, *Aeneid* 2.48–49, translated by Stanley Lombardo

The Fall of Troy

On the final night, the city of Troy was sacked and burned by the invading Achaeans. King Priam was slain by Neoptolemos on the palace altar, Hector's son Astyanax was thrown from the city walls to his death, while Hekabe and all the other Trojan women were seized and allotted as slaves to the conquerors. When Menelaus found his faithless wife, he was about to kill her, but Helen let her robe fall open, and Menelaus was so overcome by her beauty that he dropped his sword. And so Helen, the cause of so much suffering and so many deaths in the war, went home to Sparta unscathed. Other Greeks did not have such easy journeys home.

This is how Helen explains the Trojan War:

"Zeus has placed this evil fate on us so that
In time to come poets will sing of us."

—Homer, *Iliad* 6.357–358, translated by Stanley Lombardo

■ SOURCES FOR THIS CHAPTER

Griffin, Jasper. (1980). *Homer on Life and Death*. Oxford: Oxford University Press.

Latacz, Joachim. (2004). *Troy and Homer: Towards a Solution of an Old Mystery*. Translated by Kevin Windle and Rosh Ireland. Oxford: Oxford University Press.

Lombardo, Stanley. (Trans.). (1997). *Homer: Iliad*. Indianapolis: Hackett Publishing Company.

Lombardo, Stanley. (Trans.). (2005). *Virgil: Aeneid*. Indianapolis: Hackett Publishing Company.

Morford, Mark P. O., and Lenardon, Robert J. (2007). *Classical Mythology*, 8th ed. Oxford: Oxford University Press.

Nagy, Gregory. (1998). *The Best of the Achaeans: Concepts of the Hero in Archaic Greek Poetry*. Revised edition. Baltimore: The Johns Hopkins University Press.

Redfield, James M. (1994). *Nature and Culture in the Iliad: The Tragedy of Hector*. Expanded edition. Durham: Duke University Press.

Schein, Seth L. (1984). *The Mortal Hero: An Introduction to Homer's Iliad*. Berkeley and Los Angeles: University of California Press.

Shay, Jonathan. (1994). *Achilles in Vietnam: Combat Trauma and the Undoing of Character*. New York: Scribner.

Strauss, Barry. (2006). *The Trojan War: A New History*. New York: Simon and Schuster.

Winker, Martin M. (Ed.). (2007). *Troy: From Homer's Iliad to Hollywood Epic*. Oxford: Blackwell.

Wood, Michael. (1998). *In Search of the Trojan War*. Berkeley and Los Angeles: University of California Press.

◼ POPULAR CULTURE REFERENCES

Film

Helen of Troy (1956). Director: Robert Wise.
Troy (2004). Director: Wolfgang Petersen.

Television

In Search of the Trojan War (1985). BBC documentary written by Michael Wood.
Helen of Troy (2003). Directed by John Kent Harrison for the USA Network.
Helen of Troy (2005). PBS documentary presented by Bettany Hughes.

Online

Greek Mythology Link (www.maicar.com/GML)
Timeless Myths (www.timelessmyths.com/classical/trojanwar)

Self-Quiz for Chapter 19

1. What is the traditional date of the Trojan War?

   _____

   _____

   _____

   _____

2. Who are the parents of Helen?

   _____

   _____

   _____

   _____

3. Which three goddesses are involved in the Judgment of Paris?

   _____

   _____

   _____

   _____

4. What is Achilles' one vulnerable spot and why?

   _____

   _____

   _____

   _____

5. What happens at Aulis?

   _____

   _____

   _____

6. Why does Achilles drop out of the war?

_____

_____

_____

_____

7. Who is the champion of Troy?

_____

_____

_____

_____

8. Who is Cassandra?

_____

_____

_____

_____

9. How does Patroklos die?

_____

_____

_____

_____

10. Who devised the Trojan Horse?

_____

_____

_____

_____

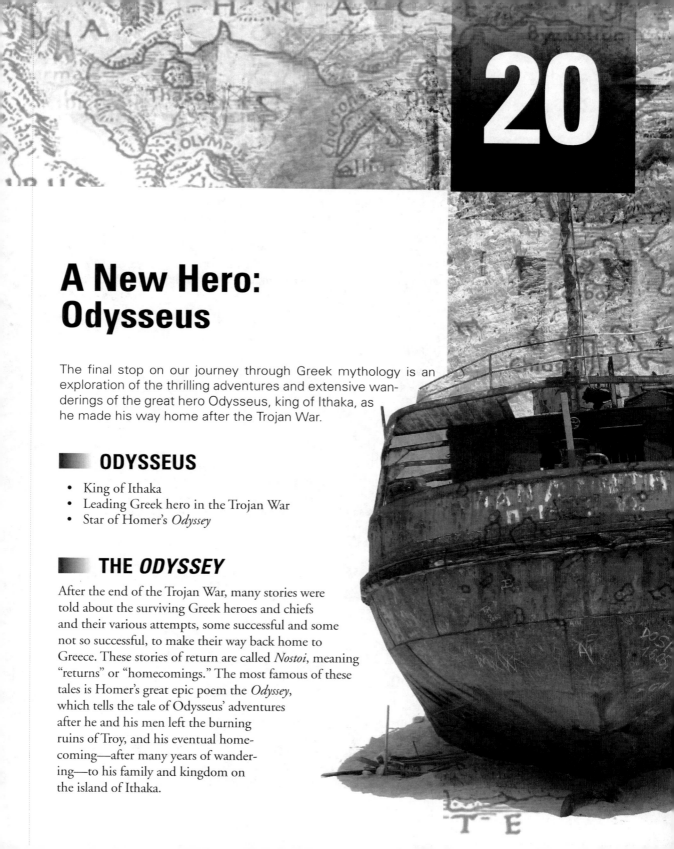

A New Hero: Odysseus

The final stop on our journey through Greek mythology is an exploration of the thrilling adventures and extensive wanderings of the great hero Odysseus, king of Ithaka, as he made his way home after the Trojan War.

ODYSSEUS

- King of Ithaka
- Leading Greek hero in the Trojan War
- Star of Homer's *Odyssey*

THE *ODYSSEY*

After the end of the Trojan War, many stories were told about the surviving Greek heroes and chiefs and their various attempts, some successful and some not so successful, to make their way back home to Greece. These stories of return are called *Nostoi*, meaning "returns" or "homecomings." The most famous of these tales is Homer's great epic poem the *Odyssey*, which tells the tale of Odysseus' adventures after he and his men left the burning ruins of Troy, and his eventual homecoming—after many years of wandering—to his family and kingdom on the island of Ithaka.

> ### *Nostos* = "Return, Homecoming"
> Stories of Greek heroes returning home after the Trojan War are *nostos* tales.
>
> *Nostalgia* in English means "a longing to return."

The Character of Odysseus

As we have seen, Odysseus was a great warrior in the Trojan War. As a hero, Odysseus is well known for his intelligence and resourcefulness. During the war, Odysseus was the "go-to guy" when the task at hand demanded a high degree of creativity, ingenuity, strategy, and cunning. For example, Odysseus' "big idea" was the design and implementation of the Trojan Horse, the trick that won the Trojan War for the Greeks. While the other heroes are compared to lions and wolves, the mastermind Odysseus is compared to an octopus, a slippery creature of great versatility and inventiveness. With his patron goddess, Athena, always by his side, Odysseus meets challenges through a combination of intelligence, courage, and strength of character.

Odysseus *"Polytropos"*

- "Man of many turns"
- "Having many ways to do things"
- "Resourceful"
- "Much-traveling"

Odysseus, King of Ithaka

The hero Odysseus is the king of Ithaka, a small island off the western coast of Greece. He is traditionally the son of Antikleia and Laertes, although some accounts of his paternity say that the wily Sisyphus was his father. Odysseus wooed and won the hand of Penelope, daughter of Icarius, brother of Tyndareus, and so she was first cousin to the famous Helen. Penelope bore Odysseus one child, a son, Telemachos, who grew up on Ithaka while his father was away at Troy.

> ### Best Movie "Odysseus"
> George Clooney in *O Brother, Where Art Thou?* (2000):
>
> "Damn, we're in a tight spot!"

The Wanderings of Odysseus

After the Trojan War, it is said that Odysseus was the last Greek hero to return home alive. Even though he was favored by Athena, Odysseus' journey home was made extremely difficult because he incurred the wrath of Poseidon, god of the sea, which obviously made it a challenge to cross the waters. So after fighting for ten years at Troy, Odysseus spent another ten years wandering, as he tried to make his way home to Ithaka. On his travels, Odysseus encountered many dangers, and he met several gods and monsters, all the while remaining nostalgic for his wife and son. When Odysseus finally made it home, it had been twenty years since he last saw his family! The story told in the *Odyssey* is a rousing tale of adventures narrated in successive episodes, full of folktale elements and romantic legends that are mingled with what was possibly the historical saga of a real king's journey home from a great ancient war.

> *Odyssey* in contemporary English usage means
>
> an extended, eventful trip,
>
> an intellectual or spiritual journey:
>
> "They experienced an *odyssey* of discovery."

Ismarus

After Odysseus and his men set sail from Troy, their first stop was at Ismarus in Thrace, where they were attacked by the inhabitants, so they sacked the city and enjoyed the spoils. Odysseus spared the life of the Priest of Apollo, who in gratitude gave him twelve jars of very potent wine—this wine would prove useful on a later adventure.

Land of the Lotus-eaters

Next, the ships of Odysseus and his men were driven way off course to a mystical place called the Land of the Lotus-eaters. There they received a friendly welcome from the cheerful locals who invited them to partake of the lotus fruit, a narcotic substance that some believe may have been the opium poppy. This posed a great danger, since anyone who experimented with the lotus would forget everything in his life and just want to stay eating lotus forever. So, with Athena's help, Odysseus had to drag his men away to continue on their journey.

Land of the Cyclops

Odysseus and his men reached another strange land, this one inhabited by the one-eyed giants known as the Cyclopes. One of them was Polyphemus, son of Poseidon, who was out pasturing his sheep when Odysseus and a few of his men entered his cave. There they helped themselves to food and supplies, until Polyphemus returned and barricaded the door of the cave with a great stone. The Cyclops was angry at the intrusion and ate some of the men before Odysseus could figure out what to do. First, Odysseus used the Ismarian wine to get the Cyclops drunk, and then he told him his name was *Outis*, or "Nobody." When Polyphemus fell asleep in a drunken stupor, Odysseus stabbed his eye out with a sharpened stick made red-hot in the fire. Polyphemus screamed in pain, "Nobody is killing me!" and so none of his brothers came to the rescue. In the morning, the blind Polyphemus rolled away the stone to let out his sheep, but Odysseus devised another trick: he and his men tied themselves to the bellies of the sheep in order to escape the cave safely. As he boarded his ship to sail away, Odysseus gloated in his triumph and shouted out his true name to the Cyclops.

> ### Polyphemus' Revenge
> The wounded Cyclops calls on his father Poseidon to curse Odysseus
> with many years of wandering, much trouble, and sorrow.

Aeolia

Odysseus and his men now arrived at Aeolia, the land of Aeolus, god and keeper of the winds. Aeolus presented Odysseus with a bag confining all the winds except the west wind, which was left free to blow Odysseus home to Ithaka. On board his ship, Odysseus did not tell his crew what was in the bag, so the men grew suspicious. Just as they were nearing Ithaka, while Odysseus slept the men opened the bag, releasing a torrent of winds that blew them farther off course than they had ever been before.

Laestrygonians

At their next landing, Odysseus and his men were attacked by giant cannibals called the Laestrygonians, who crushed all his ships but one. The curse of Polyphemus was clearly in full force against Odysseus.

Circe's Land

With only one ship left, Odysseus and his crew reached Aeaea, the home of the goddess Circe, a sorceress and the daughter of the Sun. This time Odysseus sent a scouting party ahead, but the men were turned into pigs by the crafty sorceress. One man escaped, and informed Odysseus of what had happened. As Odysseus went to rescue his men, the god Hermes appeared and gave him an herb to protect him from Circe's magic spells. Circe was so impressed with Odysseus that she turned his men back into humans and invited Odysseus to her bed. Odysseus became Circe's lover and stayed with her for one year, and had a son by her, Telegonus.

> The visit to Circe is important because she directs Odysseus
> to visit the Underworld to speak to the prophet Teiresias
> so he may get information about how to return home.

Visit to Hades

On Circe's directions, Odysseus and his men sailed to the western end of the world, where they found the entrance to the Land of the Dead. Alone, Odysseus went inside the entrance, where he performed a ritual sacrifice in order to speak to the shades of the dead: any ghost who drank the blood of the sacrifice was able to speak. Odysseus met the ghosts of his lost companions and his fellow warriors from the Trojan War, and also his beloved mother who had died longing for him to return home. Most important, Odysseus spoke to the shade of Teiresias, the old blind prophet, who told Odysseus of the many disasters he still must face on his journey. Teiresias also warned Odysseus that when he arrived home, he must deal with a dreadful situation: a hundred suitors were encamped in his house, harassing his wife and son. Teiresias informed him that only if he used caution and self-control would he succeed in taking back his kingdom.

Visit to the Underworld

Called the *Nekuia* in Greek, this is another example of the conquest of death motif and is the climax of Odysseus' adventures.

Sirens

After they sailed away from the entrance to Hades, Odysseus and his men had to sail past the Sirens, dangerous nymphs, half woman and half bird, who lured sailors to their island with their beautiful singing. Ships would be wrecked on the rocks, where the Sirens would then pick their victims' bones clean. Warned by Circe, Odysseus stuffed the ears of his crewmen with wax, and then had them bind him to the mast of the ship. As the men rowed past, Odysseus heard the irresistible song and begged his men to untie him—but the men could hear neither their captain nor the Sirens' lethal song. In this way, Odysseus was able to sail past the Sirens, hear their forbidden song, and still survive.

Scylla and Charybdis

Next Odysseus had to get his ship through the perilous narrow straits that lay between two horrifying monsters, Scylla and Charybdis. On the one side was Charybdis, a giant sucking whirlpool, which would completely destroy the last remaining ship of Odysseus. On the other side was Scylla, the sea nymph who had been turned into a monster by jealous Amphitrite, wife of Poseidon. Scylla had six hungry dogs' heads around her waist, which would snatch sailors out of their ships and eat them. On Circe's instructions, Odysseus sailed closer to the predator Scylla and lost six men, but he avoided total destruction in the whirlpool.

Scylla and Charybdis

The location of these monsters is traditionally identified as the narrow Strait of Messina between the eastern tip of Sicily and southern tip of Calabria (mainland Italy).

Contemporary English usage: the phrase *between Scylla and Charybdis* means "between a rock and a hard place"—that is, between two equally dreadful options.

Island of the Sun God

Circe's final warning was about the Island of Thrinacia, where her father, the sun god, pastured his huge herds of cattle. Circe gave strict instructions to Odysseus not to touch a single cow of her father's herd. When Odysseus and his last few men landed here, they were forced to linger for a month because of adverse winds. One day while Odysseus slept, the ravenous men killed and ate some of the cattle. The men set sail, but the sun god demanded justice, so Zeus zapped the ship with a thunderbolt and sent it to the bottom of the sea. All the men were lost and drowned, but Odysseus was saved by clinging to a piece of the ship's keel.

Island of Calypso

Odysseus, all alone, finally floated ashore at the Island of Ogygia, home of the beautiful goddess Calypso, an Oceanid. Calypso fell in love with Odysseus and wanted to make him her husband, promising he would be immortal all of his days. Odysseus remained with Calypso for seven years, but after a while started longing for his true home and family. Athena complained to Zeus about the situation, so Zeus sent Hermes down with orders for Calypso to let Odysseus go home to his real wife. Calypso had no choice but to help Odysseus build a raft, and so he sailed away.

Calypso = the "Concealer"

"She Who Enfolds, Embraces, Conceals"

Symbol of Grasping Female Sexuality

Scheria

When Poseidon caught sight of Odysseus on his newly built raft, he sent a storm to smash the vessel to pieces. Naked and half-drowned, Odysseus came ashore at the beach of Scheria, the land of the wealthy, sophisticated, and kindly Phaeacians. On the beach he is discovered by the lovely Princess Nausikaä, who gave him some clothing and instructed him to go into the city to her parents' royal palace. There he is welcomed by King Alkinoos and Queen Arete, who entertained the stranger for several days with lavish banquets. After some prodding, Odysseus revealed his identity and told tales of his many harrowing adventures. The Phaeacians gave Odysseus an abundance of rich gifts and then escorted him back to Ithaka on one of their splendid ships.

And so the curse of Polyphemus came true:

Odysseus finally reached his home in Ithaka,

but only after many years and much trouble,
all alone, and on someone else's ship!

Arrival at Ithaka

So his wanderings were over, but Odysseus still had to face one last trial in dealing with the sorry situation at his home. The suitors—one hundred noble men from the regions surrounding Ithaka—were courting his wife, Penelope, seeking to take his place and rule the kingdom, since his son, Telemachos, at barely twenty years of age, was considered too young to rule. What was worse, the suitors and their retinues had set up camp at Odysseus' palace, and were eating up his stores, drinking his wine, corrupting his maids, and generally trashing the place.

Faithful Penelope

For twenty years, Penelope had remained faithful to her husband, even when it appeared he had to be dead. Penelope, as clever, cunning, and eloquent as Odysseus, had devised a trick to stall the suitors until either her husband could return or her son Telemachos could gain enough maturity to inherit the throne. She promised the suitors she would choose one of them as soon as she finished weaving a fine burial shroud for her father-in-law, Laertes, Odysseus' elderly father. For some years she wove the shroud by day, and by night she would unweave the work she had done. Penelope's brilliant delaying tactic went long unnoticed by the drunken suitors, until one of her maids gave her up, so the angry suitors demanded that she choose among them.

The "Beggar"

Once they had assessed the situation, Athena helped Odysseus by disguising him as an old beggar, so he could enter the palace undetected and make his plans of attack. Odysseus revealed himself only to a few servants and to Telemachos, who gladly joined his father in the fight to keep his throne. In the palace, Odysseus endured many insults from the suitors, but the hero used all his caution, strategy, and self-control to achieve his goal. With the help of his son and a handful of loyal servants, Odysseus quietly made preparations for attack, stripping the great hall of weapons and stashing them in the storeroom for later use.

Argos, Odysseus' Dog

Argos was a puppy when Odysseus left for Troy, and so waits twenty years to see his master.

Argos recognizes Odysseus in the "beggar" disguise, wags his tail one last time, and dies!

Interview with Penelope

Still wearing the disguise of the old "beggar," Odysseus spoke privately with Penelope, telling her he knew Odysseus from his travels, and expressing his belief that her husband was very near. Impressed and cheered by his heartfelt words, Penelope confided in him that she had finally decided to choose a suitor by setting a contest for her hand the next day.

Soon after, the old nurse Eurykleia, who had nursed Odysseus when he was a baby, recognized a scar on his thigh that he had received from a boar's tusk while hunting, but she is sworn to silence by Odysseus for one day more.

The Contest of the Bow

The next morning, Penelope invited the suitors to compete for her hand in the trial of the bow. First, the suitors had to try to string the great bow of Odysseus, and then shoot an arrow straight through a row of twelve standing ax heads. Not a single one of the suitors could even string the great bow, much less attempt a shot through the ax heads. Then the old "beggar" asked for a try, and of course, Odysseus easily strung the bow and made the shot. Next he shot the chief suitor, and with the help of Telemachos and the loyal servants, the rest of the suitors were slain until the great hall ran with their blood. And so the interlopers were punished.

Athena joins the fight disguised as Mentor,

the old tutor of Telemachos.

Mentor in English signifies a wise, trusted, experienced counselor or guide.

Reunion of Penelope and Odysseus

But one final test still awaited Odysseus. Penelope could not believe that her husband had really returned to her after all these years, so she challenged him with the knowledge of a secret only she and her husband shared. She directed the servants to move her great bed from her chamber out into the hallway for her guest to sleep on. At this, Odysseus lost his last vestiges of hard-earned self-control, and he exploded, telling Penelope that the bed could not be moved, since he himself had built it with one of the bed posts made from a tree trunk growing out of their bedroom floor. Hearing their secret from Odysseus, Penelope leapt into his arms, and wife and husband were blissfully reunited. They spent the long night together, made longer by a pleased Athena, talking, laughing, and making love.

End of Odysseus

In later years, it is said, Odysseus was reconciled with Poseidon by building a splendid shrine for the sea god in the interior lands where nobody knew about him. Odysseus lived for many years as king of Ithaka, until one day, as the story goes, his son Telegonus, the son of Circe, came to the island in search of his father. There, during a cattle raid, Odysseus defended his herds and Telegonus, not knowing it was his father, accidentally shot Odysseus with an arrow made from a stingray spine. Telegonus was overcome with remorse when Odysseus died from the wound. But Teiresias had warned Odysseus that his death would come from the sea.

> **Odysseus**
>
> A New Kind of Hero
>
> A Man of Many Possibilities

⬛ SOURCES FOR THIS CHAPTER

Clay, Jenny Strauss. (1983). *The Wrath of Athena: Gods and Men in the Odyssey.* Princeton: Princeton University Press.

Cohen, Beth. (Ed.). (1995). *The Distaff Side: Representing the Female in Homer's Odyssey.* Oxford and New York: Oxford University Press.

Griffin, Jasper. (2004). *Homer: The Odyssey,* 2nd ed. Cambridge: Cambridge University Press.

Lombardo, Stanley. (Trans.). (2000). *Homer: Odyssey.* Indianapolis: Hackett Publishing Company.

Morford, Mark P. O., and Lenardon, Robert J. (2007). *Classical Mythology,* 8th ed. Oxford: Oxford University Press.

Schein, Seth L. (Ed.). (1996). *Reading the Odyssey: Selected Interpretive Essays.* Princeton: Princeton University Press.

Segal, Charles. (1994). *Singers, Heroes and Gods in the Odyssey: Myth and Poetics.* Ithaca: Cornell University Press.

Shay, Jonathan. (2002). *Odysseus in America: Combat Trauma and the Trials of Homecoming.* New York: Scribner.

Tracy, Stephen V. (1990). *The Story of the Odyssey.* Princeton: Princeton University Press.

⬛ POPULAR CULTURE REFERENCES

Film

Ulysses (1955). Director: Mario Camerini (starring Kirk Douglas).

2001: A Space Odyssey. (1968). Director: Stanley Kubrick.

O Brother, Where Art Thou? (2000). Directors: Joel and Ethan Coen.

Cold Mountain (2003). Director: Anthony Minghella.

Television

The Odyssey (1997). Directed by Andrei Konchalovsky for Hallmark Entertainment.
Hercules: The Legendary Journeys (1995–2000). Syndicated series.
Xena: Warrior Princess (1995–2001). Syndicated series.

Online

Greek Mythology Link (www.maicar.com/GML)
Odysseus Unbound (www.odysseus-unbound.org)
Under Odysseus (www.underodysseus.blogspot.com)

Self-Quiz for Chapter 20

1. What is a *nostos*?

   _____

   _____

   _____

   _____

2. What does Odysseus *polytropos* mean?

   _____

   _____

   _____

   _____

3. Who is Penelope? Who is Telemachos?

   _____

   _____

   _____

   _____

4. Who is Polyphemus and what happens in his cave?

   _____

   _____

   _____

   _____

5. Who is Circe and what instructions does she give to Odysseus?

   _____

   _____

   _____

   _____

6. Who is Teiresias and what does he tell Odysseus?

_____

_____

_____

_____

7. What are Scylla and Charybdis?

_____

_____

_____

_____

8. Who is Calypso and what does she do to/for Odysseus?

_____

_____

_____

_____

9. Who is Nausikaä and how does she help Odysseus?

_____

_____

_____

_____

10. What happens in the contest of the bow?

_____

_____

_____

_____

Greek Mythology: Exam I

1. _____
   _____

2. _____
   _____

3. _____
   _____

4. _____
   _____

5. _____
   _____

6. _____
   _____

7. _____
   _____

8. _____
   _____

9. _____
   _____

10. _____
    _____

11. _____
    _____

12. _____
    _____

13. _____
    _____

14. _____
_____

15. _____
_____

16. _____
_____

17. _____
_____

18. _____
_____

19. _____
_____

20. _____
_____

21. _____
_____

22. _____
_____

23. _____
_____

24. _____
_____

25. _____
_____

Extra Credit:

Greek Mythology: Exam II

1. _____
_____

2. _____
_____

3. _____
_____

4. _____
_____

5. _____
_____

6. _____
_____

7. _____
_____

8. _____
_____

9. _____
_____

10. _____
_____

11. _____
_____

12. _____
_____

13. _____
_____

14. _____
_____

15. _____
_____

16. _____
_____

17. _____
_____

18. _____
_____

19. _____
_____

20. _____
_____

21. _____
_____

22. _____
_____

23. _____
_____

24. _____
_____

25. _____
_____

Extra Credit:

GLOSSARY

Acastus Son of Pelias; exiled Jason and Medea for the murder of his father.

Achaeans Homeric term used to refer to the Greeks.

Achelous River god defeated by Herakles for the hand of Deianira.

Acheron River in Hades; the "River of Woe."

Achilles Son of Peleus and Thetis; prince of Phthia; leader of the Myrmidons; greatest warrior of the Trojan War.

Actaeon Hunter punished by Artemis.

Adonis Gorgeous youth; lover of Aphrodite; turned into an anemone flower.

Aeacus Judge in the Underworld; sometimes the gatekeeper of Hades.

Aeaea Land of Circe.

Aeëtes King of Colchis; father of Medea; owner of the Golden Fleece.

Aegeus King of Athens; father of Theseus; helps Medea in her hour of need.

Aegis Magic goat-skin shield of Zeus; given to his favorite daughter, Athena.

Aeneas Trojan hero; son of Aphrodite and Anchises; escaped the fall of Troy and went on to found the city of Rome.

Aeolus God and keeper of the Winds; tried to help Odysseus on his journey.

Aeson King of Iolcus; father of Jason.

Aetion Ancient Greek word meaning origin, cause, or reason.

Agamemnon King of Mycenae; brother of Menelaus; leader of the Achaean expedition to Troy to recover Helen.

Agave Mother of Pentheus; tore him apart in a Dionysian frenzy.

Ajax (also **Aias**) King of Salamis; son of Telamon; leading Greek warrior in the Trojan War.

Alkinoos King of the Phaeacians; husband of Arete; father of Nausikaä.

Alkmene (also **Alcmena**) Wife of Amphitryon; lover of Zeus; mother of Herakles.

Alpheius River near Olympia used by Herakles to clean the Augean stables.

Amaltheia Magic goat who nursed baby Zeus.

Amazonomachy A battle against the Amazons.

Amazons Legendary tribe of fierce warrior women in northern Asia Minor.

Ambrosia Food eaten by the gods; the word means "immortal stuff."

Amphitrite A Nereid; Queen of the Sea; wife of Poseidon.

Amphitryon Husband of Alkmene; father of Iphikles.

Anauros River crossed by Jason on his way to Iolcus; carried a disguised Hera across.

Anchises Trojan hero; lover of Aphrodite; father of Aeneas.

Andromache Daughter of Eëtion; wife of Hector; mother of Astyanax.

Antaeus Giant; son of Gaia; slain by Herakles.

Anthropomorphism The attribution of human characteristics to the gods.

Antikleia Wife of Laertes; mother of Odysseus.

Aphrodite One of the Olympians; goddess of love and beauty, born from the castrated genitals of Ouranos; in some accounts, daughter of Zeus and Dione.

Apollo (also **Phoebos**) One of the Olympians; god of light, music, and prophecy; son of Zeus and Leto.

Apsyrtus Prince of Colchis; son of Aeëtes; brother of Medea, slain by her during her escape from Colchis with Jason.

Arachne Expert weaver punished for boasting of her skill and challenging Athena to a contest; turned into a spider.

Ares One of the Olympians; god of war; son of Zeus and Hera.

Arete Queen of the Phaeacians; wife of Alkinoos; mother of Nausikaä.

Argo Ship on which Jason and the Argonauts sailed.

Argonauts Crew of the *Argo*.

Argos Shipwright who designed and built the *Argo* with Athena's help; sailed as one of the Argonauts.

Argus Hundred-eyed servant of Hera; slain by Hermes during Io affair; his eyes placed Hera's bird, the peacock.

Artemis One of the Olympians; goddess of the hunt; daughter of Zeus and Leto.

Asklepios Great physician; son of Apollo; punished by Zeus for raising the dead.

Astyanax Son of Hector and Andromache; heir to the throne of Troy; thrown from the walls and killed after the sack of Troy.

Atē Madness or moral blindness that follows *hubris.*

Athena One of the Olympians; goddess of wisdom; born from the head of Zeus.

Athlos (plural **athloi**) "Contest for a prize," Greek word for the labors of Herakles.

Atlas Brother of Prometheus; fought with the Titans against the Olympians; punished by having to hold up the world.

Augeas Owner of stables cleaned by Herakles on his fifth labor.

Aulis Gathering point of the Achaean fleet before the expedition to Troy.

Bacchae (also **Bacchantes**) Female followers of Dionysus.

Briseis Prize of Achilles; seized by Agamemnon.

Busiris Egyptian king slain by Herakles.

Caduceus Winged herald's staff, symbol of Hermes.

Calais A Boread, or son of Boreas; brother of Zetes; sailed as one of the Argonauts.

Callirhoë An Oceanid; wife of Chrysaor.

Callisto Companion of Artemis; punished for her affair with Zeus; turned into a bear.

Calypso Sea goddess, an Oceanid; name means the "Concealer"; lover of Odysseus.

Cassandra Princess of Troy; daughter of Priam and Hekabe; priestess of Apollo whose prophecies were never believed.

Castor One of the Dioscuri; mortal son of Leda and Tyndareus; later shared immortality with his brother Polydeuces; sailed on the *Argo*.

Centauromachy A battle against the Centaurs.

Centaurs Rowdy nature spirits, half human and half horse.

Cerberus Three-headed hound of Hades; sought by Herakles on his final labor.

Chalciope Daughter of Aeëtes; sister of Medea.

Chaos First principle in the Greek cosmogony; a great yawning void.

Charites Three Graces; companions of Aphrodite.

Charon Boatman on the River Styx in Hades.

Charybdis Monstrous sucking whirlpool; she and Scylla form dangerous narrow straits passed by Odysseus on his journey.

Chimaera Triple monster with lion front, goat middle, and snake tail.

Chiron Good and wise centaur; trainer of heroes.

Chrysaor He of the "Golden Sword"; born from Medusa's severed neck; father of monsters.

Chryseis Prize of Agamemnon; daughter of priest of Apollo; given back to her father.

Chthonian (also **chthonic**) Category of underworld deities.

Circe Sorceress; daughter of the Sun; lover of Odysseus.

Clytemnestra Daughter of Leda and Tyndareus; sister of Helen; wife of Agamemnon; mother of Iphigeneia; killed Agamemnon upon his return from the Trojan War.

Cocytus River in Hades, the "River of Wailing."

Colchis Land at the eastern end of the Black Sea; home of Medea.

Cosmogony A creation myth; the word means "birth of the universe."

Creon King of Corinth; exiled Medea from his city; slain by her in revenge.

Cronos Youngest of the Titans; castrated his father Ouranos and seized the throne of Heaven; father of the original Olympians, including Zeus, who deposed him.

Cyclopes One-eyed monsters, offspring of Gaia and Ouranos: Brontes, Steropes, and Arges.

Cyparissus Boy loved by Apollo; turned into a cypress tree.

Cyprus Island sacred to Aphrodite.

Cythera Island sacred to Aphrodite.

Daedalus Master craftsman who designed the Labyrinth in Crete; created wings of feathers and wax and lost his son, Icarus, who flew too close to the sun.

Daphne Nymph loved by Apollo; turned into a laurel tree.

Deianira Wife of Herakles, who unintentionally caused his death.

Deidamia Lover of Achilles, by him mother of Neoptolemos.

Deimos Spirit of Terror; companion of Ares.

Delos Island; sacred birthplace and important cult site of Apollo.

Delphi Oracular shrine of Apollo; most important pan-Hellenic sanctuary in Greece.

Demeter One of the Olympians; goddess of agriculture; mother of Persephone.

Deucalion Son of Prometheus; survived the great flood with his wife, Pyrrha.

Diomedes King of Argos; favorite of Athena; leading Greek warrior in the Trojan War.

Dione An Oceanid; lover of Zeus; in some accounts, mother of Aphrodite.

Dionysus One of the Olympians; god of wine; son of Zeus and Semele.

Dioscuri "Sons of Zeus" Castor and Polydeuces; heroes who shared immortality; sailed on the *Argo*.

Dodona Oracular shrine of Zeus in northern Greece.

Dryads Tree nymphs.

Echidna Monster, half snake and half woman; mother of many monsters, including Cerberus, Orthus, and the Hydra.

Eileithyia Goddess of childbirth; daughter of Zeus and Hera.

Ekstasis Standing outside oneself in the Dionysian ritual.

Electra An Oceanid; wife of Thaumas.

Eleusis Sacred site of Demeter and Persephone; home of the Eleusinian Mysteries.

Elysian Fields (also **Elysium**) Paradise of the Underworld.

Enthousiasmos Possession by the god in the Dionysian ritual.

Eos Goddess of the dawn and sunrise.

Epimetheus Brother of Prometheus; his name means "Afterthought"; husband of Pandora.

Erichthonius Legendary first king of Athens; born from Gaia after Athena and Hephaestus mingled their essences.

Erinyes The Furies; divine agents of vengeance.

Eris Goddess of strife; companion of Ares; threw the golden apple at the wedding of Peleus and Thetis.

Eros God of sexual desire; one of the first principles; in some accounts, the son of Aphrodite and Ares.

Eurydice Dryad loved by Orpheus; after her untimely death, Orpheus tried to rescue her from Hades, but lost her again.

Eurykleia Old nurse of Odysseus; recognized her master and helped him defeat the suitors.

Eurystheus Weakling king of Argos for whom Herakles performs his twelve labors.

Eurytus King of Euboea; father of Princess Iole; denied his daughter to Herakles, so is slain by him.

Gaia Mother Earth; one of the first principles.

Galanthis Maid of Alkmene; tricked Eileithyia into allowing her mistress to go into labor.

Ganymede Trojan prince loved by Zeus; taken to Mt. Olympus to be his cup bearer.

Gegeneis Another name for the Giants, meaning "Earth-born Ones."

Geryon Triple-bodied monster; slain by Herakles on his tenth labor.

Gigantomachy A battle against the Giants.

Glaukopis "Grey-eyed" or "Owl-eyed"; epithet of Athena.

Gorgons Three female monsters: Stheno, Euryale, and Medusa; daughters of Phorcys.

Graiae Three sea goddesses, the Spirits of Old Age; daughters of Phorcys.

Hades (also **Pluto**) One of the original Olympians; Lord of the Underworld. Also, the Underworld itself, the Realm of the Dead.

Halioi Gerontes Sea gods; Old Men of the Sea.

Harpies Monsters, half bird and half woman; daughters of Thaumas and Electra.

Hebe Goddess of youthful bloom; daughter of Zeus and Hera; last wife of Herakles.

Hecatoncheires Three hundred-armed monster offspring of Gaia and Ouranos: Cottos, Briareos, and Gyes.

Hector Crown prince of Troy; son of Priam and Hekabe; great champion of the Trojans; husband of Andromache; father of Astyanax; slain by Achilles in one-on-one combat.

Hekabe Queen of Troy; wife of Priam; mother of Hector and Paris.

Hekate Goddess of witchcraft; patrolled the pit of Tartaros.

Helen Daughter of Zeus and Leda; queen of Sparta; favorite of Aphrodite; most beautiful woman in the world; wife of Menelaus; mother of Hermione; eloped with Paris to Troy, thereby causing the Trojan War.

Helios God of the sun.

Hellen Son of Deucalion and Pyrrha; eponymous ancestor of the Hellenes, or Greeks.

Hephaestus One of the Olympians; the blacksmith god; son of Zeus and Hera or, in some accounts, Hera's son by parthenogenesis.

Hera One of the Olympians; queen of the gods; wife of Zeus; goddess of marriage.

Herakles Greatest Greek hero; son of Zeus and Alkmene; performed twelve labors and many other deeds, after which he became a god on Mt. Olympus.

Hermaphroditus Offspring of Hermes and Aphrodite; had both male and female sexual body parts.

Hermes One of the Olympians; the messenger god; son of Zeus and Maia.

Hermione Daughter of Helen and Menelaus.

Hesperides Daughters of Evening, or more commonly of Atlas; lived in the western garden of the Golden Apples, sought by Herakles on his eleventh labor.

Hestia One of the original Olympians; goddess of the hearth.

Hieros Gamos "Sacred marriage," in which an earth goddess is joined with a sky god.

Hippolyte Amazon queen whose belt was sought by Herakles on his ninth labor.

Hubris Sin of audacity, arrogance, or presumption.

Hyacinthus Boy loved by Apollo; turned into a hyacinth flower.

Hydra Nine-headed water snake slain by Herakles on his second labor.

Hyllus Son of Herakles and Deianira; married Iole.

Hypnos God of sleep; twin brother of Thanatos, god of death.

Hysipyle Queen of Lemnos; lover of Jason; mother of twins by him.

Icarus Son of Daedalus; wore wings of feathers and wax made by his father; flew too close to the sun and fell into the sea.

Ichor Divine substance that flowed through the veins of the gods.

Iliad Homer's epic poem set in the final year of the Trojan War.

Io Priestess of Hera; lover of Zeus; turned into a white cow.

Iolaus Son of Iphikles; assisted his uncle Herakles on his labors.

Iolcus Land in northern Greece; home of Jason.

Iole Daughter of Eurytus; princess loved by Herakles; later married his son, Hyllus.

Iphigeneia Daughter of Agamemnon and Clytemnestra; sacrificed by her father to appease Artemis before the Trojan War.

Iphikles Son of Alkmene and Amphitryon; mortal half-brother of Herakles.

Iphitus Son of Eurytus; slain by Herakles.

Iris Goddess of the rainbow; daughter of Thaumas and Electra.

Ismarus Odysseus' first stop after the Trojan War, where he got twelve jars of wine.

Ithaka Island kingdom of Odysseus.

Ixion Punished for seducing Hera; celebrity sinner in Tartaros, bound to an ever-rolling wheel of fire.

Jason Son of Aeson and Polymede; heir to the throne of Iolcus; led the quest of the Argonauts for the Golden Fleece; husband of Medea.

Labyrinth Maze built by Daedalus that housed the Minotaur on the island of Crete.

Ladon Dragon who guarded the Golden Apples of the Hesperides; son of Phorcys.

Laertes Husband of Antikleia; father of Odysseus.

Laestrygonians Giant cannibals who attacked Odysseus and his men.

Leda Queen of Sparta; wife of Tyndareus; lover of Zeus; mother of Helen, Clytemnestra, and the Dioscuri.

Lemnos Island sacred to Hephaestus; stop made by the Argonauts.

Lethe River in Hades; this "River of Forgetfulness" flowed in the Elysian Fields.

Leto Daughter of the Titans Coeos and Phoebe; lover of Zeus; mother of Apollo and Artemis.

Linus Son of Apollo; music teacher of Herakles, who accidentally killed him.

Macaria Daughter of Herakles and Deianira.

Maenads Nymphs, followers of Dionysus.

Maia Daughter of Atlas; eldest of the Pleiades; lover of Zeus; mother of Hermes.

Marsyas Satyr who challenged Apollo to music contest; punished and flayed alive by Apollo.

Medea Daughter of Aeëtes; princess of Colchis; priestess of Hecate; wife of Jason.

Medusa Most famous Gorgon; lover of Poseidon; mother of Pegasus and Chrysaor.

Megara First wife of Herakles, who unknowingly kills her in a fit of madness.

Meleager Hero of the Calydonian boar hunt; sailed as one of the Argonauts; brother of Deianira.

Menelaus King of Sparta; brother of Agamemnon; husband of Helen, who left him for Paris.

Mentor Old tutor of Telemachos; disguise worn by Athena as she helped Odysseus and Telemachos defeat the suitors.

Merope Wife of Sisyphus.

Metis Goddess of practical wisdom; lover of Zeus, who swallowed her and gave birth to Athena from his head.

Minos King of Crete; husband of Pasiphaë; later a judge in the Underworld.

Minotaur Monster, half man and half bull; offspring of Pasiphaë, queen of Crete, and the Cretan Bull; lived in the Labyrinth.

Mnemosyne Goddess of memory; mother of the Muses.

Moirae Three Fates, goddesses of destiny: Clotho, Lachesis, and Atropos.

Mopsus Seer; sailed as one of the Argonauts.

Morpheus God of dreams; son of Hypnos, god of sleep.

Mt. Olympus Home of the Olympian gods.

Muses Nine daughters of Zeus and Mnemosyne; goddesses of artistic and intellectual inspiration: Cleio, Euterpe, Thaleia, Melpomene, Terpsichore, Erato, Polyhymnia, Urania, and Calliope.

Myrmidons "Ant-men"; troops led by Achilles in the Trojan War.

Myrrha Mother of Adonis; turned into a tree.

Mythos Ancient Greek word meaning "utterance, something spoken"; a tale, story, or speech.

Naiads Nymphs of freshwater springs.

Nausikaä Daughter of King Alkinoos and Queen Arete; princess of the Phaeacians; helped Odysseus when he washed up on the beach of Scheria.

Nectar Drink of the gods.

Nekuia Visit of Odysseus to the Underworld.

Nemean Lion Monstrous lion slain by Herakles on his first labor.

Nemesis Retribution or punishment; also the goddess of retribution.

Neoptolemos Son of Achilles and Deidamia; played major part in the sack of Troy.

Nereids Fifty daughters of Nereus; salt-water nymphs.

Nereus Sea god; Old Man of the Sea; father of the Nereids.

Nessos Centaur who sought vengeance against Herakles.

Nike Goddess of victory; companion of Athena.

Nostos (plural **nostoi**) Greek word meaning "return" or "homecoming."

Oceanids Daughters of Oceanos; nymphs of rivers and waterfalls.

Oceanos One of the Titans; the stream of ocean that surrounded the Earth.

Odysseus King of Ithaka; son of Antikleia and Laertes; husband of Penelope; father of Telemachos; leading Greek warrior in the Trojan War. After ten years at war, spent another ten years wandering on his way home.

Odyssey Homer's epic poem about the return of Odysseus after the Trojan War.

Oedipus Hero of Thebes who conquered the Sphinx; unknowingly killed his father and married his mother.

Oenone Mountain nymph with the gift of healing; first wife of Paris.

Ogygia Island of Calypso.

Olympia Sacred shrine of Zeus in southern Greece, where Herakles founded the Olympic Games.

Omophagia Sharing the communal sacrifice in the Dionysian ritual.

Omphale Queen of Lydia; served by Herakles for a three-year sentence.

Oreads Mountain nymphs; companions of Artemis.

Oreibasia Running away to the woodlands by worshippers of Dionysus.

Ornithomorph Bird used as a symbol of a deity.

Orpheus Expert musician; son of Apollo and the Muse Calliope; in some accounts, son of the river god Oeagrus; tried to rescue Eurydice from Hades, but failed.

Orphism Mystery religion associated with the myth of Orpheus.

Orthus Two-headed hound of Geryon.

Ortygia Island sacred to Artemis.

Ouranos Father Sky, or Heaven; husband of Gaia.

Pan Pastoral god; most commonly, son of Hermes; companion of Dionysus.

Pandora First woman; given as punishment to humankind; opened her jar and introduced evil things into the world.

Pantheon All the gods considered as a group, the Olympian pantheon.

Parergon (plural **parerga**) "Side-deed" performed by Herakles outside the main twelve labors.

Paris (also **Alexander**) Prince of Troy; son of Priam and Hekabe; eloped with Helen to Troy, thereby causing the Trojan War.

Parthenogenesis Process by which the female gives birth without insemination by the male; the word means "maiden birth."

Patroklos Best friend of Achilles; one of the Myrmidons; put on Achilles' armor and was slain by Hector.

Pegasus Winged horse; born from Medusa's severed neck.

Peleus King of Phthia; husband (briefly) of the Nereid Thetis; father of Achilles; sailed as one of the Argonauts.

Pelias Brother of Aeson; seized the throne of Iolcus; sent Jason on his quest for the Golden Fleece.

Penelope Daughter of Icarius; wife of Odysseus; mother of Telemachos.

Penthesilea Amazon queen slain by Achilles in the Trojan War.

Pentheus King of Thebes punished for denying Dionysus; torn apart by Bacchantes.

Persephone (also **Kore**) Goddess of spring; daughter of Zeus and Demeter; seized by Hades to be his wife and queen of the Underworld.

Petasos Wide-brimmed traveler's hat, symbol of Hermes.

Phaeacians Kindly people of Scheria; helped Odysseus on the final leg of his journey.

Phaëthon Son of Apollo; drove the chariot of the sun recklessly; zapped by Zeus.

Philoctetes Son of Poeas; used the bow of Herakles to kill Paris at the end of the Trojan War.

Phineus Old blind prophet; tormented by Harpies; helped by Jason.

Phobos Spirit of Fear; companion of Ares.

Phorcys Sea god; Old Man of the Sea.

Phrixus Husband of Chalciope; rode the golden ram to Colchis from Greece.

Poeas Shepherd who lit Herakles' funeral pyre; given the hero's bow as reward; gave the bow to his son, Philoctetes.

Polydeuces (also **Pollux**) One of the Dioscuri; immortal son of Leda and Zeus; later shared immortality with his brother Castor; sailed on the *Argo*.

Polymede Queen of Iolcus; mother of Jason.

Polyphemus One-eyed Cyclops; son of Poseidon; blinded by Odysseus.

Polytropos Homeric epithet of Odysseus, meaning "man of many turns," "having many ways to do things," and "much-traveling."

Polyxena Princess of Troy; virgin daughter of Priam and Hekabe; sacrificed on the tomb of Achilles after the fall of Troy.

Poseidon One of the original Olympians; great god of the sea.

Priam King of Troy during the Trojan War; father of Hector and Paris; slain on the high altar during the sack of Troy by Neoptolemos, son of Achilles.

Prometheus Son of the Titan Iapetos; his name means "Forethought"; rebelled against Zeus to help humankind and was punished.

Proteus Sea god; Old Man of the Sea.

Psychopompos "Guide of Souls"; epithet of Hermes, who guided the souls of the newly dead down to Hades.

Pyriphlegethon River in Hades; this "River of Fire" encircled Tartaros.

Pyrrha Daughter of Pandora; wife of Deucalion; survived the great flood.

Pythia Priestess of Apollo who delivered his words at Delphi.

Python Dragon slain by Apollo at Delphi.

Rhadamanthus Judge in the Underworld.

Rhea One of the Titans; wife of Cronos; mother of Zeus and the original Olympians.

Salmoneus Punished for impersonating Zeus; celebrity sinner in Tartaros.

Satyrs Male nature spirits; companions of Dionysus.

Scheria Land of the Phaeaecians; last stop of Odysseus on his journey home.

Scylla Sea monster with six dogs' heads around her waist; she and Charybdis form dangerous narrow straits passed by Odysseus on his journey.

Scyros Island where Thetis tried to hide Achilles before the Trojan War.

Selene Goddess of the moon.

Semele Princess of Thebes; lover of Zeus; mother of Dionysus.

Silenus Elderly male nature spirit; caretaker of baby Dionysus.

Sirens Sea nymphs, half bird and half woman; daughters of Phorcys.

Sisyphus Punished for cheating death; celebrity sinner in Tartaros; forced to push a rock up a hill eternally.

Sparagmos Ripping apart the sacrificial animal in the Dionysian ritual.

Sphinx Winged monster, half woman and half lion; conquered by Oedipus.

Styx River in Hades; shades must cross the "River of Hate" to enter the Underworld.

Symplegades "Clashing rocks" that destroyed ships passing through; after the *Argo* went through, rocks stuck together forever.

Tantalus Punished for offending the gods at table; celebrity sinner in Tartaros; tempted with food and drink but never satisfied.

Tartaros Deep pit of Hades; place of punishment for the worst sinners.

Teiresias Old blind prophet whose shade is consulted by Odysseus in the Underworld.

Telamon Father of Ajax; sailed as one of the Argonauts.

Telegonus Son of Odysseus and Circe; accidentally killed his father with an arrow shot.

Telemachos Son of Odysseus and Penelope; heir to the throne of Ithaka; helped his father defeat the suitors and secure the kingdom.

Tethys One of the Titans; sister and wife of Oceanos.

Thanatos God of death; twin brother of Hypnos, god of sleep.

Thaumas Sea god; Old Man of the Sea; brother of Phorcys.

Themis Titan goddess of justice; mother of the Moirae.

Theogony A divine genealogy myth; the word means "birth of the gods." The *Theogony* is a long poem by the Greek poet Hesiod.

Theseus Hero of Athens; killed the Minotaur on Crete.

Thespian Lion Lion slain by Herakles as one of his early *parerga*.

Thetis A Nereid, sea goddess; married (briefly) to Peleus, by him mother of Achilles.

Thiasos Sacred band of worshippers of Dionysus.

Thrinacia Island where the sun god, Helios, kept his herds of cattle.

Thyrsos Magic wand/weapon used by followers of Dionysus.

Tiphys Helmsman of the *Argo*; sailed as one of the Argonauts.

Titanomachy A battle against the Titans.

Titans Twelve gods, offspring of Gaia and Ouranos: Oceanos, Coeos, Crios, Hyperion, Iapetos, Theia, Rhea, Themis, Mnemosyne, Phoebe, Tethys, and Cronos.

Tityos Punished for seducing Leto; celebrity sinner in Tartaros; stretched out on the ground where vultures eat his liver every day.

Triton A merman sea god; son of Poseidon and Amphitrite.

Troy (also **Ilion**, or **Ilios**) Great city on north coast of Asia Minor; site of the famous ten-year conflict known as the Trojan War.

Tyndareus King of Sparta; husband of Leda; stepfather of Helen.

Typhon (also **Typhoeus**) Dragon; offspring of Gaia and Tartaros; slain by Zeus.

Zetes A Boread, or son of Boreas; brother of Calais; sailed as one of the Argonauts.

Zeus King of the gods; chief Olympian; son of Cronos and Rhea.

Index